SCOTS LAW FOR JOURNALISTS

SCOTS LAW FOR JOURNALISTS

SIXTH EDITION

BRUCE MCKAIN
Law Correspondant, The Herald

· ALISTAIR J. BONNINGTON
Solicitor to BBC Scotland and Lecturer at Glasgow University

GEORGE A. WATT, M.B.E.,
Former Court of Session Correspondent, The Herald

W. GREEN/Sweet & Maxwell
EDINBURGH
1995

First published 1995
Reprinted 1995

© 1995
BRUCE MCKAIN AND ALISTAIR J. BONNINGTON

ISBN 0 414 01005 1

A catalogue record for this book is
available from the British Library

W. GREEN The Scottish Law Publisher *would like to thank:*

BBC Scotland
Daily Record
Evening News
Evening Times
Forth FM
Max AM
Radio Clyde
Scottish Television
The Scotsman
The Herald

for kindly granting permission to reproduce their logo on the cover of this book.

Computerset by Wyvern Typesetting, Bristol
Printed in Great Britain by Antony Rowe Ltd, Chippenham, Wiltshire

FOREWORD

By The Right Honourable Lord Hope Lord President of The Court of Session and Lord Justice General of Scotland

The task of the journalist, and especially that of the court reporter, has never been more important, or more difficult, than it is today. As Lord President Emslie said in his Foreword to a previous edition of this book, it is in the best interests of the courts that what they do, and how they do it, should be as widely known as possible. But the growing complexity of modern life, and increasing pressures in the market place, have affected journalism as much as they have affected every other business activity. There have been significant improvements in recent years in the technology which assists the rapid transmission from place to place of words and images. But the volume of cases coming before the courts, and the variety and complexity of the issues raised by them, have increased just as dramatically. The processes of selection and editing are more important than ever, as time and space are at a premium. Yet the task of informing the public with the fairness and accuracy which confidence in the judicial process demands grows ever more demanding for those engaged in this work.

The importance of this book cannot be understated in these circumstances. A sound knowledge of the basic structure of our institutions and of the framework of our law can be derived readily by reading it. The book has been prepared against the background of many years' experience of the work of our courts, and there is much good advice here as to how the best traditions of those who report what goes on there can be maintained. I am confident that the publication of this latest edition of Scots Law for Journalists will continue to uphold the high standard of journalism in Scotland, which has contributed so much to the quality of life in this country and on which so much depends.

EDINBURGH   DAVID HOPE
JANUARY 1995

PREFACE TO THE SIXTH EDITION

Since this book was first published in 1965 there have been wide-ranging changes in the law as it affects the media. However, the aim of the book remains broadly the same—to provide journalists with a basic guide to the Scottish legal system as it affects their daily working lives.

In that sense it serves a twofold purpose—as a text book for the trainee and as a reference book for the working journalist. It also aims to provide valuable assistance for members of the legal profession involved with the law and the media.

The book outlines the main areas of Scots law with which both print journalists and those working in radio and television should be familiar if they are to carry out their work competently and safely. It also details the pitfalls that lie in wait for the unwary.

Although the fifth edition was published only 6 years ago the intervening period has seen a number of major changes in the law affecting the media, which have made it vital for the book to be brought up to date.

The notorious catch-all s2 of the 1911 Official Secrets Act has been repealed by the Official Secrets Act 1989. The Copyright Designs and Patents Act 1988 makes important changes for journalists in this area of the law. The Court of Session has clarified the law on identification of children in civil cases, an area which was in doubt for many years.

The chapters on defamation and contempt of court have been extensively rewritten to take recent developments into account, and we examine the ramifications of the *Spycatcher* and Inside Intelligence cases.

There is also a completely new section dealing with the structure of broadcasting in the United Kingdom and the special problems faced by broadcast journalists in areas such as contempt of court, defamation and freedom of speech.

Since the last edition the Press Council has been abolished to be replaced by a Press Complaints Commission following the Report on Privacy by Sir David Calcutt QC. The Calcutt Committee has also raised the threat that unless the media put their own house in order, criminal law sanctions will be introduced to deal with what is seen as unwarranted intrusion into private lives.

The Press Complaints Commission introduced a code of conduct for the media which is reproduced as an appendix at the end of the book.

It can safely be said, therefore, that there has never been a more important time for journalists to have a sound knowledge of their rights and duties under the law. The law is stated as at January 1995.

CONTENTS

Contents

ABBREVIATIONS

The following abbreviations are among those most frequently found in the Court of Session rolls:

AG	Against (between names of parties in Calling List)
Alit	Aliment
(a.p.)	Assisted person (under the Legal Aid Scheme)
C.B.	Curator bonis
C.R.&P.	Count, reckoning and payment
cy-pres	"As near as possible" (see Glossary)
Dec. of Null.	Declarator of nullity
Diss. of Marr.	Dissolution of marriage
Eosd. (eosdem); eund. (eundem)	"Same as in case above" (with reference to names of counsel)
I.P.D.	*In prasenti Dominorum* (in their Lordships' presence)
J.F.	Judicial factor
Min.	Minute
MP	Multiplepoinding (see Glossary)
N.P.	Notary-public
p(per)	"Represented by" (with reference to counsel after name of party
Pet.	Petition
R.M.	Reclaiming motion (see Glossary)
Sep. & Alit	Separation and aliment
S.&I.	Suspension and interdict
S.M.& A.	Summons, minute and answers
Trs.	Trustees
* (asterisk)	Preceding name of case in the motion roll, indicates counsel will appear (the absence of an asterisk indicates there will be no appearance).

CHAPTER 1

INTRODUCTION

THE LEGAL FRAMEWORK

01–01 Scots law is a distinct system, largely based on Roman law while English law is essentially a home-grown product. The basic differences between the two systems were preserved by the Act of Union of 1707 which provided that no alteration was to be made in Scottish private law "except for the evident utility of the subjects within Scotland."

01–02 Today, although Scots law retains many distinct features such as the not proven verdict and the 110-day rule (the time within which an accused person in custody must be brought to trial), the laws of the two countries are much more similar than they were in 1707.

There is a constant tendency towards harmonisation. Many Acts of Parliament apply to the whole United Kingdom and great stretches of the law, particularly in the fields of taxation and commerce, are the same on both sides of the Border.

01–03 An important development in the reform of the two systems along the same lines began with the setting up in 1965 of the Scottish Law Commission and the Law Commission for England and Wales. Under the Law Commissions Act of 1965 the Scottish Law Commission has the duty of keeping under review all the law of Scotland "with a view to its systematic development and reform." It has a full-time chairman, who is a Judge, seconded for a term of five years, and two full-time and two part-time commissioners. In pursuit of its law reform projects it issues consultative documents exploring areas of possible reform, seeks reactions from people and organisations with specialised knowledge as well as from the general public and prepares draft Bills for submission to Parliament.

01–04 In several important respects Scots law has led the way in recent years both in development of the common law and through legislation. This revival has been accompanied by growing support for the publication of Scottish law books, giving Scots lawyers better access to the sources they require for practice, research and teaching.

01–05   Since 1971, for example, Scotland has pioneered and developed the modern shift in the approach to children in trouble, from punishment towards care and protection. The passing of legislation to combat alcohol abuse and crowd violence at sports meetings originated here—as did, centuries earlier, the system of independent local prosecutors under the Crown now emulated in England and Wales. England's abandonment of its insistence upon the unanimous jury verdict goes part-way at least towards acceptance of what has been the position north of the Border for centuries.

01–06   A central element in recent reforms of the law of contempt of court—which aims at allowing legitimate publicity for crime while affording the accused protection from unfairness—had its origin in a judgment of the High Court of Justiciary. Scotland meanwhile has followed England's example in simplification of divorce procedures.

01–07   The other great and growing influence on Scots law stems from our membership of the European Community. Jacques Delors, former President of the European Commission, has stated that in the 1990s 80% of economic and social law will come from Brussels and it is clear that in areas such as agriculture, fishing, immigration, commercial and tax law, Europe is already exercising a profound influence on legal systems in the United Kingdom.

This even extends to our traditional views on the sovereignty of Parliament. In the Factorfame case in 1991 the European Court of Justice ruled illegal and unenforceable provisions of the 1988 Merchant Shipping Act, legislation which had been validly introduced at Westminster. The European Court said the Act discriminated against people from other Member States on the ground of nationality and was therefore contrary to Community law.

For journalists in particular, the European Court of Human Rights has also issued decisions of major importance in recent years, especially in areas such as freedom of speech and contempt of court. (See chapter 9.) Although decisions of the Human Rights Court are not binding on our judges, the UK

Government is committed to complying with the obligations laid down by the Convention on Human Rights.

Sources of law

01–08 There are four main sources of legal rules—legislation, precedents, writers and custom.

01–09 Legislation or enacted law is the first and most important. This includes Acts of Parliament and subordinate legislation made under powers conferred by Parliament. Acts of Parliament may apply to the whole of the United Kingdom or to part of it. Many apply to Scotland alone. Others, such as the Defamation Act, have sections which apply exclusively to Scotland. Subordinate legislation may take the form of Orders in Council (made in theory by the Queen in Council; in fact by the Government), regulations made by Government Ministers, or rules of procedure made by courts.

The term statutory instruments is used to describe most such legislation. In Scotland the rules made by the Court of Session to regulate procedure in civil cases are known as "Acts of Sederunt," while the rules made by the High Court of Justiciary for regulating procedure in criminal cases are known as "Acts of Adjournal." Subordinate legislation also includes the bye-laws of local authorities and other bodies.

01–10 Precedent or case law is the second source of legal rules. Any body having to make decisions over a period of time tends to seek consistency. Courts of law are no exception. The decisions and opinions of judges in important cases are recorded in law reports and constitute "precedents" if a similar case arises again.

01–11 The general rule is that a court is bound to follow a previous decision of itself and any higher court in the same hierarchy. However, the House of Lords, the highest court in a Scottish civil case, does not now regard itself as absolutely bound by its own previous decisions. Within the Court of Session there is a very convenient procedure whereby a case can be referred to a larger court when it may be necessary to overrule an awkward precedent.

01–12 Not everything said in a case is equally authoritative. A judge may make incidental comments which are not necessary for the decision of the case before him. Statements made "by the way" in this manner are known as *obiter dicta* and are not binding on other judges.

01–13   Writers are the third source of legal rules. Their authority varies. Some, such as Stair (seventeenth century) and Erskine (eighteenth century), are known as "institutional writers" and enjoy a very high authority in Scotland. English law too has its great writers, such as the eighteenth century Blackstone, but they carry less weight than their Scottish counterparts.

01–14   Custom is a subsidiary source of law. The Scottish institutional writers took customary rules and amalgamated them with Roman law to form a coherent system. Custom therefore played an important part in the development of Scots law. In comparatively rare cases custom may still be recognised as a source of law, provided it is certain, fair and not contrary to a definite legal principle. The courts, for example, have applied a custom of the Stock Exchange and a local custom of Caithness regulating the rights of tenants against their landlords.

Two meanings of "common law"

01–15   The journalist may often come across a reference to the phase common law, which can have two meanings. Firstly, it can refer to all law other than that introduced by legislation. Rules derived solely from custom, precedents and the institutional writers, are rules of common law. Secondly, common law is often used in the sense of "English common law." A common law system is one, as in Australia, deriving its inspiration from the English common law.

Two meanings of "civil law"

01–16   Civil law sometimes means Roman law. A civil law system is one, like that of France or, to a lesser degree, Scotland, deriving its inspiration from Roman law. In this sense, civil law is constrasted with the second meaning of common law given above.

01–17   The term civil law is more often used in contrast to criminal law. The civil law is concerned with, for example, divorce, contract, property and actions for damages. The criminal law deals with wrongful acts which are harmful to the community as a whole and which are punished by the State. The same act, for example, careless driving, may give rise to both a criminal prosecution and a civil law claim for damages.

Private and public law

01–18 We have already used the term private law in quoting from the Act of Union. Broadly speaking private law regulates relations between subject and subject while public law regulates relations between State and subject. The law of divorce is a branch of private law. Criminal law is part of public law.

KEY POINTS

Scots Law is a distinct system with the basic differences from England preserved by the Act of Union. UK-wide legislation in areas such as company law means that the two systems now share common features, but Scots law returns many distinctive characteristics such as the children's hearing system, the not proven verdict and the 110-day rule. European law is also an increasing influence.

CHAPTER 2

THE LEGAL PROFESSION

02–01   The legal profession in Scotland is divided into two main branches—solicitors and advocates. Solicitors deal directly with clients and handle all sorts of legal business. Although they plead on behalf of clients in the sheriff and district courts on a daily basis, traditionally they could not, with certain limited exceptions, appear in the Court of Session or in the High Court of Justiciary.

02–02   The privilege of appearing in the Supreme Courts was reserved for members of the Faculty of Advocates. However, this was changed under the Law Reform (Miscellaneous Provisions) Act 1990 which granted solicitors with the required qualifications and experience rights of audience in the higher courts. Under rules drawn up by the Law Society of Scotland and approved by the Lord President, solicitors wishing to plead in the House of Lords, High Court or Court of Session have to lodge an application with the Law Society and undergo a course of "induction training" at the Court of Session to familiarise themselves with procedural rules.

They may also be required to "sit-in" on cases for a specified number of days. The rules also provide for examinations to test the suitability of would-be pleaders and Supreme Courts training courses, including lectures and practical sessions, for solicitors seeking extended rights of audience.

Although solicitor-advocates are a relatively recent phenomenon, they have made significant inroads into work, particularly criminal cases, which had previously been passed by solicitors to the Faculty of Advocates.

02–03   The solicitor intending to practise must have completed the three or four year university LL.B. course or passed the professional examinations set by the Law Society of Scotland. He or she must also attend a post-graduate course for one year and pass examinations to qualify for the Diploma in Legal

Practice. The diploma course supplements the degree studies with emphasis on the practical day-to-day aspects of work in a law office and is followed by two years of practical office training. Practising certificates are issued by the Law Society, the governing body of Scottish solicitors.

02–04   There are various societies of solicitors whose names may cause confusion. Writers to the Signet (W.S.s) and Solicitors in the Supreme Courts (S.S.C.s) are based in Edinburgh and at one time had special privileges in Court of Session work. Other local societies include the Royal Faculty of Procurators in Glasgow and, particularly confusing, the Society of Advocates in Aberdeen. In spite of the diverse names, members of these societies are simply solicitors. The advantages of membership include widows' pensions and library facilities.

02–05   Many solicitors are also notaries public (N.P.s). This privilege, obtained by presenting a petition to the Court of Session, enables the solicitor to act as an official witness to important formal documents.

02–06   Advocates, also referred to as counsel, are not allowed to deal directly with clients and must, as a rule, rely on solicitors for their cases. The solicitor takes the litigant's instructions, interviews witnesses and does all the background work in the case. The advocate may advise on points of law and frame some of the documents involved but his main function is to plead in court.

02–07   To be admitted as an advocate an intrant must have passed, or gained exemption from, certain examinations. He must also have completed a period of professional training in a solicitor's office, and a period as a "devil" or, more accurately, pupil to a practising advocate.

02–08   If the advocate builds up a successful practice he may, after some years, apply to become a Queen's Counsel (Q.C.). This is known as taking silk. He is then a senior counsel and will frequently appear only in cases where a junior appears with him. He will tend to be engaged in fewer, but more difficult and more rewarding, cases.

02–09   Advocates are called barristers in England. Their training is in some respects more colourful than that of their northern brethren. They must join one of four Inns of Court and eat a prescribed number of dinners each term for three years—a system surviving from the days when the main part of the barrister's training consisted of discussion with his peers and superiors at table. Recently, quite a number of Scottish advocates have "taken chambers" under the English system and have qualified by "eating dinners" to become qualified barristers in England. It is perfectly possible to be an advocate in Scotland and a barrister in England at the same time.

Nowadays this, valuable as it may be, is supplemented by more formal instruction, culminating in the sitting of the Bar examinations.

The traditional monopoly enjoyed by barristers of audience before the English High Court of Justice was for the first time broken when, on May 14, 1986, Mr Leo Abse, M.P., made a brief appearance before Mr Justice Caulfield in London. He read an agreed statement in settlement of a libel action which he and 24 other M.P.s brought against Mr Cyril Smith, M.P., for an alleged statement by him during the Falkland Islands conflict accusing them of treason on opposing the Government.

This was followed by the Courts and Legal Services Act 1990 which aimed to allow solicitors much wider rights of audience in the higher courts than they had previously enjoyed. However, the development of the English equivalent of the solicitor-advocate has lagged significantly behind the pace of change in Scotland.

02–10   Barristers tend to specialise much more than advocates and several of those specialising in a particular field often share one set of chambers and one clerk. In Scotland the system is different. Counsel's chambers are generally in their own houses in Edinburgh. They are not, as in England, in the nature of "offices" shared by a group. In Scotland clerical and secretarial services are provided centrally at Parliament House, Edinburgh (where the Court of Session sits), by a small number of advocates' clerks and by an organisation called Faculty Services Ltd.

KEY POINTS

The two main branches of the legal profession are advocates and solicitors. Senior advocates can apply to take silk and become Queen's Counsel. Generally, the solicitor deals directly with the client and instructs the advocate who appears in court. Solicitors with the required training and experience have now been granted the right to plead in the High Court and Court of Session.

Chapter 3

CRIMINAL COURTS AND PROCEDURE

Scottish Criminal Courts

Jurisdiction

03–01 In dealing with courts the word jurisdiction constantly occurs. Its basic meaning is simply a power to hear and decide. A court has appellate jurisdiction if it has power to hear and decide appeals, original jurisdiction if it has power to hear and decide cases coming before it directly, at first instance, and not on appeal from another court.

Summary and solemn jurisdiction

03–02 Courts of summary jurisdiction deal with the less serious crimes. Proceedings begin with a complaint and there is no jury. The punishment which can be awarded is limited. The courts of summary jurisdiction in Scotland are the sheriff courts and district courts.

03–03 Courts of solemn jurisdiction deal with the more serious crimes. Proceedings take place on an indictment and there is always a jury of 15. The sheriff courts and the High Court of Justiciary are the only courts of solemn jurisdiction in Scotland. The sheriff court has both summary and solemn jurisdiction, the sheriff sitting alone in summary cases and with a jury in solemn cases.

District courts

03–04 District courts sit in each local government district or islands area unless the Secretary of State directs, in view of the likely lack of business, that no district court shall be established for a particular district. As from May 1975 they replaced the former justice of the peace courts, burgh courts and police courts. The judges are either lay justices of the peace or legally qualified stipendiary magistrates. Most justices of the peace are appointed by the Secretary of State for Scotland but, in addition, each local authority can nominate up to one quarter of its members to serve as *ex officio* justices for its area. A stipendiary magistrate is appointed by the local authority. He must have been an advocate or a solicitor for at least five years. Only a few district courts have stipendiary magistrates. The majority consist of justices of the peace. Normally the court consists of one or two justices.

03–05 The district courts have jurisdiction over a wide range of minor offences, such as breach of the peace and many offences under local authority bye laws. Except where particular statutes provide otherwise, their powers of punishment are limited to a fine of up to £1,000, or 60 days' imprisonment or both. A district court when constituted by a stipendiary magistrate has, in addition to the above jurisdiction and powers, the summary criminal jurisdiction and powers of a sheriff.

03–06 Prosecutions are conducted by the procurator fiscal who must comply with directions given by the Lord Advocate regarding prosecutions in the district court and must report to the Lord Advocate, if called upon to do so, on matters concerning the discharge of his functions. The clerical work of the court is the responsibility of the clerk of the district court, who is appointed and employed by the local authority. He may be full-time or part-time, and must be an advocate or a solicitor. The clerk also acts as legal assessor in the court, advising the justices about the law and procedure. In busy district courts such as Glasgow, the clerk carries out this function through part-time depute assessors.

03–07 The procedure and rights of appeal in district courts are similar to those in summary procedure in the sheriff courts and will be considered later.

03–08 It has been said that justices need to be "fatherly rather than grandfatherly". For this reason, justices over the age of 65 are put on a supplemental list and cannot perform judicial functions. The Secretary of State has power to place justices under the age of 70 on the supplemental list in certain circumstances—for example, if they decline or neglect to take a proper part in the exercise of their judicial or other functions or to attend suitable courses of instruction.

Children's hearings

03–09   Children's hearings are not really courts at all, although they do in fact deal with most offences committed by children. (See also Chapter 12.) "Children" for this purpose means anyone under the age of 16 and certain children over that age who are already subject to a supervision requirement or who have been referred to the hearing from another part of the United Kingdom. The policy behind the Social Work (Scotland) Act 1968, which introduced children's hearings, is based on therapy rather than punishment.

03–10   In certain circumstances children may be "in need of compulsory measures of care". These circumstances include cases where the child is beyond the control of his parent; where through lack of parental care he is falling into bad associations or is exposed to moral danger; where he has been the victim of certain offences (such as cruelty); or where he has failed to attend school regularly without reasonable excuse.

03–11   The circumstances also include the commission of an offence, and in fact a large proportion of the cases brought before children's hearings are brought on the offence ground. The hearing does not, however, conduct trials. If the grounds of referral are accepted by the child and his parent the hearing proceeds to decide what course would be in the best interests of the child; it may, for example, decide to place him under the supervision of a local authority social work department, or it may decide to send him to a residential establishment. But if the grounds are not accepted—as would be the case if the referral was on an offence ground and the child denied committing the offence—the children's hearing does not proceed. Instead it must either discharge the referral or have the case referred to the sheriff for a finding as to whether the grounds are established.

03–12   A referral hearing before a sheriff takes the form of a proof as in a civil court. Witnesses are put on oath and their evidence is subject to cross-examination. The standard of proof which the sheriff applies is the same as in civil courts—on a balance of probabilities. It is important to note that the sheriff does not dispose of the case himself even if he is hearing a referral. If he finds the facts established he simply remits the case back to the children's hearing for disposal. To use a criminal analogy (although it is not entirely appropriate) the sheriff decides on conviction, but not sentence.

03–13 The same result follows if the hearing considers that the grounds have not been understood by the child. This can be a case where the child is too young to understand. In some cases new-born babies have been taken into care if the social work authorities believe the parents are not capable of taking care of the child or if the child is in some form of danger. For example, an elder brother or sister may have been assaulted or abused in the past. If the sheriff finds the ground established the case goes back to a children's hearing for the appropriate measures to be taken. Hearings also have power to deal with cases referred under the Solvent Abuse (Scotland) Act 1983.

03–14 The people who sit on children's hearings are lay volunteers drawn from carefully selected children's panels. The organisation of hearings and the referral of cases to them are the responsibility of an officer called (rather confusingly) "the reporter", who is appointed and paid by the local authority. Procedure at the hearings is quite informal. The public is not admitted, but *bona fide* press representatives may attend. There is a strict ban on identifying any child in any way concerned in a hearing. This is dealt with in more detail in Chapter 12.

03–15 Appeal from any decision of the children's hearing lies to the sheriff. Appeal from any decision of the sheriff in relation to the children's hearing lies to the Court of Session by way of stated case (explained later) on a point of law or in respect of any irregularity in the conduct of the case.

03–16 The rôle of the media in covering children's hearings was a central issue in the long-running inquiry, beginning in August 1991, into allegations of child sex abuse on Orkney. Some sections of the media were severely criticised for "taking the side" of parents whose children were said to have been abused. The conduct of the media was given as one of the reasons why place-of-safety orders could not continue in force and children had to be returned home. The case illustrated the extreme difficulties of producing balanced reports in this type of case where one side, the reporter, feels unable to comment because of confidentiality. Because of what happened in the Orkney case, submissions were made to Lord Clyde, the judge in charge of the inquiry, that the media should no longer be allowed to attend children's hearings.

Sheriff courts

03–17 The sheriff courts deal with most criminal cases in Scotland. The judge is either the sheriff or the sheriff principal. Both are appointed by the Crown on the recommendation of the Secretary of State for Scotland who in turn acts on the advice of the Lord Advocate. Both must be advocates or solicitors of at least 10 years' standing. There are six sheriffdoms in Scotland—Grampian, Highland and Islands; Tayside, Central and Fife; Lothian and Borders; Glasgow and Strathkelvin; North Strathclyde; and South Strathclyde, Dumfries and Galloway. Each is headed by a sheriff principal who, in addition to his judicial functions, has a general duty to secure the speedy and efficient disposal of business in the sheriff courts of his sheriffdom and who has correspondingly wide administrative functions.

03–18 The sheriff courts have a very wide criminal jurisdiction, both solemn and summary. There are three limitations. Firstly, the jurisdiction is limited geographically. As a general rule a sheriff can deal only with crimes committed within his sheriffdom. Secondly, the jurisdiction does not extend to certain crimes, of which the most important are treason, murder and rape. Thirdly, the sheriff's powers of punishment are limited to three months' imprisonment in most summary cases and three years' imprisonment in solemn cases. In its "Firm and Fair" White Paper (a review of Scottish criminal procedure published in 1994 the Government did not support the idea of increasing the sentencing powers of the Sheriff at present—but it is clear that this is still under review. The increasing pressure on the High Court points towards increased powers for Sheriffs at some point.

03–19 The prosecutor in the sheriff court is the procurator-fiscal or his depute. The administrative work is done by the sheriff-clerk and his deputes.

High Court of Justiciary

3–20 The judges of the High Court of Justiciary are the Lord Justice-General (who is the same person as the Lord President of the Court of Session), the Lord Justice-Clerk and 24 Lords Commissioners of Justiciary. All are also judges of the Court of Session and Senators of the College of Justice. They are appointed by the Crown on the advice of the Lord Advocate and can be removed from office only for gross misconduct. The 1990 Law Reform Act also made provision for "temporary" High Court judges, leading to the appointment of two leading Q.C.'s and two sheriffs. The number of temporary judges soon increased to eight.

3–21 The seat of the High Court is at Parliament House in Edinburgh, but it also goes on circuit to other parts of Scotland. All of the judges do not, of course, sit in each case. Normally there is only one but difficult cases can be heard by two or more.

3–22 The High Court deals with the most serious crimes and is the only court which can try treason, murder or rape. Prosecutions are conducted by the Lord Advocate, the Solicitor-General, or, more usually, an advocate-depute.

3–23 The High Court also has jurisdiction to hear appeals from and review the decisions of cases heard on summary procedure. When sitting for this purpose it consists of at least three judges and is commonly referred to as the Justiciary Appeal Court. It has the important duty of reviewing proceedings in all inferior criminal courts with a view to seeing that justice is done.

Court of Criminal Appeal

3–24 Strictly speaking, there is no such court in Scotland. However, the "Scottish Court of Criminal Appeal" is a convenient term frequently used instead of the more correct but cumbersome "High Court of Justiciary sitting as a Court of Criminal Appeal". The court hears appeals against conviction or sentence in trials heard on solemn procedure. It is the highest Scottish criminal court. There is no appeal to the House of Lords. Three judges form a quorum but in difficult cases more may sit. In its White Paper "Firm and Fair" in June 1994, the Government proposed a system of weeding out worthless appeals by means of a single judge "sift." Only if he granted leave would the case proceed to the appeal court. This would apply in both solemn and summary cases. The White Paper, whose aim was to improve the delivery of justice in Scotland, also proposed that appeals against sentence would be heard by two judges rather than three.

SCOTTISH CRIMINAL PROCEDURE

03–25 Although the details of criminal procedure can be left to the lawyer, the journalist should know the steps in outline so that he can tell what is happening and what is about to happen. In this field the laws of Scotland and England are very different. To take only one example, private prosecutions are common in England but very rare in Scotland. An outstanding case occurred in 1982 when, after the Crown had decided not to prosecute three youths following a particularly vicious attack upon a woman in Glasgow, the High Court granted her authority to bring a private prosecution (by the old process of issuing a bill for criminal letters). The case went to trial and resulted in convictions for rape against one youth and for indecent assault against two others. It was the first private prosecution to have been allowed and to have succeeded under this procedure in Scotland since 1909. The three judges who authorised the private prosecution described the case as strange and unique, the Crown having earlier dropped proceedings against the youths following a psychiatric report that the risk of damage to the victim's health if she appeared in court made it inadvisable that she be called as a witness. The court's decision to allow her to proceed was reached after the judges were satisfied that she would after all be able to appear and give evidence, without which it was originally thought a prosecution could not succeed. The court ruled that there was no doubt the woman had the necessary title and interest to prosecute privately, and this course was not opposed by the Lord Advocate.

03–26 The Lord Advocate, assisted by the Solicitor-General for Scotland, is responsible for the investigation and prosecution of crime in Scotland. Both are appointed by the Crown. It is usual, but not always possible, for at least one of them to have a seat in Parliament. In practice the Lord-Advocate delegates most of his responsibility in criminal matters to advocates-depute who work, along with a staff of officials, at the Crown Office in Edinburgh. The procurators-fiscal investigate crime at the local level under the general supervision of the Crown Office. In the case of minor offences the procurator-fiscal has a discretion whether or not to prosecute, or to issue a formal written warning, with the implied sanction of a prosecution if the warning is not heeded. He reports more serious crimes to the Crown Office which decides whether to prosecute and, if so, in which court.

3–27   Two general principles should be noted at this stage. The first is that everyone is innocent until he is proved guilty beyond reasonable doubt (and in Scotland the proof must normally be by the evidence of at least two witnesses). The second is a principle of great importance to journalists which will be dealt with in more detail later. It is that there must be no publicity which may seriously prejudice a person's trial. (See Chapter 9.)

3–28   There are two types of criminal procedure—summary and solemn. Different rules apply but the preliminary steps are the same. The first stage is generally the police investigation under the authority of the procurator-fiscal. Newspapers have sometimes played an active part in the exposure of crime but there is a grave risk of contempt of court if anything is published after arrest has been made or a warrant granted for arrest which creates a substantial risk of seriously prejudicing or impeding the course of justice.

3–29   The police often enlist the help of the media in their inquiries and there is probably no danger in assisting as requested. In certain cases, however, it may be wise to check that the request has been cleared by the procurator-fiscal. This would be advisable, for example, if the request is to publish a photograph of a wanted man in a case where the question of identification could arise at a later stage. Even if the Crown approves the release of a photograph, or an identikit likeness, it should be remembered that the defence can independently raise the issue of contempt. However, a finding of contempt would be extremely unlikely in these circumstances.

03–30   The investigations may result in an arrest. Normally a warrant is required but some statutes allow arrest without warrant. A policeman can arrest without warrant when he finds a person committing or attempting to commit a serious crime or when he is told by the victim or a credible eye-witness that this has just occurred. He can also arrest without warrant in cases of breach of the peace or threatened violence or in certain circumstances when he finds a person in possession of stolen goods and unable to give a satisfactory explanation.

Summary procedure

03–31   Where the accused has not been arrested, but has simply been cited to appear, he may plead in person, through a solicitor or by letter. If he pleads guilty in his absence, he may, subject to certain safeguards, be sentenced there and then. If he pleads not guilty a date will be fixed for a trial.

03–32   The procedure at the trial is straightforward. The prosecutor calls his first witness and examines him. The defence can cross-examine, after which the prosecution has a limited right to re-examine. After all the evidence for the prosecution has been led, the evidence for the defence is led. Then the prosecutor addresses the court, followed by the accused or his agent and the judge pronounces his finding. This may be either guilty, not guilty or not proven. A finding of not proven has the same effect as a finding of not guilty. It is used where the court is not satisfied that the man is innocent but the prosecution has failed to prove that he is guilty. If the accused is found guilty he is allowed to address the court before sentence is pronounced.

Criminal Justice (Scotland) Act 1980

03–33   Criminal procedure was consolidated in the Criminal Procedure (Scotland) Act 1975, amended in a number of important respects by the Criminal Justice (Scotland) Act 1980. The 1980 Act introduced several novelties into the criminal law with which journalists should be familiar. The most important of these are noted in summary here. Provision made under s.22 of the 1980 Act for anonymity of children in criminal cases is dealt with in Chapter 12.

03–34   The Act gives police powers to detain a suspect for up to six hours while they make investigations to enable them to decide whether there is sufficient evidence to arrest him. The strict liability rule under the contempt of court law (outlined in Chapter 9) does not come into operation until the arrest stage is reached or a warrant is granted but the journalist must still exercise great caution about what he reports at the detention stage. Publication of information which creates a serious risk of prejudice to any future trial before an arrest is made or a warrant issued may be regarded as contempt at common law.

03–35   There are safeguards for the detainee: he is not obliged to answer any questions other than those intended to find out his name and address; he has to be told the nature of the suspected offence; he is entitled to have his detention intimated to a solicitor and one other person of his choice; and if not arrested at the end of six hours' detention he must be released and cannot again be detained on the same grounds. If he is arrested he is entitled to have this fact intimated to a person named by him without unnecessary delay. There are special safeguards for children.

03–36   Under section 4 of the 1980 Act a constable may search a person without warrant if he has reasonable grounds for suspecting he carries an offensive weapon, and can arrest anyone who obstructs the search or conceals such a weapon. By section 5 a constable with power to arrest without warrant, who suspects a person is drunk, may take him to a place designated for drunken persons which has been selected by the Scottish Secretary. The person is not liable to be detained there but may be charged with an offence.

03–37   The Act gives an accused the right to petition the sheriff to have an identification parade held where the prosecutor has not already made arrangements for one and the sheriff considers it reasonable.

03–38   In summary cases an accused who is refused bail by the court and is kept in custody must not be detained for more than 40 days after his initial court appearance. The court, however, has power to grant an extension for reasons similar to those provided under solemn procedure (referred to below), and subject to a right of appeal by either side.

03–39   District courts have power, under section 7, to try certain classes of motoring offence, including endorsable offences but not those which involve automatic disqualification, and a large range of other offences including theft or reset, falsehood, fraud or wilful imposition, breach of trust or embezzlement involving an amount not exceeding £1,000.

Solemn procedure

03–40 In solemn procedure the accused's first appearance in court is on petition in chambers before a sheriff, and all that can be published about the proceedings at this stage, besides the identity of the accused (unless he is a child) is a general indication of the nature of the charges, supplied usually by the procurator-fiscal. It is important to remember that the fiscal may later proceed on an amended charge, or charges, or even drop proceedings altogether, although this is unusual.

03–41 Under the 1980 Act, the first pleading diet, 10 days before trial, is no longer mandatory. However in 1994 the Government proposed the introduction of a mandatory intermediate diet. This was an attempt to cut down on the number of trials postponed at the last minute, causing great inconvenience to witnesss and jurors. The mandatory diet was to be introduced for summary and sheriff and jury cases. If the accused is pleading not guilty he must give notice of any special defences such as alibi, self-defence, incrimination (accusing someone else of the crime charged) or insanity at the time of the crime.

03–42 The Act revives judicial examination as a method of discovering, at a hearing in chambers before a sheriff, what explanation or comment the suspect may have on any incriminating statement he is alleged to have made. He can be questioned by the fiscal under the control of the sheriff who must ensure questioning is fair. The accused has a right to be represented by a solicitor and to consult him before answering any question, and the solicitor may ask him questions to clear up any ambiguity. A shorthand record is kept of the examination and a copy of the transcript must be made available to the accused. The record, or any part of it, may be used in evidence. The journalist is not allowed into these proceedings and will have to rely on the procurator-fiscal or the defence agent for information as to what took place. In that situation, particular care must be taken with any report.

03–43 The Act requires that a trial under solemn procedure must start within 12 months of the accused's first appearance on petition; otherwise he must be discharged and cannot be charged again with the same offence—unless delay has been caused by his failure to appear or an extension has been granted by the court. The Act also requires that an accused must not be kept in custody for more than 80 days before being served with an indictment, and the trial must commence within 110 days of his appearance in court at his full committal. Full committal usually takes place one week after the first appearance of the accused. These periods can be extended if the court is satisfied (in regard to the 110-day rule) that this is justified because of illness of the accused or a judge, absence or illness of a necessary witness, or other "sufficient cause". The grant or refusal of an extension is subject to appeal.

03–44   If during the trial the court decides that, because of the accused's misconduct, a proper hearing cannot take place unless he is removed, it may order that the trial proceed in his absence, although he must be legally represented.

03–45   In court the accused is called "the panel". The trial takes place before a judge and a jury of 15. The 1980 Act reduces from five to three the number of challenges of jurors allowed to each side without giving any reason. Any additional objections must be supported by a reason related to the particular juror. In its 1994 White Paper on criminal procedure "Firm and Fair" the Government proposes the abolition of challenges without reasons given. It intends to allow challenges only "on cause shown". The clerk of court informs the jury of the charge and administers the oath. Evidence is led for the prosecution, followed by evidence for the defence. In rare cases, the Crown can lead what is known as evidence in replication after the defence case has closed. This evidence can rebut defence evidence which the Crown could not reasonably have anticipated.

03–46   The prosecution and the defence address the jury in turn and the judge charges the jury. The general principle is that the jury are masters of the facts and the judge master of the law. His main duty in charging the jury is to set out the law applicable to the case but he may also make fair and impartial comments on the evidence. After the charge the jury retire to consider their verdict, which may be by a majority, even 8–7, and will be "Guilty", "Not Guilty" or "Not Proven". In the rare case where the accused is found to have been insane at the time of the alleged crime, he will be found not guilty on the ground of insanity.

03–47   If the verdict is "Guilty" then, after the prosecutor has moved for sentence and any previous convictions have been admitted or proved, the accused or his counsel or solicitor may make a plea in mitigation of sentence. The judge will then pronounce sentence, but if the trial has been in the sheriff court and the sheriff thinks the offence merits a heavier sentence than he can impose, he can remit to the High Court for sentence.

03–48   The accused may inform the Crown that he wants to plead guilty and have his case be disposed of as quickly as possible. He gets a shortened form of indictment and appears for sentence on what is known as a section 102 hearing. (The procedure is provided under section 102 of the Criminal Procedure (Scotland) Act 1975.)

03–49   The only sentence for murder is life imprisonment except where the person convicted is under 18, in which case the sentence is detention without limit of time in a place and under conditions to be directed by the Scottish Secretary. If he is over 18 but under 21, the sentence is detention for life at first in a young offenders' institution and then in prison. Where the sentence passed is for life the judge may recommend the minimum term to be served and must give his reasons if he does so; a recommendation is appealable as part of the sentence.

03–50   No prison sentence may be imposed on a person over 21 who has not previously been so sentenced to detention, unless the court thinks no other course is appropriate. No one under 21 may be sent to prison, and borstal training is replaced by detention in a young offenders' institution.

03–51   At the close of the prosecution evidence in either solemn or summary procedure the accused is entitled (in solemn procedure in the absence of the jury) to submit a plea that there is no case to answer. If the plea is sustained the accused is acquitted, if refused the trial proceeds to defence evidence. Any report of submissions made on such a plea can be safely published only after the proceedings have ceased to be "active" (see Chapter 9, "Contempt of Court").

03–52 The 1980 Act creates the new category of offence known as vandalism, which it defines as wilfully or recklessly destroying or damaging anyone else's property without reasonable excuse.

03–53 It also provides that it is no longer an offence for consenting parties over 21 to perform a homosexual act in private provided no more than two persons are present and it does not take place in a public lavatory.

03–54 Offenders can be ordered to pay compensation to their victims, either instead of or in addition to any other method the court may select for dealing with them, for personal injury, loss or damage caused by their offences. The provisions do not apply to loss resulting from death or from a road accident unless caused by the convicted person. There is no limit to compensation under solemn procedure, but in summary cases the limits are set by statute. Where the convicted person's means are insufficient to meet a fine besides compensation, priority is given to compensation. A compensation order is treated as a sentence for appeal purposes.

03–55 Part of the Act is designed to control violence at or in connection with sporting events. It is illegal to carry alcohol on public service vehicles, or other vehicles adapted to carry more than eight passengers, taking spectators to or from games held at grounds designated by the Scottish Secretary, to be in possession of alcohol when entering such a ground or have any firework, flare or smoke bomb or container for liquid which could be used as a missile, or to be drunk at the ground or when entering it.

03–56 The main differences between summary and solemn procedure can be summed up as follows. In summary procedure there is no petition for committal. Proceedings begin with the complaint. In solemn procedure there is usually a petition for committal and proceedings are on indictment. Cases of summary procedure are heard in the sheriff courts or district courts. There is no jury. Cases on solemn procedure are heard in the sheriff or High Court and there is a jury. Appeal in summary procedure is by stated case or bill of suspension to three judges sitting as the Justiciary Appeal Court. Appeal in solemn procedure is to at least three judges of the High Court sitting as a Court of Criminal Appeal.

Summary appeals

03–57 The 1980 Act made some important changes to the procedure for appeals in summary cases. The initial step is an application for a stated case, note of appeal (against sentence only) or bill of suspension, which must take place within one week of the decision under appeal (the stage at which the proceedings again become active under the Contempt of Court Act 1981: see Chapter 9).

03–58 The draft stated case prepared by the sheriff or justice is subject to adjustments proposed by either side if they are agreed at a hearing arranged for this purpose. The judge stating a case for appeal must give his reasons if he refuses any adjustments, and these may be taken into account by the appeal court, which also has power to hear additional evidence or order that this be heard by a person it appoints for the purpose. The appeal court may also appoint an assessor with expert knowledge to assist in deciding an appeal.

03–59 There is also a right of appeal against conviction by way of bill of suspension where the stated case procedure would not be appropriate or competent. The prosecutor may appeal against acquittal or sentence on grounds, in either case, of alleged miscarriage of justice. The court may remit a case back with directions to affirm the verdict, quash the verdict and authorise a new prosecution (to be begun within two months) on the same or similar charges as before. Where an appeal against acquittal is sustained the court may convict and sentence the respondent, remit the case back to the court below with instructions to do so, or remit back to the lower court with the appeal court's opinion and direction.

Solemn appeals

03–60 Where the appeal court in solemn procedure has allowed an appeal against conviction on the ground that there has been a miscarriage of justice, a new prosecution may be brought within two months charging the accused with the same or any similar offence arising out of the same facts. However, no sentence may be passed which could not have been passed in the original proceedings.

03–61 In the first case to be brought under this provision, a man who had been charged in 1982 with the murder of his wife's lover was convicted of culpable homicide in the High Court at Inverness. He appealed successfully, on the ground that a misdirection by the trial judge had led to a miscarriage of justice. Under the old law he would have been freed, but under the 1980 Act the Lord Advocate was granted authority by the appeal court to bring a fresh prosecution. This time, the man was charged with culpable homicide and the second trial took place at Edinburgh to avoid the risk of prejudice from local knowledge in Inverness of the original hearing and conviction. The charge was found not proven and the accused was released. Evidence at the two trials was for the most part identical.

03–62 While in theory there is no limit to the number of retrials in any case, in practice more than one is unlikely. The new trial procedure is used only where a conviction at the first trial is quashed on what amounts to a technicality.

03–63 The procedure is exceptional, compared to practice in England where retrials are relatively common, but the 1980 Act brought to an end the fundamental rule in Scotland that an accused could not be tried more than once on the same charge. In such a case the proceedings remain active under the Contempt of Court Act from the time authority for a new prosecution is granted by the court, until a new trial is concluded or a decision is taken to drop further proceedings.

03–64 An accused may appeal against conviction, sentence, or both, on grounds of alleged miscarriage of justice, and formal notice has to be lodged at the Justiciary Office in Edinburgh within two weeks. This has special significance when the question of publicity arises after the end of a trial. The appeal court may uphold the verdict, quash the conviction, substitute an amended verdict of guilty (and pass a different sentence from that already passed), or, as we have seen, set aside the verdict and grant authority for a new prosecution. Where the appeal is against sentence the court has power not only to reduce but also to increase the original sentence.

03–65 Where some important point of law arises during a case where an accused has been acquitted, the Lord Advocate may refer it to the High Court for its opinion, although this will not affect the acquittal. From October 1993 the Crown has had a right of appeal against (what it feels) are unduly lenient sentences in solemn cases; S42 of the Prisoners & Criminal

Proceedings (Scotland) Act 1993. An appeal can be taken by the Crown against a sentence imposed by either a Sheriff or a High Court Judge. The legislation will be extended to allow the Crown a similar right in respect of summary cases if and when the Secretary of State for Scotland chooses to make an order to that effect. To date he has not done so. In September 1994 the Crown appealed against a sentence of probation and community service imposed by the Sheriff at Ayr on a drug dealer who had supplied LSD to schoolgirls. The Court of Criminal Appeal increased the sentence to three years' detention.

03–66   In both solemn and summary appeals there is provision for the hearing of additional evidence not available at the trial, and in either situation the Crown may appeal by bill of advocation. The High Court also has power under section 252 of the Criminal Procedure (Scotland) Act 1975 to allow the hearing of new evidence of any witnesses whether or not they were called at the trial.

03–67   This procedure was used in 1983 when two Ayrshire youths convicted of rape were acquitted after the appeal court considered fresh evidence from a psychiatrist. He stated that the supposed victim had a history of sexual fantasies and was prone to making unwarranted accusations of rape and sexual interference. The Crown had reportedly been unaware of this condition of the alleged victim at the time of the trial. The appeal court held there had been a miscarriage of justice and the youths were released. The effect on publicity of the law of contempt in such a situation does not appear to be specifically covered by the Contempt of Court Act. However, where a hearing of new evidence is allowed, it is safe to assume the case is in the same position as where the appeal court "remits the case to the court below" and remains active from conclusion of the appeal proceedings until the hearing of the new evidence and ultimate disposal of the case.

Bail

03–68   A man is presumed innocent until he is proved guilty and should not, without good reason, be deprived of his liberty before conviction. It is reasonable, however, that if he goes free he should be required to give some security that he will appear at later stages in the proceedings. Bail is a means to this end.

03–69 Until the passing of the Bail etc. (Scotland) Act 1980, the normal security took the form of a payment of money under a bail bond, but the Act effectively abolished money bail except in special circumstances. Bail is now granted subject to conditions, laid down by the court or the Lord Advocate, to which the bail applicant must subscribe.

03–70 These will, for example, be that he will appear at a court diet when required, does not commit an offence while on bail or interfere with witnesses or obstruct the course of justice in any other way. He may also be required to make himself available to enable inquiries to be made or a report prepared to assist the court, or be required to report regularly at a police station, or stay away from his wife or family or other person(s) specified in the conditions attached to his bail. In special circumstances either the accused or someone on his behalf may be required to lodge money in court to ensure his attendance at a future hearing. The money may be forfeited if he fails to attend.

03–71 Liberation on bail may also be granted by the police after arrest on a summary charge, and if the accused is refused bail at this stage he may apply to the court for bail. Because the conditions of bail are contained in a document, a copy of which the accused must receive, and which must show also his normal place of residence, access to the addresses of accused persons is more readily available to the media under the terms of the Bail Act than before it, when the accused was frequently cited at the sheriff-clerk's office.

03–72 In deciding whether or not to grant bail the court may take into account the type of crime charged—whether, for example, it involves alleged interference with witnesses—or whether the applicant has a criminal record, and if so what bearing that may have upon the possibility of his being in breach of conditions attached to bail. In each case the court has to balance the right of the untried person to the presumption of innocence against the risk of justice being frustrated by his failure to keep his part of the bargain.

03–73 For breach of his undertaking the person granted bail may be fined and jailed for a maximum of three months in a summary case in the sheriff court or a similar sum and 60 days in

the district court. If he is charged on indictment, he is liable
to a fine (with no maximum laid down) and imprisonment up
to two years. Any penalty imposed may be in addition to the
sentence passed by the court in respect of the original offence.

03–74   The only crimes not bailable are murder and treason, except
by the authority of the Lord Advocate or the High Court.

03–75   In addition to the provisions for pre-trial bail, anyone convicted and sentenced to jail or detention may be granted bail
pending disposal of an appeal.

03–76   There is a right of appeal against refusal or against the conditions attached to the granting of bail. The Crown may
appeal against the granting of bail. In either case the appeal
is normally heard by a High Court judge in chambers. The
proceedings are kept private to protect the accused from possible prejudice arising from publicity given to statements
made as a necessary part of information required by the judge.
These may relate to the accused's record or other matters
likely to influence the minds of potential jurors or witnesses
at a subsequent trial. This kind of information must not
appear in any report at this stage. Reporters, however, have a
right of access to the decision, and this information is usually
supplied by the Justiciary Office.

English Courts

03–77   Mainly for the benefit of Scottish journalists who sometimes
have to cover cases taking place in England, we have included
a brief guide to the court structure south of the Border.

03–78   At the lowest level are about 700 magistrates' courts which
handle more than two million cases a year, both civil and
criminal. On the criminal side they resemble district courts,
but also deal with more serious cases such as assault which
would normally be dealt with by a sheriff in Scotland. On the
civil side magistrates handle a variety of cases such as claims
for maintenance payments and childcare.

03–79   The Crown Court tries all serious crimes such as murder
and rape. There are 94 Crown Courts in six Crown Court
areas. Four types of judges sit in Crown Courts—High Court
judges, circuit judges, recorder's and assistant recorders. High
Court judges are referred to as, for example Mr Justice Jones,

circuit Judges as Judge Jones Appeals are heard by the Court of Appeal (Criminal) headed by the Lord Chief Justice. From there a further appeal can be taken to the House of Lords.

03–80 No matter how serious the charge, criminal proceedings in England and Wales normally start in the magistrates' court. The defendant in England has more control over the method of trial, for example in choosing to be tried by a jury, than the accused in Scotland. In Scotland the method of trial, in so far as the law allows a choice, is within the discretion of the prosecution, the only minor exception being the accelerated trial procedure noted above.

03–81 English criminal procedure differs from Scottish in a number of important ways. There is a preliminary inquiry by the justices into indictable offences to see whether or not a person should stand trial. This inquiry is in public but there are restrictions on publicity, designed to avoid the risk of prejudice to the defendant.

These are dealt with in detail in Chapter 30, but the general principle is that the evidence called by either side cannot be published until after the trial, if the defendant is committed for trial, or until after the committal proceedings, if he is not. The Criminal Justice Act 1991 established youth courts to deal with young people who were under 18 when they committed an offence.

03–82 A criminal jury in England consists of 12 and not, as in Scotland, 15 jurors. The verdict is either "Guilty" or "Not Guilty". English law regards a unanimous verdict as normal and desirable, but since 1967 has made provision for a majority verdict. A majority verdict must be supported by at least 10 jurors (or nine if the number of the jury has been reduced to 10 by death, illness or other cause). The Crown Court cannot accept a majority verdict unless it appears to the court that the jury have had a reasonable time for deliberation. The time can vary according to the nature and complexity of the case, but in any event must be at least two hours. In England there is no verdict of "Not Proven".

03–83 At the actual trial an important difference is that in England the prosecutor begins by making an opening speech instead of, as in Scotland, simply leading his evidence. Although useful for the media, this practice has been criticised on the ground that counsel may make allegations which are not fully supported by the subsequent evidence but which may make a profound impression on the minds of the jury.

03–84   Finally, in England applications for bail are often dealt with in public by the justices conducting the preliminary inquiry into indictable offences. In Scotland privacy is the general rule.

03–85   In 1986 English criminal procedure took an important step towards the Scottish model by transferring the conduct of prosecutions from the police to a network of centrally-funded Crown prosecutors under the authority of the Director of Public Prosecutions, who reports to the Attorney-General and who deals with difficult or sensitive cases involving a political element. In Crown Courts the prosecution is handled by barristers in private practice briefed by Crown Prosecution Service solicitors or barristers directly employed by the service.

KEY POINTS

03–86   There are three criminal courts—High Court, sheriff and district. The Lord Advocate is responsible for the investigation and prosecution of crime. Private prosecutions are extremely rare. Solemn procedure (dealing with the most serious cases) begins by way of a petition and cases are heard by a judge or sheriff and a jury of 15. Maximum sheriff court sentence is three years. Certain cases such as murder and rape must be taken in the High Court. There is no opening speech and the verdict can be by a simple majority. Summary cases start with a complaint and are heard by justice or sheriff sitting alone. Appeal is to three High Court judges. In certain cases the Appeal Court can grant authority for a retrial.

CHAPTER 4

CIVIL COURTS AND PROCEDURE

SCOTTISH CIVIL COURTS

Sheriff court

04–01 The sheriff court has a very wide civil jurisdiction extending to almost all types of action. Exceptions are actions of reduction of deeds and actions to prove the tenor of lost documents. Legislation introduced in 1982 gave sheriffs jurisdiction to deal with divorce actions (see Chapter 11). They already had power to handle actions for judicial separation, separation and aliment, or affiliation and aliment. Actions involving amounts under £1,500 must be brought in the sheriff court. They cannot be heard by the Court of Session. There is no upper limit to the value of cases which can be dealt with in the sheriff court. Civil jury trial in the sheriff court was abolished in 1980.

04–02 An important part of the sheriff court's work is its commissary jurisdiction involving the appointment and confirmation of executors to administer the estates of people who have died. Only when he has obtained confirmation is an executor entitled to uplift and administer the estate.

04–03 Procedure in civil cases in the sheriff court was modified by the introduction of the summary cause in 1971 and again by the introduction of the small claims procedure in 1988. Certain cases, including all actions for payment of sums of money between £750 and £1,500 (excluding interest and expenses) are known as summary causes. They are begun by filling in a printed form of summons. Evidence is not recorded. Appeal lies from a final judgment of the sheriff to the sheriff principal on any point of law, and then from the sheriff principal to the Inner House of the Court of Session if the sheriff principal certifies the case as suitable for such an appeal.

04–04 The small claims procedure applies to actions where the money value does not exceed £750. It was introduced after criticism of court procedures by the consumer lobby, which claimed that even the summary cause procedure was too difficult for lay people to understand. In small claims cases both pursuers and defenders are encouraged to "do it yourself". There is a preliminary hearing at which the sheriff tries to determine the issue between the parties. This takes the form of an informal discussion involving the sheriff, pursuer and defender of their representatives. If matters cannot be resolved at this stage the case is adjourned for a proof hearing at which, again, the emphasis is on informality. There is a right of appeal on a point of law to the sheriff principal, although appeals in small claims cases are extremely rare. The system seems to have been based on the arbitration procedure used for low value cases in the English county courts. The early impression among sheriffs, solicitors and the consumer lobby appeared to be that the system was not working satisfactorily.

04–05   The procedure in ordinary causes, including actions for amounts over £1,500, is more formal and follows the lines of Court of Session procedure, with some modifications noted later. Appeal is either to the sheriff principal and from him to the Inner House of the Court of Session, or else direct to the Inner House of the Court of Session.

The Court of Session

04–06   The Court of Session sits in Edinburgh and consists of the Lord President, Lord Justice-Clerk and 24 other judges. As we have seen, the personnel is the same as that of the High Court of Justiciary. Because of pressure of business, the 1990 Law Reform Act provided for temporary judges to sit in the High Court and Court of Session. The first four appointments were two leading Queen's Counsel and two sheriffs. They sit on the Bench dressed as QCs, and do not wear the traditional judges' robes.

04–07   The court is divided into an Inner House which is largely an appeal court, and an Outer House which deals with cases at first instance. The Court of Session remains one court, however. The division between Inner and Outer House is not a strict one. Judges from the Inner House may sit as single judges in the Outer House to help with pressure of work, and judges from the Outer House may be brought in to make up an additional appellate bench, known as the Extra Division. In theory, the court could still sit as a whole court to hear cases of particular difficulty but the raising of the number of judges and limitations of space have made this impracticable.

04–08 The Inner House is in turn divided into two divisions of equal status, the First Division and the Second Division. The First Division consists of the Lord President and three judges. The Second Division consists of the Lord Justice-Clerk and three judges. The Outer House consists of judges who sit singly and are known as Lords Ordinary. The reason for this peculiar name is that at one time there were two types of judges in the Court of Session, Ordinary Lords and Extraordinary Lords, the latter being nominees of the King and needing no legal qualifications. The power of appointing Extraordinary Lords was lost in 1723.

04–09 The Inner House is mainly an appeal court, hearing appeals from the sheriff courts and from the Outer House as well as from various other special courts and tribunals. It also has an original jurisdiction in certain types of petition including many petitions to the *nobile officium.*

04–10 The Court of Session has a general power to review the judgments of inferior courts and tribunals on the ground that they have exceeded their jurisdiction or have failed to observe fundamental rules of justice, such as the rule that both parties must be heard before a decision is given.

The House of Lords

04–11 There is an appeal from the Court of Session to the House of Lords. An appeal must be lodged within three months of the judgment appealed from.

PROCEDURE IN CIVIL CASES IN SCOTLAND

04–12 What follows is merely an outline designed to give a general picture of the steps involved in getting a case into court. The person who brings an ordinary civil action is called the pursuer, the person against whom it is brought, the defender.

04–13   In the case of ordinary actions in the Court of Session, the first step is for the pursuer's solicitor or counsel to prepare a *summons*. This is, in essence, a document summoning the defender to appear at court, setting out the pursuer's claim and asking the court to give judgment in his favour. A copy of the summons is served on the defender, usually by recorded delivery or registered post. There is then a period of grace, known as the *induciae*, to give the defender time to take legal advice and decide on his course of action.

04–14   When this period expires, the pursuer's solicitor lodges in the court offices what is known as the *process*, which consists of the summons and various other documents which will be needed later in the proceedings.

04–15   The next stage is that the case appears in the *calling list* of the Court of Session. This is the first public announcement of the action. The only details given are the names and addresses of the parties and the names of the pursuer's solicitors.

04–16   If the defender does not defend, the court will give judgment for the pursuer—a decree in absence. In divorce and other actions affecting status, however, decree will not be given until the grounds of action have been proved by sufficient evidence. If the defender does wish to defend, he must enter appearance and lodge *defences* containing his answers to the pursuer's allegations.

04–17   In an action for divorce or separation, however, there is no open record; the parties merely note their adjustments on the summons and defences.

04–18   After the parties have completed their adjustments, the court makes an order closing the record. A *closed record* is then printed and added to the process.

04–19   The next steps in the procedure vary. There may be a preliminary dispute about further procedure and this may have to be decided by a judge. In the normal course of events, the case will eventually be heard by a judge alone or, much more rarely, by a judge and jury. An action for damages which involves difficult questions of fact and law may be regarded as unsuitable for a jury. In civil cases, the jury numbers 12 and may return a majority verdict. The procedure in court is dealt with later in the section on court reporting (see Chapter 13).

04–20   To sum up, the procedure in an ordinary civil action in the

Court of Session is, in rough outline, summons—lodging of process—case in calling list—appearance—defences—open record—closed record—proof or jury trial.

04–21   The procedure in an ordinary civil action in the sheriff court is broadly similar. The pursuer's solicitor draws up an *initial writ* instead of a summons and a copy is served on the defender. There is no calling list as such and the defender must, if he wishes to defend, enter appearance *within* the *induciae*. Thereafter he must lodge defences. Adjustments are now exchanged between parties only. They are not lodged in court. When adjustments are complete the sheriff closes the record and the case will proceed to debate or proof. Anxiety about the length of time being taken for ordinary actions to reach their conclusion in the Sheriff Court, led to the introduction of a new set of rules as from January 1994. Basically, the aim is to cut down the length of proceedings by allowing the Sheriff a greater managerial role over the conduct of actions. The 'Options Hearings' introduced by the new Rules may well prove a rich source of copy for court journalists, as they will often contain a brief discussion of the essential elements of the case.

Optional procedure

04–22   Following criticisms of delays in personal injury cases, a committee chaired by Lord Kincraig recommended reforms aimed at simplifying procedure and giving the court more control over the conduct of cases. The result was the introduction in the Court of Session in 1986 of an optional procedure in such cases. The written pleadings are in a short, simplified form and a closed record is not obligatory. At an early stage the case is sent to a diet roll where a judge decides what course it will take. For example, he may order a hearing on the amount of damages alone, or, if the law is not in dispute, an inquiry only into the facts of the case. In September 1994 Lord Penrose was appointed for a three-year period as a full-time judge in commercial cases in the Court of Session.

04–23   There are, of course, special procedures in special types of case. The points of most interest to journalists are dealt with later in the section on court reporting. For the present, it is worth noting that the procedure for cases brought by petition differs from that outlined above. The person presenting the petition is called the petitioner and the person opposing it is known as the respondent.

Judicial Committee of the Privy Council

04-24   The Judicial Committee of the Privy Council is a body of distinguished lawyers, including senior judges and former judges, acting as a court of appeal from the supreme courts of Commonwealth countries. It was formerly the final court of appeal in the British Empire, and still decides appeals from New Zealand, Hong Kong, Singapore, the Channel Islands and most of the Caribbean countries. In June 1993 seven lawlords sat to consider an appeal from Jamaica involving two men who had been on death row awaiting execution since 1980. The condemned men argued that this long delay breached the Jamaican constitution. In theory its decision is merely advice to the Crown on whether to allow or refuse the appeal. Within the United Kingdom, the Judicial Committee hears appeals from the decisions of English ecclesiastical courts and various professional disciplinary bodies such as the Disciplinary Committee of the General Medical Council.

EUROPEAN COURT OF JUSTICE

04-25   The court's powers are laid down in the European Economic Community Treaty, and one of the consequences of the United Kingdom joining the Community in 1972 was that the court assumed jurisdiction to give preliminary rulings on any question raised before a Scottish or English court, criminal or civil. A domestic court may in certain circumstances request the European Court to give a preliminary ruling. The national court must be satisfied that a decision by the European Court is necessary to enable it to give a judgment in the case before it.

04-26   The national court or tribunal may take this course either at the instance of any party in the case or on its own initiative. Once the ruling has been given the case returns to the court or tribunal where it began. The procedure is likely to be adopted in situations where the national law appears to be incompatible with Community law. The proceedings before the originating court are halted meantime.

04–27   The first case referred from a Scottish court under this procedure was a claim for a student's grant made by a Frenchman which had been refused by the Scottish Education Department. A question requiring an interpretation of Community law was referred to the European Court from the Court of Session by Lord Clyde in 1986. The applicant, born in France of an English father and a French mother, claimed he was entitled to a grant in light of certain provisions of EEC law.

EUROPEAN COURT OF HUMAN RIGHTS

04–28   Not to be confused with the European Court of Justice, which deliberates in Luxembourg, is the European Court of Human Rights which sits in Strasbourg. Whereas the Court of Justice is concerned with the interpretation of European Community rules, often of a highly technical nature, the Court of Human Rights handles a broad range of cases frequently of great constitutional significance. A list of some of the cases referred from the United Kingdom confirms this. The court has been asked to rule on issues such as corporal punishment in schools, the closed shop, pensioners' rights, contempt of court, the use of "plastic bullets" and telephone tapping. For journalists the *Lingens* v. *Austria* decision in 1986, is of interest as it recognised that public figures (such as politicians) must expect and accept vigorous criticisms. Domestic Scots law, however, may not be so generous to journalists.

04–29   The court is part of the machinery set up under the European Convention on Human Rights in 1950. Where a breach of human rights is alleged a state or an individual can make a complaint to the European Commission of Human Rights in Strasbourg. This can be done only after all remedies in the applicant's own country have been exhausted. The commission investigates the circumstances and may refer the case to the Court of Human Rights.

04–30   The commission comprises a member from each of the states which signed the convention, the members being elected by the Committee of Ministers of the Council of

Europe. The court consists of judges elected by the Consultative Assembly of the Council of Europe.

04–31 If a case goes to the court there will normally be a public hearing in Strasbourg to elaborate on written submissions. The court's final judgment is delivered in public, usually by the reading of a summary of the decision. A full text of the judgment is made available outside the court. In May 1994 the signatories to the Convention entered into the 11th Protocol. Once ratified the Protocol will have the effect of merging the Commission and the Court. The Commission will cease to exist as an independent body. The new Court will comprise three tiers. One of the principal aims of the 11th Protocol is to accelerate the time taken for disposal of applications—which is currently running at around six years.

CIVIL CASES IN ENGLAND

04–32 In England the less serious civil cases, for example small claims for money, are heard by some 290 county courts where legally-trained circuit judges preside. More important cases are dealt with by the High Court. There are more than 80 High Court judges who sit in three Divisions—Queen's Bench, Family and Chancery. Apart from its civil functions, the Queen's Bench Division deals with some criminal appeals from magistrates' courts. As its name suggests, the Family Division deals with issues such as divorce and the Chancery Division with matters such as tax, wills and companies.

04–33 The Court of Appeal (Civil) is headed by the Master of the Rolls and hears appeals from the High Court and County Courts. Again, there is an appeal to the House of Lords.

KEY POINTS

04–34 Civil cases are dealt with in the Court of Session and Sheriff Court. Sheriffs can now deal with divorce cases. The Inner House of the Court of Session (three judges) hears appeals, and there can be a further appeal to the House of Lords. The opposing sides in a civil action are the pursuer and defender. The Scottish system is based on written pleadings and the main documents involved are the summons or initial writ, open record and closed record. Civil cases are heard by a sheriff or judge sitting alone and, much more rarely in the Court of Session, by a jury of 12.

Chapter 5

MISCELLANEOUS SPECIAL COURTS

05–01 Journalists should be aware that they run the risk of contempt in the reporting of some of the miscellaneous special courts listed here just as much as in the reporting of the normal criminal and civil courts. The Contempt of Court Act 1981, s.19, applies the law of contempt to "any tribunal exercising the judicial power of the State."

05–02 This vague phrase was inserted by Parliament when it was found to be impossible to draw up a list of the tribunals and other courts to which contempt law should apply. Deciding whether or not a court or tribunal has the power to punish for contempt is a very complex matter, and the journalist writing a controversial story arising out of the proceedings of an inferior court or tribunal should take legal advice.

05–03 The issue was fully discussed in the case of *Attorney-General* v. *BBC* in 1981 when the House of Lords decided that the Lands Valuation Court was not a tribunal within the meaning of the 1981 Act and did not have contempt powers.

05–04 It should also be noted that even if a court or tribunal does not itself have the power to punish for contempt, a contempt power may still be exercisable over a report of such a court or tribunal. It could be exercised by the High Court which has a supervisory jurisdiction over all inferior tribunals and courts.

The Lands Valuation Appeal Court

05–05 If a business is dissatisfied with the valuation of its property for rating purposes, it can appeal to the local valuation appeal committee. There is a further right of appeal on a point of law by way of stated case to the Lands Valuation Appeal Court which consists of three judges of the Court of Session.

RESTRICTIVE PRACTICES COURT

05–06   All restrictive agreements between manufacturers or traders must be registered with an official known as the Registrar of Restrictive Trading Agreements. If he thinks they are not in the public interest he may bring them before the Restrictive Practices Court. The burden is then on the parties to the agreements to show that they are in the public interest.

05–07   When sitting in Scotland the Restrictive Practices Court usually consists of one judge of the Court of Session and at least two lay members qualified by experience in, or knowledge of, industry, commerce or public affairs. There is appeal to the Court of Session on points of law by way of stated case.

05–08   When sitting in other parts of the United Kingdom the court is similarly composed of a judge and two or more laymen. There is appeal on a point of law to the Court of Appeal or the Court of Appeal of Northern Ireland.

ELECTION COURTS

05–09   The function of these courts is to hear petitions, rare now, but at one time common, complaining against irregularities in the conduct of elections. In Scotland the election court in the case of a parliamentary election consists of two judges of the Court of Session. In the case of a local government election, it consists of the sheriff principal of the sheriffdom in which the election took place.

05–10   Election courts can try prosecutions for corrupt and illegal practices. Corrupt practices are the more serious and include bribery and treating, that is, treating people to "meat, drink or entertainment" to influence votes. One glass of beer may not justify the charge but a large number may, and "giving drink to women that they may influence the votes of their fathers, brothers or sweethearts" has been held to be treating. It is also a corrupt practice to exert undue influence on voters—by force or threats of force or injury. Illegal practices include such offences as paying or receiving money to transport electors to or from the poll, voting when disqualified or inducing a disqualified person to vote.

05–11   In England election courts consist, in the case of a parliamentary election, of two High Court judges and, in the case of a local election, of a senior barrister.

Registration Appeal Court

05–12   Appeals over the registration of voters can be taken in the first instance to the sheriff and from there to a special Registration Appeal Court consisting of three judges of the Court of Session. The type of case which the court deals with can be illustrated by its decision that a minister of the Church of Scotland who had been summoned to the General Assembly and who would accordingly be unable to vote at the polling station allotted to him, was entitled to be registered as an absent voter.

The Scottish Land Court

05–13   The Scottish Land Court consists of a legally qualified chairman who enjoys the same rank and tenure of office as a judge of the Court of Session, and up to six other members of whom one must speak Gaelic. It decides various questions under the Acts concerning agriculture in Scotland. Its approval is often necessary, for example, before a landlord can serve an effective notice to quit on a farm tenant.

The Land Court also deals with the exercise by the Secretary of State for Scotland of his powers under the Agriculture Acts. If a person is aggrieved by a proposed exercise of these powers he may have the matter referred to the Land Court. There is a right of appeal to the Inner House of the Court of Session by way of stated case, but only on a point of law.

The Lyon Court

05–14   The Lyon Court is held by the Lord Lyon King-of-Arms to deal with questions of heraldry and the right to bear arms in Scotland. There is appeal to the Inner House of the Court of Session and from there to the House of Lords.

Licensing boards

05–15   Licensing boards sit quarterly and comprise members of the district or islands council. Their functions include making decisions (after considering objections) on applications for certificates for the retail sale of alcohol, and on complaints, as well as imposing and revoking conditions, giving consent to and ordering alterations to licensed premises. Certificates normally last three years. There is a right of appeal to the sheriff by either an applicant or objector or by a licence holder or a complainer, and a right of appeal to the Court of Session against the sheriff's decision.

Church courts

5–16   The Courts of the Church of Scotland have a statutory jurisdiction going back to 1592 and extending over the whole range of church affairs, including discipline. So long as matters are within the jurisdiction of the church courts, the civil courts cannot interfere.

The Courts of the Church of Scotland are the Kirk Session consisting of the minister and elders of a particular church, the Presbytery consisting of the ministers and representative elders from the parishes within its bounds, the Synod consisting of the members of the several Presbyteries within its bounds and finally the General Assembly with representatives from the whole church. Certain appeals concerning character and conduct are heard by a Judicial Commission of the General Assembly, which can decide at any stage of the proceedings whether they will be heard in public.

5–17   The courts of other churches in Scotland, including the Episcopal Church, have no statutory powers, their jurisdiction, like that of a club committee, depending on agreement between the members. The civil courts can intervene if there is a breach of this agreement affecting property interests just as in any other case of breach of contract. The courts can intervene also where there has been a denial of natural justice within the courts of a church in dealing with a complaint against a minister or a member or where those courts have exceeded their powers.

In 1986 the Court of Session ruled that the Synod of the Free Presbyterian Church of Scotland had erred in suspending two ministers for life on grounds of contumacy (wilful disobedience). In his judgment in favour of the ministers, Lord Ross, Lord Justice-Clerk, said that the court had a limited jurisidiction to interfere with decisions of the governing body of a church. There could be no question of the court reviewing the merits of the synod's decision, but it would entertain an action where a religious body had acted clearly beyond its constitution or where procedure was grossly or fundamentally irregular.

The church had failed to show that the two ministers were ever given an order they had disobeyed. They were also entitled to know what the case against them was; they were convicted of contumacy before given any hearing and without any charge being put to them.

Courts-martial

05–18   There are three types of military courts-martial—a general court-martial which consists of at least five officers and can try officers as well as other ranks, a district court-martial which consists of at least three officers and cannot try an officer or award more than two years' imprisonment and a field general court-martial which normally consists of at least three officers and is, in effect, an emergency general court-martial for the trial of offences committed on active service.

In the case of a general court-martial there must be, and in the case of other courts-martial there may be, a judge-advocate—a qualified lawyer whose function is to advise the court on the law and summarise the facts. He does not take part in the actual decision of the court.

Procedure at a court-martial follows that in an English criminal court, even when it sits in Scotland to try a Scottish soldier.

A finding of "not guilty" is final, but if the finding is "guilty" both decision and sentence are subject to confirmation by the confirming officer—usually the officer who convened the court-martial or any officer superior to him. This is no mere formality. Findings may be quashed or sentences greatly reduced.

To give just one example, a Scots Guards officer was sentenced by a court-martial at Edinburgh Castle to be dismissed the service for fraudulently appropriating £1.30 from the sergeants' mess fund. The confirming officer commuted the sentence to a severe reprimand.

Reports must always state that "findings and sentence are subject to confirmation." The Contempt of Court Act 1981 provides that criminal proceedings before a court martial are not concluded until the completion of any review of the finding or sentence.

Air force courts-martial are very similar and naval courts-martial consist of five to nine officers of or above the rank of lieutenant. Their findings and sentences are not subject to confirmation but take effect immediately. The authorities do, however, go over the record of the proceedings at a later date and may quash the conviction or reduce the sentence if there has been some irregularity.

A person who had been tried by an ordinary court is not liable to be re-tried by a court-martial. Under the Armed Forces Act 1966 a person who has been tried by a court-martial cannot be tried later by an ordinary court for the same, or substantially the same, offence.

Courts-martial meet at irregular intervals. The practice regarding notice varies. In some cases, the media are sent notice of pending trials but usually notice is simply posted at the service headquarters.

There is appeal from the findings of a court-martial to the Courts-Martial Appeal Court, which consists of the judges of the English Court of Appeal together with nominated judges from the English High Court, the Scottish High Court of Justiciary and the Supreme Court of Judicature of Norther Ireland. The Lord Chancellor can also appoint other persons of legal experience to be judges of the court. Three judges normally sit but there may be a larger uneven number.

Application for leave to appeal must first be made to the Courts-Martial Appeal Court. There is no appeal against sentence, but the court may vary the sentence incidentally if, for example, it finds that the accused was wrongfully convicted on one charge but that he was properly convicted or should have been convicted on another. Where a point of law of general public importance is at stake there can be a further appeal to the House of Lords. This is the only case where the decision of a criminal court sitting in Scotland may eventually be heard by the House of Lords.

Standing civilian courts

5–19 These operate outside the United Kingdom for the trial of people employed by the armed forces or accompanying them but not subject to military law. They comprise an assistant judge-advocate-general, sometimes with two assessors. A civilian convicted by such a court has a right of appeal to a court-martial or may petition a reviewing authority against conviction or sentence or both.

KEY POINTS

The law of contempt of court applies to reports of any tribunal exercising the judicial power of the State. Scotland has a number of special courts to deal with disputes over, for example, heraldry and the right to bear arms, business rates, the conduct of elections and the registration of voters. There is usually an appeal against their decisions to the Court of Session on a point of law.

Courts-martial follow English criminal procedure even when a Scottish soldier is being tried in Scotland. Reports should always state that a finding of guilty, and the sentence which follows it, are subject to confirmation.

CHAPTER 6

OTHER BODIES

TRIBUNALS

6–01 There are a large number of tribunals which exercise judicial-type functions but which are not courts. Tribunals are designed to achieve a quicker, cheaper and more informal kind of justice in specialised areas than the ordinary courts. Tribunals enable individuals to seek independent decisions on administrative decisions with which they disagree. While the operation of tribunals varies considerably, the system is based on the principles of openness, fairness and impartiality. In all there are about 70 different types of tribunal dealing with a wide variety of subjects such as complaints against doctors and solicitors, national insurance, immigration, fair rents, social security and war pensions. Some are open to the public while others are normally held in private. There is space here to mention briefly only a few of the more important ones to which the media normally have access.

6–02 Since 1958 most tribunals have operated under the supervision of the Council on Tribunals and the Council's Scottish Committee has direct supervision over the operation and procedure of about 25 tribunals. The Council and its Scottish Committee operate under the Tribunals and Inquiries Act 1971 which introduced important reforms in this area of law by providing for the possibility of appeal to the courts on points of law from the most important tribunals. The Act also provided that tribunals should, if requested, give reasons for their decisions.

6–03 Since most tribunals are set up under the authority of Parliament, a fair and accurate report of tribunal proceedings will normally be protected by qualified privilege. However, many tribunals are, as they are intended to be, informal, with the result that witnesses or parties are frequently allowed to make allegations which would not be allowed in a court of law. For example, hearsay evidence is admissible and it is not normal practice for people involved in tribunal hearings to be placed under oath.

06–04   The journalist should always consider whether some wild allegation would form part of a fair and accurate report, bearing in mind that the protection of privilege does not cover anything which is not of public concern and the publication of which is not for the public benefit.

06–05   It is not always easy to answer the question of whether a journalist can be in contempt of a tribunal. It depends on the tribunal. The Contempt of Court Act states that a court includes any tribunal or body exercising the power of the State. An industrial tribunal would probably come under this category. Judges in England have held that the purpose of a local valuation court is essentially administrative and not therefore protected by the law of contempt. However, a mental health review tribunal has been held to be a court. Lord Donaldson, the Master of the Rolls, stated that the power of mental health tribunals to affect a person's liberty was a classic example of the exercise of judicial power. (See Chapter 9).

Industrial tribunals

06–06   Industrial tribunals are a regular source of copy. They deal with questions of redundancy, equal pay, sexual and racial discrimination at work, contracts of employment, trade unions and labour relations and health and safety at work. In particular, they deal with complaints by employees of unfair dismissal and have power to order the reinstatement of the employee or an award of compensation.

06–07   The tribunals normally consist of a legally qualified chairman and two other members selected from a panel with specialist knowledge or experience. The Employment Protection Act 1975 provided for the setting up of a special Employment Appeal Tribunal to hear appeals on questions of law from industrial tribunals. This consists partly of nominated judges, at least one being from the Court of Session, and partly of members having special knowledge or experience of industrial relations.

6–08   Industrial tribunals normally sit in public but can take evidence in private in the interests of national security or to prevent a breach of the law, a breach of confidence or to stop information being revealed which would damage the interests of an employer.

    Since 1993 Industrial Tribunals have had the power in cases involving allegations of sexual misconduct to make an order preventing the media from naming certain witnesses. The power was first exercised in Scotland in December 1993 in a case brought against Aberdeen Journals Limited by a female employee. It is good practice for journalists to check with the tribunal clerk as to whether such a 'restricted reporting order' has been made. The order ceases to have effect when the tribunal decision is released.

National Health Service tribunals

6–09   The National Health Service (Scotland) Act 1947 provided for the setting up of a tribunal to investigate cases where it is claimed that a doctor, dentist, pharmacist or optician should be removed from the National Health Service list.

6–10   The tribunal consists of a legally qualified chairman and two other members. If it decides that the practitioner should not be removed from the list, the matter is at an end. There is no appeal. If it decides for removal, the practitioner can appeal to the Secretary of State and has also an appeal to the Court of Session on a point of law. The tribunal meets in private unless the practitioner otherwise requests but its decisions are generally made public.

Transport

6–11   The traffic commissioners of an area (a full-time chairman and two others) deal with road passenger traffic. They grant road service licences and public service vehicle licences. Appeal from their decisions in these matters is to the Secretary of State for Scotland and from him on a point of law to the Court of Session. They also deal with public service vehicle drivers' and conductors' licences. Appeal in these cases is to the sheriff. The traffic commissioners sit in public. The licensing authority for an area (in fact the chairman of the traffic commissioners) issues operators' and transport managers' licences for the carriage of goods by road and also grants special authorisations for the use of large goods vehicles. There is appeal from its decisions to the Transport Tribunal. It is also responsible for the issuing of heavy goods vehicles drivers' licences and in this case appeal is to the sheriff.

06–12   The Transport Tribunal consists of a legally qualified president, and four other members experienced in finance, commerce or transport. Appeals on road haulage matters are heard by the Road Haulage Appeals Division of the Tribunal, which consists of the president and two of the members. The Transport Tribunal sits in public. When considering a Scottish case, it sits in Scotland and there is an appeal to the Court of Session on a point of law.

Lands Tribunal

06–13   The Lands Tribunal for Scotland deals with disputes over compensation for the compulsory acquisition of land, with the variation and discharge of certain obligations contained in the titles to land, and with the valuation of land for certain tax purposes. Parties may also voluntarily refer a matter to the tribunal as an arbiter. The tribunal consists of both lawyers and valuers, with a legally qualified president. Appeal on a point of law lies to the Court of Session. The tribunal sits in public, except when it is acting as arbiter under a voluntary reference, when it may, if requested, sit in private.

INQUIRIES

06–14   Inquiries into matters of national importance can take three forms—a tribunal of inquiry, a committee of inquiry or a royal commission.

Tribunals of inquiry

06–15   Tribunals of inquiry are appointed by Parliament to inquire into matters of "urgent public importance". Their findings are laid before Parliament and published by the Stationery Office.

06–16   Tribunals of inquiry sit in public, unless they think privacy is in the public interest in view of the subject-matter of the inquiry or the nature of the evidence to be given. They can exclude the public for part only of the proceedings.

6–17 There is power to order witnesses to attend and give evidence. There is also power to refer cases of contempt of the tribunal to the High Court in England or Court of Session in Scotland for consideration and, if necessary, punishment.

Committees of inquiry

6–18 Either House of Parliament may set up a committee of inquiry to investigate any matter of public importance. The committee may include people who are not members of Parliament. Committees of inquiry were widely used at one time but have now been superseded in practice by tribunals of inquiry. Their main disadvantage is that it is difficult to exclude the suspicion, or indeed the actual presence, of political bias.

Royal commissions

6–19 Royal commissions are often set up where the object is not so much to find out facts as to consider a situation with a view to reform. There have been royal commissions on, among other things, the Press, capital punishment, the law of marriage and divorce and legal services in both Scotland and England and Wales. The most recent was the Royal Commission on Criminal Justice in England and Wales under the Chairmanship of Lord Runciman which reported in July 1993. Commissioners are appointed by the Crown and given power to summon witnesses and demand information. Their report is generally published as a Command Paper.

6–20 In practice royal commissions often sit in public but may hear evidence in private and may receive written evidence which need not be published. The bodies submitting such evidence may send it to the media for publication.

Local inquiries

6–21 Local inquiries are held, generally in public, under various statutes. Planning inquiries are among the most common and deal with questions such as proposed motorway routes and the building of "superstore" developments. Local inquiries are also held when there are objections to a proposed Private Act of Parliament.

06–22   In Scotland inquiries are held by reporters who are often practising advocates. The reporter makes his findings and recommendations to the appropriate minister who then gives his decision.

Fatal accidents and sudden deaths inquiries

06–23   The law on these inquiries is contained in the Fatal Accidents and Sudden Deaths Inquiry (Scotland) Act 1976. Public inquiries are held (a) in the case of fatal accidents at work, (b) in the case of deaths in legal custody (in, for example, a police station or prison) and (c) in any case in which the Lord Advocate considers that it is in the public interest that an inquiry should be held on the ground that the death was sudden, suspicious or unexplained, or occurred in circumstances such as to give rise to serious public concern.

06–24   Even in cases (a) and (b) an inquiry will not be held if the Lord Advocate is satisfied that the circumstances of the death have been sufficiently established in criminal proceedings. The inquiry is held by the sheriff, without a jury. The fact that a person is examined as a witness at an inquiry does not prevent criminal proceedings later being taken against him but the sheriff's determination as to the cause of death and other relevant facts is not admissible in evidence in any judicial proceedings arising out of the death or accident.

06–25   The sheriff may ban publication in any newspaper or broadcast of any identifying particulars (including a picture) of any person under 17 involved in the inquiry in any way. (See Chapter 12.)

Shipping and railway inquiries

06–26   There is statutory provision for inquiries into deaths at sea, shipping casualties and railway accidents. These are again in no way trials or civil actions. Their sole purpose is to find out the facts.

06–27   Where there is a death on board any foreign-going British ship, an inquiry is held, generally in public, by a Department of Transport superintendent at the next port of call if in the United Kingdom or by a British consul if in a foreign port. If it is thought that death was caused by violence or other improper means the department can if need be "take steps for bringing the offender or offenders to justice."

6–28   Department of Transport shipping casualty inquiries are held when a ship is lost, abandoned or materially damaged if at the time of the casualty the ship was registered in the United Kingdom or was in the United Kingdom or its territorial waters.

6–29   A preliminary inquiry may be made by a person appointed by the Secretary of State for Transport. If a formal inquiry is considered desirable it is held by a court of summary jurisdiction (the sheriff court in Scotland) assisted in each case by one or more assessors who are experts in nautical engineering or other relevant matters. In practice shipping casualty inquiries in Scotland are held in public. The questions for the opinion of the court must be stated in open court. In practice the rest of the proceedings are also in public. After hearing the case the court must report to the Secretary of State for Transport. The court has power to cancel or suspend the certificate of a master, mate or engineer, if it finds that the casualty was due to his "wrongful act or default". Its decision on this matter must be announced in open court.

6–30   The Secretary of State for Transport has power to order inquiries into train accidents. These are held by an Inspecting Officer of Railways who has a wide discretion as to the procedure. In practice the public are admitted but may be excluded if, for example, evidence would be likely to prejudice an accused at a subsequent criminal trial.

The Ombudsman

6–31   On the model of the Scandinavian Ombudsman, the office of Parliamentary Commissioner for Administration was created in 1967, to investigate complaints by the public against actions of the Executive or of bureaucratic incompetence giving rise to injustice. Appointed by Parliament, the Commissioner is independent and his duty is to act impartially between government and the individual. A separate Commissioner with particular and similar duties in relation to the administration of the National Health Service came into being in 1973. The journalist is most likely to be concerned, however, with the work of the Local Commissioners for Administration—one for England and Wales (created in 1974) and another for Scotland (1975). As in the case of the Parliamentary Commissioner, the local ombudsmen are entirely independent, their main function being to investigate complaints by members of the public who consider they have been victims of injustice as a result of maladministration by a local authority.

06–32   The majority of complaints are concerned with matters of housing, planning and building control, education and environmental health. The Commissioner issues an annual report, which is published, and his report on each individual complaint is also made public through the media. The identity of the complainant is not usually disclosed, but the local authority concerned is named.

06–33   Complaints are normally made in the first instance through a councillor, but in the event of his failure or refusal to pass it to the Commissioner, the complainant may submit his grievance direct, provided it is made in writing. The Commissioner will not usually look into any complaint which can be taken to a court, tribunal or Minister, unless for some reason the person who feels aggrieved is unable to follow that course. In carrying out his inquiries, the Commissioner has the same powers to compel attendance of witnesses and insist on production of documents as has the Court of Session.

06–34   The procedure is informal and private, and he prepares a draft report for the chief executive of the local authority concerned, for comment. In this way any dispute on the facts is established before the formal report is prepared and published. If there is a finding of maladministration resulting in injustice the local authority has to indicate to the Commissioner what action they propose to take to rectify matters. If he is not satisfied (as happens in a small minority of cases) he presents a further report.

06–35   The weakness of the system is that, apart from issuing his finding and pointing the direction in which he holds the remedy lies, the Commissioner is powerless to do more. But the pressure his efforts bring to bear on defaulting authorities through the publicity his reports receive in the media should not be underestimated. His functions are seen as concerned with settling questions of principle rather than dealing with disputes involving issues of compensation. Even without powers of enforcement, his watchdog and investigative role for the most part achieves its essential purpose in producing a solution without recourse to law.

PROFESSIONAL DISCIPLINARY BODIES

6–36 There are various bodies set up under statute to supervise discipline in the professions. Broadly speaking, they all have power to strike members off the respective registers if (a) they have been convicted of a criminal offence or (b) they have been guilty of "infamous or disgraceful conduct in a professional respect". In the case of doctors, it used to be said that conduct of this type was usually one of the five As—adultery, abortion, alcohol, addiction or advertising.

6–37 The professional disciplinary bodies dealing with doctors, dentists, opticians and pharmacists must be clearly distinguished from the National Health Service tribunals dealt with earlier. The former are concerned with discipline in the profession, the latter with breach of the terms of employment in the National Health Service. The former can remove a name from the register of members of the profession, the latter only from the list of those members of the profession employed in the National Health Service.

6–38 The general rule is that proceedings of these bodies take place in public, but that they may exclude the public in the interests of justice or for other special reason.

6–39 Professional disciplinary bodies fall into two classes, those from which appeal is to the Privy Council and those from which appeal is to the Court of Session. Reports should always state that the name will be removed "failing the entry of an appeal to the Privy Council within twenty-eight days" or as the case may be. Even where the name is removed it is generally possible for the person concerned to apply after a suitable period for restoration to the register.

6–40 Bodies from which appeal lies to the Privy Council within 28 days are the Disciplinary Committee of the General Medical Council, the Disciplinary Committee of the General Dental Council, the Disciplinary Committee of the Council of the Royal College of Veterinary Surgeons and the Disciplinary

Committee of the General Optical Council all of which generally meet in public.

06–41   Bodies from which appeal lies to the Court of Session or the High Court in England within three months are the Statutory Committee of the Pharmaceutical Society which must open in public and announce its decisions in public but can if it thinks fit hold any other part of the hearing in private, and the Disciplinary Committee of the Architects Registration Council which appears to have discretion as to meeting in public.

06–42   The Scottish Solicitors' Discipline Tribunal can strike a solicitor off the roll, suspend him and, in cases of professional misconduct, fine him up to £10,000. There is a right of appeal to the Court of Session within 21 days.

06–43   The tribunal meets in private but under the Law Reform (Miscellaneous Provisions) (Scotland) Act 1990 the decision, including the name of the solicitor, is made public whether or not professional misconduct is established. The only exception is where, in the opinion of the tribunal, publicity might damage the interests of someone other than the solicitor against whom the compaint was made, his partners or their families. The Law Society must keep available for inspection without payment a copy of every decision of the tribunal.

06–44   The tribunal is an independent body, not an offshoot of the Law Society of Scotland. The majority of its members at any hearing are solicitors but lay members make up not less than 25 per cent of the numbers. Members of the tribunal are appointed by the Lord President of the Court of Session. Complaints are prosecuted by fiscals, who are private practitioners independent of the Council of the Law Society. Although the majority of complaints are brought by the society, private prosecutions may be taken.

06–45   In July 1991, Mr David Morrell was appointed as Scotland's first Legal Services Ombudsman. The appointment was made under the Law Reform (Miscellaneous Provisions) (Scotland) Act 1990, with the intention of strengthening procedures for dealing with complaints against members of the legal profession.

06–46   The new post replaced that of the Lay Observer but the Ombudsman was given a wider remit. His basic function is to consider the way that professional bodies providing legal services in Scotland handle complaints against their members. The bodies include the Law Society of Scotland and the Faculty of Advocates.

6–47 The work of the Ombudsman includes examining written complaints from, or on behalf of, members of the public who are unhappy with the way in which a professional body has dealt with a complaint about alleged professional misconduct or inadequate legal work.

6–48 The Legal Services Ombudsman submits an annual report to the Secretary of State for Scotland who lays it before Parliament.

6–49 Disciplinary measures against members of the Scottish Bar are taken in private by the Dean of the Faculty of Advocates. Rarely a disciplinary body chaired by a retired Judge is used in serious cases. Robert Henderson, QC, was disciplined in 1993 for releasing confidential information from a client to others. In 1994 Raymond Fraser was fined for bringing the Bar into disrepute because of flippant remarks he made to the media after his conviction for drink driving at Haddington Sheriff Court. He was also suspended from practice for a while.

Complaints about judges

6–50 Under section 12 of the Sheriff Courts (Scotland) Act 1971, the Lord President of the Court of Session and the Lord Justice-Clerk have power, either on their own initiative or at the request of the Secretary of State for Scotland, to carry out a joint investigation into the fitness for office of any sheriff principal or sheriff and to report to the Secretary of State if they consider that the judge is unfit for office by reason of inability, neglect of duty or misbehaviour.

6–51 The Secretary of State may order the removal of the sheriff from office. The order seeking the sheriff's removal must be placed before both Houses of Parliament.

6–52 The procedure for removing judges of the High Court and Court of Session is uncertain.

6–53 In England, High Court judges under the Act of Settlement hold office during good behaviour, subject to removal on an address to both Houses of Parliament. The Lord Chancellor, a political appointee, is not subject to this procedure. He has authority to remove a circuit judge on grounds of incapacity or misbehaviour.

KEY POINTS

06–54 Tribunals are designed to achieve speedier and less formal justice than courts. They deal with a wide range of social issues, generally sit in public, and a fair and accurate report of proceedings is normally protected by qualified privilege. However, care must be taken with wild allegations that would not be allowed in a court of law. Privilege protects only matters of public concern, publication of which is for the public benefit. A journalist can be in contempt of a tribunal which is exercising the judicial power of the State (Contempt of Court Act 1981). Fatal Accident Inquiries are held by a sheriff sitting without a jury. He has power to ban identification of anyone under the age of 17 involved in the inquiry.

CHAPTER 7

THE COURT REPORTER

RIGHTS AND RESPONSIBILITIES

7–01   The aim here is to present a guide, for quick reference, to cover the situations most likely to cause difficulty or raise doubts in the minds of journalists reporting the courts in Scotland. Over the years, there have been statements by judges on many important aspects of the court reporter's work, but these are only pieces in the jigsaw. Decisions of the courts and Acts of Parliament leave unanswered vast areas of difficult and dangerous territory. Commonsense is as important as a detailed knowledge of the law.

7–02   Few members of the public have the time to attend and see for themselves that justice is being done. In the civil courts in particular—including the Court of Session, the supreme civil court in the land—the public are often entirely absent. The desire to ensure that justice is not only done, but seen to be done, can hardly be achieved if the only people present in court are counsel and solicitors and the judges themselves.

7–03   Perhaps no one has expressed the rôle of the court reporter and the need for open justice better than the distinguished English judge, Lord Denning. He said it was fundamental that proceedings in courts of justice should be public unless there were overwhelming reasons to the contrary. A judge, when he tried a case, was himself on trial to see that he behaved properly, conducted the case properly, and that his reasons, when given, justified themselves at the bar of public opinion. How could that be done if the case was heard in private?

7–04   Lord Denning added: "The great principle should always be that cases must be heard in open court when the newspaper reporters are there to represent the public and there to see everything is rightly done. They are indeed, in this respect, the watchdogs of justice, but a free press has its responsibilities. Its freedom must not be abused".

07–05   Where so much may be at stake—not only the reputations of people named in his reports but possibly also his own career—the court reporter must have a sound grasp of what information he can safely use. This is preferable to muddling along, hoping to pick up bits of advice from court officials or lawyers. The reporter will find it difficult to insist on his rights if he does not know what they are.

Fairness and accuracy

07–06   The essential ingredient of a court report is that it is fair and accurate. This is important not just from the point of view of fair play to everyone involved in the case—parties, witnesses, counsel and the judge. A fair and accurate report of proceedings held in open court is also protected from a defamation action even though it contains defamatory information. It also cannot be a contempt of court.

07–07   The reporter must not fall into the trap of believing that as long as his report is accurate it is safe—that is, protected by privilege. It must also be fair. Fairness implies not only that there should be a proper balance between the claims of both sides, but also that there should be no unfair allegations about third parties who are not present or represented in court and therefore have no opportunity to reply.

07–08   The classic example is the plea in mitigation made by counsel on behalf of an accused person, based on information from the accused. Counsel has no opportunity himself to check the truth of these statements, and it is part of his duty to his client and to the court to bring them out. Where statements of this kind form an essential part of the story and must be published, it should be made clear in any report that they are allegations and not necessarily statements of fact.

07–09   Denials made out of court by someone offended by the plea, or demands for a right to reply, must be treated with great care since publication of these would not be protected by privilege.

07–10   The great majority of civil cases are argued in the presence of both parties and their lawyers. Normally, claims made by one side against the other will be answered, and the reporter has the opportunity (which he will miss at his peril) of giving the reply where one is given. But if one side makes an allegation in the presence of the other, and there is no reply, the newspaper is as free to publish the allegation as if a reply had been made. The point is that there was an opportunity to reply which was not taken. In that situation, justice would be on the side of the journalist, provided, of course, that the report was fair and accurate. It would probably be appropriate to indicate in the report that no reply was made.

Balance

07–11 A court report should also include more than information which makes it a good hard news story, amusing or out of the ordinary. It should leave out nothing which is essential for a balanced report, viewed from the position of both sides in the case. To achieve this balance, the court reporter may have to include in his story dull or uninteresting information. For example, it may be important to say in an interim interdict hearing that one side was not represented in court, otherwise it may look as if he has no defence to put forward.

07–12 The reporter should always remember, however, the important distinction between details which could lead to a court action and information which merely causes annoyance or irritation. Many complaints about Press reports have no merit, and the journalist has to be ready for, and to recognise, the groundless protest when it arises. He should also remain detached, because if he falls into the trap of feeling sympathy for one side he will be in danger of causing prejudice to the other.

07–13 Depending on the kind of organisation the reporter works for, he may not always find it necessary to report every piece of information the law allows. As a matter of taste rather than law it might, for example, be preferable in certain circumstances not to identify someone who was insane or mentally defective. When the reporter does decide to omit from a report information which would normally be regarded as newsworthy, whether the name of a party or an allegation, he must be able to justify his decision. Otherwise, he may be accused of suppressing information without good reason.

07–14 If a reporter is approached by someone involved in a court case with the suggestion that details of the case should not be published, he should inform the news editor. In the meantime the report should be written up as if no approach had been made. The duty to write the story is the reporter's, that of deciding whether to publish it is the editor's. Requests by interested parties to publish an explanation or correction in a case before the court should be treated with great caution. This might suit the interests of one side but interfere with those of the other. It would also not be privileged if it was not part of the court proceedings.

Closed doors

07–15   While proceedings are sometimes held behind closed doors in special circumstances, it is one of the fundamental principles of the Scottish system that the judicial process is public. It is only in this way that justice may not only be done but may be seen to be done. Two Acts of the Scottish Parliament—the Evidence Act 1686 and the Court of Session Act 1693—are still in operation. The first of these lays down that there shall be "publication of the testimonies of witnesses". The second provides that "in all tyme comeing all bills, reports, debates, probations, and others relating to processes shall be considered, reasoned, advised, and voted by the Lords of Session with open doors. . . but with this restriction, that in some speciall cases the said Lords shall be allowed to cause remove all persons except the parties and their procurators".

07–16   The types of "speciall cases" that are in practice taken in private are few. In criminal law, for example, bail appeals, although they may be heard in court, are usually heard in chambers because the judge deciding whether to grant bail may be given information such as details of previous convictions. Since such applications precede trial, it is in the interests of justice that details of this kind are not made public at this stage. Appearances by an accused on petition in solemn criminal cases, both first appearance and the subsequent full committal diet, are held in private.

07–17   Cases brought in the sheriff court or the Court of Session involving the adoption of children are, with rare exceptions, heard in private. Referral hearings before a sheriff under the Social Work (Scotland) Act 1968 are held in the sheriff's chambers. The press can attend but the sheriff has a discretion to refuse to admit the media if he thinks it proper.

7–18   Actions of declarator of nullity of marriage sometimes involve evidence which can only suitably be given in private, since it would often be difficult to persuade witnesses to speak freely on matters such as sexual perversion or impotency in the presence of spectators.

7–19   The doors may be closed in any case on the order of the judge for part of the hearing where it appears to him that this is necessary for the doing of justice, but it should not be a decision which is reached lightly. He may decide on this for reasons other than the particular character of the evidence, for example, where he has reason to anticipate a demonstration in the courtroom which might disrupt the proceedings, or any conduct among members of the public which would distract the attention of the court, counsel or witnesses. It is not usual for the media to be excluded in cases of this kind.

7–20   The decision to close the doors, where not provided by statute, is a matter for the discretion of the judge, and some judges are likely to exercise it more freely than others.

7–21   The Press are also admitted to sittings of the Vacation Judge of the Court of Session, who sits during court holidays. The judge and counsel do not wear wig and gown, and the court deals with urgent business, often custody and access cases.

Summary trial procedure

7–22   There is a kind of short-cut procedure in the Court of Session known as summary trial provided for by section 10 of the Administration of Justice (Scotland) Act 1933, by which parties, by agreement, may bring their dispute before a Court of Session judge of their choice for a speedy decision, and without right of appeal. In the great majority of such cases the procedure, so far as reporters are concerned, does not differ significantly from that of a proof under the ordinary procedure: evidence and counsel's speeches are heard, and the judge delivers a judgment (which, however, is final).

7–23   In 1967, however, a petition was brought before the court to determine who was the heir male of the late Lord Sempill, and the procedure appears to have been unique in that it took place entirely in secret. The decision of the case depended on the sex of Ewan Forbes-Sempill, who was registered in infancy as female but underwent a change of sex as an adult. The petition, which was brought under the section 10 procedure, was heard by Lord Hunter in a solicitor's office, no decision or judgment was ever issued, and no Press report of the case was therefore possible.

07–24 Following Press reaction to this unusual method of avoiding publicity, the Lord Advocate said that under section 10(3) of the 1933 Act the course taken by the court was justified in view of the "purely private" nature of the matter being dealt with. It seemed to him that somewhat similar considerations to those operating in nullity cases justified the secret hearing. The view of Lord Kilbrandon, then Chairman of the Scottish Law Commission, was that section 10 was intended to provide a kind of judicial arbitration, whereby people could take their private disputes before the judge they had selected and get a final decision. The judge's opinion need not be published, any more than the deliverance of an arbiter. The Commission, he said, saw no reason to amend section 10.

07–25 Subsection 3 of section 10 provides that the judge may, on cause shown, hear and determine in chambers any dispute or question submitted for his decision under the section. Subsection 8 lays down, however, that the section shall apply to any dispute or question "not affecting the status of any person". In other words, actions of divorce or nullity of marriage cannot be dealt with by summary trial procedure. Perhaps the most remarkable aspect of the procedure, as applied to the Forbes-Sempill case, is that the choice (with the judge's consent) lies with the parties themselves. It is a device for maintaining secrecy in judicial proceedings which one would like to believe would be rarely if ever invoked since it is so directly in conflict with the principle that justice should be seen to be done.

07–26 The public are normally excluded from court when the alleged victim gives her evidence in a rape trial. Reporters are allowed to stay, on the understanding that they do not disclose the woman's identity.

07–27 Section 11 of the Contempt of Court Act 1981 gives the courts power to direct non-publication of a name "or other matter" which it already was able merely to allow to be withheld from the public during the hearing of a case. This extension of courts' powers is more fully dealt with in Chapter 9.

The reporter's privilege

07–28 While the privilege of reporting judicial proceedings in England is provided by statute, the right in Scotland originated in the common law. Lord President Inglis, put it this way in the case of *Richardson* v. *Wilson* in 1879. "The publication by a newspaper of what takes place in court at the hearing of any case is undoubtedly lawful; and if it be reported in a fair and faithful manner the publisher is not responsible though the report contains statements or details of evidence affecting the character of either of the parties or of other persons; and what takes place in open court falls under the same rule, though it may be either before or after the proper hearing of the cause. The principle on which this rule is founded seems to be that as courts of justice are open to the public, anything that takes place before a judge or judges is thereby necessarily and legitimately made public, and being once made legitimately public property may be re-published without inferring any responsibility".

07–29 But, as was pointed out in the case of *Macleod* v. *Lewis Justices* in 1892, it is only what takes place in open court which may safely be published; examples will be given later of situations in which it is not always entirely safe even to publish everything that passes in open court. Following the case of *Cunningham* in 1986, reporters may be able to claim qualified privilege to publish passages from a summons founded on in open court although these have not been read out in court.

07–30 Lord Clyde held that a summons founded on in this way is made public—a ruling of importance to court reporters, as it may be applied also to documents other than the summons, although not, as the judge observed, to court productions. An important distinction between this case and *Richardson*, quoted above, is that in *Richardson* the action had appeared on the calling list but there had been no hearing of any kind in court.

07–31 The importance of reporters keeping their notebooks for a reasonable period is of particular importance in court cases.

What is a reasonable period will vary with the circumstances, but experience suggests that one year would not be excessive. In one Court of Session case, a newspaper report quoted counsel as stating in court that a director of a company had been trying to sell the company's assets.

07–32   Eleven months after the item appeared, a director of the company, although he was not named in the report, apparently recognised himself as the person referred to in it. He wrote to the editor of the paper, alleging he had been defamed and threatening to sue the paper for damages. Fortunately the reporter was able to find his notes, which showed that the statement complained of was indeed made by counsel in court and was accurately reported. Nothing more was heard of the matter.

07–33   A report based upon a statement made in court which is privileged may lose that protection if it is not clearly attributed to the speaker. If a statement from court proceedings is quoted in a Press report without attribution, the newspaper itself will bear responsibility for the statement, and if it should prove to be actionable the defence of privilege will not be open to the paper.

07–34   The *Daily Record* reported a bigamy case in Edinburgh Sheriff Court in 1971 under the headline "Unlucky bigamist gets nine months". The report opened with the bare statement: "Robert Hogg was unlucky in his two attempts at a happy marriage. His first wife ran off with another man—and his second had a child to another man". The statement that Mr Hogg's second wife had had a child to another man was based on a submission made in court by Mr Hogg's solicitor, but it was denied by the woman in question, who sued the *Daily Record* for £2000, alleging she had been defamed.

07–35   Her complaint was that the passage in the report stood by itself as a statement of fact by the paper and was not attributed to anyone taking part in the sheriff court proceedings.

07–36   At a legal debate in the Court of Session, Lord Brand rejected an argument by counsel for the paper that the passage, if read by itself, did not identify the woman. Sending the case for trial by jury, the judge said it was one thing for a solicitor to say in court on his client's instructions that the woman had had an illegitimate child, but it was quite another matter for a newspaper to make such a claim on its own authority. In his view, the bald statement that the pursuer had a child to another man was, on the face of it, defamatory.

07–37   He accepted that the remainder of the paper's report, duly attributing to Mr Hogg's solicitor in court the statement that the pursuer had had an illegitimate child, was privileged, but said it would be for the jury to decide whether the opening passage was a fair and accurate summary of the fuller, privileged passage which followed.

07–38   The case in fact never went to trial, but Lord Brand's judgment provides a useful warning on the care to be taken in publishing possibly defamatory statements without attributing them.

Party litigants

07–39   Special care has to be taken in reporting statements made by people conducting their own case, either because they do not wish or can not afford to be represented by counsel. This is always a very difficult situation for a layman, and the judges invariably are less strict in enforcing rules of procedure than they would be with a lawyer.

07–40   The difficulty is that party litigants tend to bring in irrelevant statements and sweeping allegations which have no direct bearing on the questions before the court. The reporter may have to exclude these from his report. Where these statements or allegations implicate third parties who have not the opportunity to reply, or are patently irrelevant to the issue under consideration, they will form no part of a fair and balanced report of the proceedings.

07–41   The need to preserve a fair balance between prosecution and defence in criminal cases and between the opposing sides in a civil action, is especially important for evening papers. Where the report is incomplete in one edition and presents an unbalanced picture of the case, particular care should be taken to ensure that the balance is restored in later editions or in the issues of the following day. Statements rebutting earlier assertions by the other side must be reported.

07–42   A proper balance between opposing sides does not necessarily require the publication of equal space to each. A lengthy argument advanced by one party may be completely demolished in a single sentence.

07–43	The reporter who has some background knowledge of a case from an outside source should remember that if that information is included in his report, it will not be protected by privilege.

Interpretation

07–44	The court reporter has to be especially careful in interpreting, condensing, or translating into lay language passages from legal proceedings. It may be relatively simple to copy accurately and reproduce what a speaker says, but the exact reproduction of language used in court would rarely be acceptable, particularly for the tabloid press.

07–45	In "translating" legalese into lay terms the reporter must first be certain that he understands the meaning of the information he is dealing with and uses precisely the words which will convey the idea intended by the speaker. For example, a trust disposition and settlement can simply be called a will, and someone who alienates his heritable subjects can normally be said to be selling his house. There are many other expressions, more or less baffling to the ordinary mortal, that crop up from time to time, and the most common are included in the glossary at the end of this book.

07–46	Apart from offering a kind of translation of legal jargon, the reporter will often find it necessary to condense the normal verbosity of legal terminology, especially when his report is based upon written pleadings in a civil action. Written judgments of the court may have to be condensed from 40 or 50 pages to a few hundred words or less before they appear in print or on a news bulletin. Again, the reporter must understand what the judge's decision means and the reasoning by which he reached it.

07–47	Where the judge has had to wrestle with difficult legal questions, perhaps involving lengthy citation of cases, the reporter's job will vary according to the kind of organisation for which he works. In many cases the paper will be satisfied with the bare result, but other newspapers will wish to give their readers some sort of explanation of the reasoning which lies behind a decision. For the bald decision in a case may sometimes seem, on the face of it, unjust or unfair. A report of the reasoning which led to the decision may explain the apparent anomaly.

KEY POINTS

7–48 It is a fundamental principle of Scots law that unless there are exceptional circumstances the courts sit in public. A fair and accurate report of legal proceedings held in public is protected against defamation or contempt of court actions. This privilege may be lost if a statement that would be defamatory outside the courtroom is not clearly attributed to the person who makes it. Special types of cases, such as adoption hearings are taken behind closed dooors.

7–49 Special care is also needed in reporting statements of people conducting their own cases. It can also be highly dangerous to mix up background knowledge with what is said in court.

CHAPTER 8

ACCESS TO INFORMATION

COURT DOCUMENTS

08–01 In reporting the civil courts one of the most common problems for the journalist is gaining access to documents. In principle, the practice in the sheriff courts should be the same as in the Court of Session; although relatively few civil cases appear to be reported from the sheriff courts, which is unfortunate since this may be a rich source of news. The lack of reporting may also make it more difficult to persuade court staff to allow access to documents when an important story does come along.

08–02 The most important documents which a reporter may have to refer to before he can write a fair, accurate and balanced report of a case at its various stages are the Calling List, Court Rolls, petitions, records and judgments. The list is not exhaustive because a wide variety of other documents may come, with the permission of lawyers or court authorities, into the hands of reporters. These include copies of wills, contracts, letters and minutes. In general these may be seen and quoted only where their contents have been read out in open court, and the reporter wants to see them only to check the accuracy of his notes.

Calling List

08–03 The Calling List is published daily during the sittings of the Court of Session and on certain dates during vacations, and is an official document. It is usually the first public notice of a court action being raised, and a copy is displayed on the wall in Parliament House. It contains intimation of actions just raised, and is worth careful daily scrutiny. Each entry contains only the names and addresses of the parties to the action, and the names of the solicitors acting for the pursuer.

08–04 The Contempt of Court Act 1981 relaxed restrictions on publication of reports at the Calling List stage (see Chapter 9) and has made it possible to prepare a report based on information in the Calling List without falling foul of the contempt law.

08–05 At this stage, however, there is still the risk of defamation and unlike coverage of a case being heard in open court, a report based on inquiries at the Calling List stage will not have the protection of privilege. And, since any report at this early stage may involve access to particulars contained in the summons, special care is needed to avoid publishing defamatory allegations from that source.

08–06 The reporter in the Court of Session can use the Calling List as a guide to the cases likely to be available for reporting in the future. It is important to keep track of the major news stories of the day because many of them end up in the Court of Session and the first sign may be in the Calling List.

08–07 A notable case was the first action to be raised in Scotland by the parents of a child said to be handicapped after the mother had taken thalidomide during pregnancy. The key in this instance was the fact that the name of the defenders (Distillers Company (Bio-Chemicals) Ltd.) had been in the news in connection with the drug, and that the action was by a father as "tutor and administrator-at-law" for his child. A telephone call to the parents confirmed that it was a thalidomide case.

08–08 Another major court action which first came to light in the calling list involved an AIDS virus victim who was suing the Blood Transfusion Service, the Secretary of State for Scotland and a health board over his condition.

Summons

08–09 The appearance of a case on the Calling List is the public signal that the pursuer in the action has served a summons on the defender. The journalist must treat a summons with great caution, particularly before a hearing of any kind has taken place in court.

08–10   In the case of *Richardson* v. *Wilson* (1879), 7R. 237 the Court of Session rejected the argument that once an action appeared on the Calling List the contents of the summons could be made public. The court said that would not be a report of judicial proceedings, but of the contents of a writ which were at the time unknown even to the court.

08–11   The *Edinburgh Evening News* published a passage from a summons which had appeared on the Calling List. No further step in procedure had taken place and a party mentioned in the report sued the paper for libel. The newspaper argued, unsuccessfully, that the paragraph which was published was a *bona fide* and correct report of the claims in an action called and pending in the Court of Session and they were entitled to publish it. The pursuer in the libel proceedings maintained that statements contained in the report (reproduced from the summons) were untrue and libellous. The report was not said to be in any way unfair as a representation of the statements in the summons.

08–12   Lord Craighill said the principle, stated generally, was that what might be seen and heard in court could be published. The courts were open and accessible to all. It did not follow, however, that every step of process in a cause from the calling to the final judgment was an occasion on which everything which could be discovered from an examination of the process might be published to the world. Were this so, the world would get to know the contents of writs and productions before the court.

08–13   The public, he said, had no right and no interest to know more than could be learned by attendance in court. The public could not demand to know, and newspaper reporters who catered for the public could not insist on knowing, what was not intended to be published merely because a writ or production had been made the subject of judicial procedure. The right and the interest of the public were concerned not with the statements which one party in a cause might make against his adversary, but with the proceedings in open court, by which justice was to be administered.

08–14   The *Edinburgh Evening News* appealed unsuccessfully to the First Division. Lord President Inglis said the duty of the clerk in charge of the process was plainly not to part with the summons or give access to it, except to the parties to the case or their agents. If they made the contents of the summons public at this stage, they would undeniably be subject to an action of damages if it contained defamatory statements. If the agent of either party were guilty of publishing it in any way he would also be answerable to the court for his misconduct. At the stage where no defences had been lodged, no one except the parties or their agents could lawfully obtain access to the summons.

8–15   In the much more recent case of *Cunningham* v. *The Scotsman Publications*, 1987 SLT 698, where there had been a hearing in open court and the contents of the summons were known to the judge, Lord Clyde decided that reporters might be able to claim the protection of qualified privilege in quoting from the summons although the summons had not been read out.

8–16   Mr David Cunningham, a former advocate, sued *The Scotsman*, *Dundee Courier & Advertiser* and the *Herald* for £600,000 damages, alleging they had defamed him in reporting a hearing in the Court of Session in 1984, when interim interdict was granted in his absence to ban him from dealing in certain shares. (That action was later abandoned.)

8–17   Mr Cunningham complained that the reports contained passages from the summons which had not been read out in court and were thus not covered by privilege. He argued that privilege protected only reports of the factual details of what went on in court—the identity of the parties and the judge, the nature of the proceedings, what was said by counsel and the judge and what the court actually did. Putting a document before a judge did not amount to publishing it in open court.

8–18   The newspapers argued that the summons was before the court, it was referred to by counsel, the allegations in it were founded on by counsel and the court granted an interdict in terms of one of the conclusions in the summons.

8–19   Lord Clyde, upholding the newspapers' plea that their reports could be protected by qualified privilege, said that previous Scottish cases (including *Richardson*) did not support the argument that a report must always be limited to what was said and read aloud in open court. Courts sat to hear cases and give judgment "with open doors", and it was evident that for public confidence in the administration of justice to be maintained the public must be able to see and hear proceedings for themselves.

08–20   The proceedings must also be intelligible. Lord Clyde added: "The public must have at least the opportunity of understanding what is going on and if they do not have the opportunity I do not consider that the hearing is a public one. If the hearing is a public hearing then it does not seem to me that that characteristic is destroyed simply because for perfectly proper reasons of convenience a document is referred to and not read out in full. Where a document has been incorporated into what counsel has said, the proceedings cannot be said to be open to the public unless the terms of the document can be seen by the public".

08–21   The danger of secrecy was regarded as so great that publicity was considered preferable even at the cost of private hardship.

08–22   There was also a clear advantage in enabling the public to know with certainty and accuracy what had passed in court rather than leaving them to rely on rumour or speculation, and the reporting of proceedings might be found to be unfair or misleading if access to the pleadings which had been founded upon in open court was not allowed. To make a realistic application of the principle to the circumstances of the *Cunningham* case, Lord Clyde said he could not restrict the availability of privilege to a report of what was actually read out in court. Lord Clyde continued: "The test is not what is actually read out—although all that is read out is published—but what is in the presentation of the case intended to be published and so put in the same position as if it had been read out. If it is referred to and founded upon before the court with a view to advancing the submission which is being made, it is to be taken as published".

08–23   To decide the scope of privileged reporting by reference to the method of communication between counsel and judge seemed to Lord Clyde to involve adopting a standard which could be fixed by "chance, caprice or idiosyncrasy". One advocate might prefer to read passages of pleadings while another would summarise or merely make reference to them. Making publication depend on whether or not a document founded on in open court was or was not read out by counsel or judge might more easily invite suspicion of secrecy and the broad purpose which lay behind the principle of openness might be put at risk of frustration.

8–24 Lord Clyde's judgment was obviously a significant one for the media but its limits should be carefully noted. The decision was not appealed and the case never went to proof. This meant that the question of whether the allegations published in the newspapers were in fact privileged in this case was never decided. All that was decided was that they might be. Lord Clyde also pointed out that it might well be that documents other than pleadings, such as productions, were in a different position. The newspapers defending Mr Cunningham's action agreed that productions could not be published unless they were led in evidence.

8–25 Lord Clyde also made it clear that not all parts of a document would necessarily be safely used in a court report: "I should not wish to exclude the possibility that cases could arise where a document contained matter which was quite distinct and separable from the point in issue before the court and neither relevant to it nor necessary for its determination and where such matter might not necessarily be published where other parts were founded upon".

8–26 An example might be a preliminary procedural step such as continuing a case to allow pleadings to be amended. It seems to follow from what Lord Clyde said in *Cunningham* that a report based on the pleadings and containing defamatory allegations, for example of criminal conduct, would not be protected by privilege unless read out in open court (which is highly unlikely at that stage of the case.)

Adjustment roll

8–27 After the summons has been served and defences lodged—all of which is done in private—an action appears on what is known as the "adjustment roll". The allegations that each party intends to prove will be made into an open record and at intervals fixed by the court, the action appears on the case-list of a particular judge who has to decide whether a continuation should be allowed for one side to answer claims put by the other. At some stage he will decide that no further adjustment of the pleadings is to be allowed and order that the record be closed.

8–28 The distinction between an open record and a closed record is important for the safe reporting of civil actions. The record (containing the parties' written pleadings) remains open so long as the case is on the adjustment roll. The court reporter must check from the front cover that it is in fact a closed record before he uses extracts from it. In the sheriff court the cover of the record may not indicate whether it is open or closed and a check must be made with court officials or lawyers as to whether it has in fact been closed.

08–29   The closing of the record means that the pleadings of the parties to the action are in their final form, subject to anything that might be added by a minute of amendment. The reporter should be mindful of the fact that even when the record is closed and both parties have therefore stated their case fully he cannot necessarily quote from the record with impunity. The safest view is to regard statements contained in a record as covered by privilege only if they are supported by evidence led at a proof hearing. It should also be remembered that the closing of a record has the effect of making proceedings active in terms of the Contempt of Court Act 1981.

Open record

08–30   It was decided in the case of *Young* v. *Armour*, 1921 S.L.T. 211, that publication of the contents of an open record was an interference with the administration of justice. The action was one for damages for breach of promise of marriage and extracts from the record were published in certain English newspapers and by one Scottish paper, the *Weekly Record*, before it had been closed. Under the heading "Love on the Golf Course", the report gave a detailed account of the facts stated in the open record. Both sides agreed there had been an interference with the due course of justice, because the case might have been settled without any of the facts having been made public.

08–31   Lord Blackburn said that the appearance of the article amounted to contempt of court since the record, while still open, was not public property. The editor was ordered to appear in court personally to give an explanation.

08–32   He apologised and explained that, although he knew that the contents of an open record should not be published, he had seen the article in certain English papers and had assumed, wrongly but quite honestly, that the case had been heard in court. The apology was accepted, but the judge said that if the explanation had not been satisfactory, the fine inflicted would have been severe. The court considered that "the contempt which resulted from publication of this sort was a serious offence and one which should be met with a severe penalty".

8–33   While that case sounded a warning about the dangers of publishing details from an open record, the reporter should not take fright at the very mention of the words open record. The Contempt of Court Act has relaxed the *Young* v. *Armour* rule. It is now contempt to publish from an open record only when proceedings are active under the Act, for example at a preliminary hearing (see Chapter 9), although publication from the open record could still be contempt at common law if intended to prejudice the administration of justice.

8–34   Important points of law are often debated before the closing of the record, and if a full-scale hearing takes place in open court a report of the proceedings can be published. On the basis of the *Cunningham* decision, information from the open record could be used if it is referred to in court and the court is being asked to make a decision on it. A report based on information in the record which had nothing to do with the particular hearing would probably not be privileged.

Closed record

8–35   A closed record is sometimes referred to as a public document, but this does not mean that its contents can be freely published at any stage in the proceedings. It was made abundantly clear in a decision in 1892 that, until a case has come into open court, excerpts from even a closed record should not be published. In particular great care must be taken over information from a closed record which might in itself be actionable.

8–36   The privilege which protects a newspaper from an action of defamation over what it publishes from a closed record operates only from the time the action has come into open court.

8–37   In the case of *Macleod* v. *Lewis Justices* (1892) 20 R. 218, it was decided that publication in a newspaper of a closed record containing defamatory statements not referred to publicly in discussion in open court was not privileged. The record

contained in that case statements about two justices of the
peace which, if untrue, were grossly libellous. The justices,
who were the defenders in the case, answered the statements
with a general denial.

08–38   Immediately after the record was closed an agent for the
pursuer handed to a reporter for the *North British Daily Mail* a
record containing pursuer's contentions but not the defenders'
general denial. A summary of the record was published in
the paper and also in the *Scottish Highlander*. The papers later
published a letter from the justices stating the allegations
about them in the record were "a tissue of libellous falsehoods". The pursuer complained to the Court of Session that
the publication of these letters was contempt of court. The
court ruled that there was no contempt, but made some observations which provide useful guidance on this aspect of court
reporting.

08–39   Lord Justice-Clerk MacDonald said it might be a practice to
hand complete records to the newspapers, but it was not one
to be looked on with favour, and certainly to hand an incomplete record to anyone for the purpose of publication was a
very gross irregularity. That was quite different from the publication by newspapers of what took place in a case when it
was in open court.

08–40   Lord Young, agreeing, said it was clear that statements
made in pleadings were privileged, however libellous they
might appear, but there was no privilege whatever in the publication of pleadings. Reporting of proceedings was simply an
enlargement of the audience which heard them in court, but
which was limited by the size of the courtroom. It was therefore quite right to report, for example a debate on the relevancy of a case, and the report would be privileged if it was
fair. While a litigant was privileged in the statements he made
on record, he was not privileged if he sent his pleadings
(whether the record was closed or not) to a newspaper for
publication. If the pleadings published were slanderous, then
the paper publishing them, and the person sending them for
publication, were liable in damages for slander.

08–41   It is not surprising, therefore, that reporters sometimes find
solicitors reluctant to hand over to them closed records in
cases which have not reached the stage of a hearing in open

court. Yet, where a closed record is made available, and contains nothing which could reasonably be regarded as libellous, or the reporter is careful not to reproduce such statements if they do appear to be slanderous, there is still scope for the safe reporting of cases from this source.

8–42   The effect of the ruling in the case of *Macleod* seems to have been modified by practice in the intervening years. For example, when an action of damages opens before a judge or jury in the Court of Session it is usual for solicitors willingly to let the Press have a copy of the closed record without any reservations as to which passages may be published. They do so although at a proof or jury trial the whole, or even a major part, of the closed record may never be read out in open court. A literal reading of *Macleod* in such cases would make adequate reporting impossible.

8–43   Since the closed record is the only reliable and practicable means of preparing a complete, fair and balanced report, it is not surprising that solicitors engaged normally hand over a copy to the Press at the opening of the evidence and often at a preliminary legal debate. Indeed, it would surprise many of them to learn that by so doing they were providing the media with something they had no legal right to publish.

8–44   The case of *Macleod* seems to assume that in all cases the closed record will sooner or later be read out in open court. In fact this rarely happens, since the judge has a copy, as do counsel and instructing solicitors. There may be no need for counsel to read it out, except to draw attention sometimes to a particular passage. If the reporter had to depend solely upon such desultory readings, often out of context, from one side of a case, he would have great difficulty in ever achieving any semblance of fair or balanced reporting.

8–45   It seems a fair interpretation of the position, taking *Macleod* into account, that there is a risk in publishing the contents of a closed record if the case has not yet come into open court. From the moment a hearing has begun (whether legal debate, proof or jury trial) the journalist can safely use the record as a basis for reporting the proof hearing, even though the contents of the record itself may not be read out in open court. This must apply particularly when the judge, because he has already read the closed record in preparation for the hearing, tells counsel expressly that he need not trouble reading it out in court. In that situation the record may properly be "taken as read".

08–46   The journalist should always check, however, that the record is up to date. It is important to ensure that the amount sued for has not changed and that there has been no major change in the allegations and defences put forward by the parties to the action. For example, are the parties to the action still the same and is the pursuer still insisting on a plea of contributory negligence?

Commonsense

08–47   As in so many other aspects of court reporting, the journalist needs to exercise a high degree of care and commonsense in deciding which passages, if any, it is safe to reproduce from the record before the case is heard in open court. He must remember that if he publishes something that is libellous he cannot rely on the protection of privilege. Where the pleadings are read out by counsel during the proceedings, these passages, when published, are of course privileged, no matter how defamatory the statements they contain might be if uttered outside the courtroom.

08–48   It is safe to assume that a lawyer who hands over a closed record to a reporter without reservation is tacitly conceding that the statements, so far as his client is concerned, may be published without fear of reprisals. But the reporter has to keep in mind the interests of other parties to the case.

Open court

08–49   Once the case is in open court the situation is entirely different, and the reporter can normally expect to obtain a closed record from the solicitor for one party or the other. If he fails to do so, and the case is worth the trouble, his next step will be to approach the clerk of court. If the clerk is unable or unwilling to provide a copy, the reporter's next line of approach is to the Principal Clerk of Session. In the unlikely event of his refusal to help, he will have to ask to see the Lord President.

08–50   This situation did occur in a case where, not only did both parties to a large property dispute refuse to hand over a record, and the clerk feel unwilling to supply one to the Press, but one of the parties offered a journalist a sum of money for not publishing anything about the case. As it was impossible to report the case without access to the pleadings Lord President Cooper was approached and instructed the Principal Clerk that the court staff should provide the Press with a closed record. Otherwise, he said, the parties would be enforcing a closed-doors hearing at their own hand.

3–51 The Lord President intervened when evidence was being heard and it cannot be assumed that he would have taken the same decision had case been at a preliminary stage, such as a hearing of debate on relevancy or competency.

3–52 Journalists should also be aware that in cases where the media have asked for eminent counsel's opinion on this issue, the view has been expressed that the provision of a closed record to reporters by the court or solicitors does not mean that every allegation in the record is covered by privilege.

3–53 The transcript of evidence taken on commission (where a witness is unable to attend court) is in a similar position to the closed record when evidence is being heard. Although the evidence may not be read out because the judge will have the actual transcript, it should, for Press purposes, be taken as read, and treated as being covered by the same kind of privilege as spoken evidence. The reporter is entitled to have access to a copy of the transcript, unless it contains the type of evidence which the court would ordinarily hear behind closed doors.

Petitions

3–54 There are a wide variety of cases which are started by a petition rather than a summons. The procedure is different, and there is a separate petition department in the Court of Session.

3–55 While an ordinary action is begun by the pursuer serving a summons on the defender, who in turn replies (if he proposes to contest the case), a petition is addressed to the court which orders notification to other parties having a potential interest to lodge answers to the petition. Interdict, custody of children, authority to vary trusts, confirmation of reduction of capital of a company, presumption of death of some missing person and company liquidations or amalgamations are brought by petition.

08–56   When (and if) answers are lodged to a petition, these go through the kind of adjustment which occurs in an ordinary action, and eventually a document equivalent to a closed record (usually entitled "petition and answers') is drawn up. The journalist can normally treat this in the same way as a closed record.

Interim interdicts

08–57 An interim interdict may be granted on the basis of a summons or a petition. The only practical difference for reporting the case is that the documents are handled by a separate department.

08–58   There are also certain changes of wording. With a summons the parties are pursuer and defender, not petitioner and respondent, and time may be allowed for lodging defences, not answers, as to a petition. In cases where the court makes an *ex parte* order (in the absence of the party interdicted) a report should indicate, in the interests of fairness, that the other party was not present or represented in court and was allowed time to answer.

08–59   The use of the expression "temporary order" or "temporary ban" is not always a satisfactory way of referring to an interim interdict. "Interim" does not necessarily mean "temporary". An interim order is made to restrain someone from doing something until some further development in the case. That may not take place for weeks or for months or may never happen at all. The interim interdict could continue in operation indefinitely and could not properly be called temporary. It is also attributing to a court more power than it has, to say in a report of interdict proceedings that it has issued an order to prevent some specific act. An interdict can only prohibit it.

08–60   Because interim interdicts come to court as a matter of urgency, the summons or petition is often in a fairly basic state. Sometimes it will be in handwriting because there has not been enough time to have it typed. There is also often no opportunity for the alleged wrongdoer to be represented at the application for an interim order against him. The court's decision has to be reached upon an *ex parte* statement which, for the reporter, requires special care. Only as much of such a statement as is necessary to explain the basis of the court's decision may be safely published.

8–61 If someone has reason to think an interim interdict will be taken out against him he can, in Scotland, lodge in court what is known as a *caveat*. A *caveat* obliges the clerk of court to contact the person against whom an interdict is sought and ask whether he wishes to appear and make submissions before the judge decides whether the interdict should be granted.

8–62 Most newspaper and broadcasting organisations in Scotland lodge caveats which last for a year.

8–63 If the court refuses to grant an application for interim interdict, the case for publishing no more than is absolutely necessary is even stronger. Unless there is some compelling reason why the result should be reported—for example where the case has been reported at an earlier stage and there is an obligation to publish the result—petitions for interim interdict which fail on an *ex parte* application should be reported with extreme care. It is possible that in refusing the application for interim interdict the judge has taken the view that the allegations contained in the writ lodged by the pursuer are unfounded, but there are a number of reasons why the court might refuse interdict at this stage.

8–64 For example, the judge might feel there is a lack of specification in the pleadings or that the test of "balance of convenience" has not been satisfied. The existence of such a variety of possibilities illustrates the difficulties and dangers of reporting interim hearings.

8–65 If there is a compelling reason why the decision refusing an interim order should be published, the decision alone should be given, and it would generally be unwise to go into the detail of the allegations made by counsel in seeking the order. On the other hand, where, in refusing to grant an interim interdict, the court reaches a decision which is in itself important the reporter is justified in asking court staff for enough information about the case, including names and addresses of parties to prepare a report.

8–66 It is not unusual in an interim interdict application for counsel to put before the court a string of allegations in the hope that one of them at least, will tilt the case in his favour. The judge may uphold only one or some of the claims and reject others, and this should be made clear in any report of the case. It may be necessary to consult the clerk of court or counsel or solicitors in the case to find out precisely which part of the claim has been sustained.

Court Rolls

08–67   The Rolls of the Court of Session are published daily along with the Calling List and contain lists of cases set down for hearing before individual judges and appeal judges in the Court of Session. Cases which have come to court by way of a petition are usually indicated by 'Pet'' before the name of the petitioner. The name of the party who is suing comes first. Parties' names are followed by the names of junior counsel and solicitors for all parties represented in the case. Where a defender is appealing to the Inner House, this is indicated by: "Appeal for defender *in causa* . . ." An appeal from a single judge is known as a "reclaiming motion" and this is indicated by the the initials "R.M"

08–68   Only in a few cases do the Rolls give a clue as to what the case is about. Where, for example, the pursuer's and defender's surnames are the same, the case is likely to be a divorce action.

08–69   In the Outer House incidental motions are marked with an asterisk if counsel are due to appear to make submissions in open court. Where there is no asterisk, there is no public appearance, and the entry in the Roll indicates a formal step in procedure which is not usually reportable at all. In the Inner House motions are called "single bills" and the same asterisk rule operates. Although the two Divisions are concerned largely with appeals from the Outer House and from the sheriff courts, they also deal with a wide variety of petitions.

08–70   At the appeal stage the court will have before it not only the closed record, or petition and answers, but also usually an appendix containing a transcript of the evidence from the court below and a copy of the judgment delivered by the judge or sheriff, which is under appeal.

08–71   Where the evidence has been given in open court, it may be useful to refer to this and the judgment of the inferior court where necessary to prepare a report of the appeal.

Avizandum

3–72 After the hearing of evidence or legal debate the court may give an immediate decision or may "make avizandum", which means that it will take time to consider the case before issuing a written judgment. Occasionally the court will give its decision and produce reasons in writing later.

3–73 Strictly speaking, the judgment of the court comprises two documents—the interlocutor and the opinion of the judge(s). In practice the opinion is the source of news. The interlocutor is a minute kept by the clerk of court recording in formal style the precise terms of the decision. This is normally not of the slightest use for publication and the reporter should refer to it only as a guide to the true effect of a decision if this is not clear from a reading of the judgment.

3–74 Decisions do not come into force until the interlocutor is signed by the judge. In certain circumstances a judge will grant a decree but for specific reasons will agree to delay operation of his decision for a stated period. He does this by "superseding extract" of the decree, in other words, delaying the process by which the successful party can obtain the extract copy of the decree which will enable him to enforce it. In these circumstances, reports of the case should make it clear that the decision does not become effective immediately.

Criminal cases

3–75 In criminal proceedings the document with which the reporter is mainly concerned is, in cases dealt with in solemn procedure, the indictment, and in summary cases, the complaint or charge-sheet. In the district court the complaint contains the name and address of the accused person as well as the charge against him. In the High Court where bail has been allowed the address of the accused is normally on the indictment, and where he is in custody his address, if known, can usually be obtained from court officials.

3–76 In the case of indictments, the first point at which the media are fully entitled to publish the whole contents of the document is when it is read out to the jury at the opening of the trial, or when the accused pleads guilty to the charge(s) contained in it.

08–77   Where charges are dropped against an accused person without trial he may feel sufficiently aggrieved to threaten proceedings against the papers which published the charge at an earlier stage, for example when he appeared on petition, but there is no record of a successful complaint of this kind. The fact that proceedings have been dropped should of course be published.

08–78   When someone appears on petition the procurator fiscal will normally inform the media of the name of the accused and provide brief details of the charge for publication. Where no plea is taken from the accused and his case is continued for one reason or another, normally for further examination, these facts should be included in any report. On the question of bail, the journalist may come to have details of the submissions made to the court (e.g., the PF opposing bail on the grounds of previous convictions). Although he may have access to this information such details must never appear in a report. All that can be said is that bail was granted or refused (see 13–26).

08–79   The general practice is not to name an accused person before he appears on petition. The charge may be dropped and he may not appear in court at all and, if he does, it may be on a different charge from that originally preferred by the police.

08–80   There do not seem to be any general difficulties for the media in getting hold of indictments and complaints once a case has come into court for a trial or a guilty plea. This has not always been the case and on one occasion, when the media were refused access to a complaint at the old Burgh Court in Edinburgh, the Lord Advocate of the day, Mr John Wheatley, Q.C., was approached. His opinion was that, although reporters had no statutory right of access to complaints, it was a matter of public policy that they should have this facility in the interests of accurate reporting of cases.

08–81   The position on documents in general seems to be that while a journalist has no greater right than any member of the public to attend legal proceedings, it is recognised that the reporter requires access to certain court documents at the appropriate stage in proceedings if he is to carry out his job properly. As a matter of public policy the media are allowed access to certain papers, both in criminal and civil cases, or at least to some of the information contained in them. Where access to documents necessary for the fair and accurate reporting of a case heard in open court is refused, the reporter should raise the matter with the appropriate court authority.

Data Protection Act 1986

08–82 Data users who store information on computer must register under the Act and newspapers or others operating computer systems have to give any person named in their database access to the information they hold about him or her. Anyone who can establish damage from storage of inaccurate information may have a claim for compensation although it is a defence to prove that reasonable care was taken to ensure the accuracy of the data. The holder of data may also be liable if the information is misused, irrelevant, or kept insecurely.

08–83 The Act does allow computer users to withhold from disclosure the source of the information but this protection from disclosure may not cover the situation where the source is an organisation rather than an identifiable individual.

08–84 The right of access applies only to data held in computer files and does not afford access to written or typewritten notes taken by journalists—*e.g.* reporters' notebooks. Disclosure of obituaries of living persons can be avoided by storing these in a traditional filing system rather than on computer.

08–85 Data users may charge inquirers for information held on file and have up to 40 days to supply it. They are prohibited from altering stored information before disclosure. Main public libraries will keep copies of the register of users for public inspection.

08–86 All media organisations which store personal information about individuals on computer must register with the Data Protection Registrar. Failure to register can result in criminal proceedings. The Act applies, in addition to news or editorial comment referring to individuals, to personal data stored for sales and advertising purposes, information used in connection with customers' orders and accounts, credit checking, identification of bad debts, market research, and filed material about the employer's own personnel. It applies also to data stored on computer by freelance journalists working on their own behalf. The requirements of disclosure can be simply avoided by retaining sensitive matter on paper, typed or handwritten.

08–87   The Data Protection Registrar has power to enforce the terms of the Act by proceedings before the Data Protection Tribunal.

KEY POINTS

08–88   The most important documents in a civil action are the summons, calling list, court rolls, open and closed record and opinion of the court. Reports based on information from a calling list, summons or open record are not privileged and could lead to a defamation action. There will, however, be instances where a case can be safely reported in some detail at the calling list, summons or open record stage. The closed record can be used as the basis for a fair, accurate and balanced report once a case has come into open court. The record is not normally read out and it is important to check that it is up to date. Disclosure of information under the Data Protection Act can be avoided by storing it in notebooks or files rather than on computer.

CHAPTER 9

CONTEMPT OF COURT

9-01 Contempt of court can take several forms, but for the journalist the area that causes the greatest problem is the risk of endangering a fair trial by publishing prejudicial information.

9-02 Legal systems adopt widely contrasting approaches to the question of balancing the potentially conflicting interests of freedom of speech and the right to a fair hearing. In the USA, for example, a mass of detailed information about a case is frequently published before a trial. This can even extend, as it did in the *John De Lorean* case, to the accused being shown on television, apparently accepting a consignment of drugs. Two hundred prospective jurors then had to be asked 100 questions to decide whether they could return a fair verdict despite the pre-trial publicity. Similarly, before former American football player OJ Simpson appeared for trial on a murder charge, there was extensive and detailed publicity about the strength and weaknesses of both prosecution and defence cases. The pre-trial publicity included nationwide screening of Simpson's protracted arrest, following a car chase.

9-03 Scots law adopts the diametrically opposite view, as expressed by Lord Emslie in the case of *Vinko Sindicic* in 1988. The Lord Justice-General said: "Our system of criminal justice in Scotland depends essentially upon the proposition that jurors called to try an accused person should arrive in the jury box without knowledge or impression of facts, or alleged facts, relating to the crime charged on the indictment".

9-04 Until 1981 the law of contempt could be found in a series of decisions by the Scottish courts, but it is now largely contained in the Contempt of Court Act 1981 (see appendix). According to Lord Hailsham, the Lord Chancellor at the time, the aim of the Act was to make the law more clear and more liberal. Journalists may be forgiven for thinking that neither of these aims has been entirely achieved.

Scotland and England

09–05 The Act was also designed to harmonise the law north and south of the Border but experience has shown a wide divergence of interpretation, even allowing for the different pre-trial procedures in Scotland and England. Several stories that would have seen a Scottish editor at least heavily fined, have passed without adverse comment in England.

09–06 This has led to unfortunate results. In the *Sindicic* case, for example, the *Daily Express* was fined £30,000 for what Lord Emslie described as a disgraceful contempt. He described the story, about a shooting in a Kirkcaldy street, as painting a lurid picture of an attempted murder and giving the clear impression that the man who had been arrested by the time the article appeared had committed the crime.

09–07 Counsel for the *Express* explained that the story had been checked in Manchester by an English barrister. Lord Emslie said: "It is perhaps unfortunate, since our system depends so much on the absence of pre-trial publicity, that advice about publication should be given ultimately not by a Scottish lawyer but an English one".

09–08 The cynical journalist might pause to observe that however "disgraceful" the contempt might have been, it was not so severe as to prevent the Lord Advocate (who brought the case against the *Express*) from prosecuting Sindicic. What some would see as an application of double standards seems to be an established part of Scots law since the case of *Stuurman* (see below at paragraph 09–84).

Strict liability rule

09–09 The Act lays down a "strict liability" rule which means that a journalist can be guilty of contempt even although he did not mean to interfere with the course of justice. The risk of committing contempt under the strict liability rule applies only to a publication which creates a substantial risk that the course of justice in legal proceedings will be seriously impeded or prejudiced. A publication is defined as any speech, writing or broadcast or other communication in whatever form addressed to the public at large or any section of the public. The phrase "communication in whatever form" would include, for example, pictures, headlines and cartoons.

Active proceedings

09–10 The risk also arises only when proceedings are active, which in a criminal case in Scotland is from the moment of arrest without warrant, the grant of a warrant to arrest or the service of an indictment or summons setting out charges against an accused person, whichever comes first. Both of these measures in the 1981 Act—the kind of risk needed to constitute contempt and the starting point for contempt—are broadly in line with what the Scottish courts had already decided a few years' earlier.

09–11 In the case of *Atkins* v. *London Weekend Television Ltd.*, 1978 S.L.T. 76, the High Court said the question for the court was whether the contents of a London Weekend Television programme gave rise to a "real risk" of prejudice to a fair and impartial trial. The test of substantial risk of serious prejudice laid down in the Act is basically the same, if more precise. Lord Lane, the Lord Chief Justice, put it this way in an English case in 1983: "A slight risk of serious prejudice is not enough; nor is a substantial risk of slight prejudice".

09–12 Lord Diplock has expressed the view in the House of Lords in the case of *Attorney-General* v. *English* 1982 3 W.L.R. 278 that the word "substantial" where it occured in section 2 of the 1981 Act was to be equated with "not remote". Lord McCluskey seemed to adopt the same approach in the trial of Paul Ferris at the High Court in Glasgow in March 1992 when he said substantial risk meant a risk which was not negligible.

09–13 This would appear to mean that it would be very easy to fall foul of the Contempt of Court Act, but textbook writers have already doubted whether Lord Diplock's approach accords with the intentions of Parliament.

Examples of contempt

09–14 It is impossible to give an exact definition of what the courts will regard as a substantial risk of serious prejudice, but obvious examples are the revealing of previous convictions or publication of any implication that the person charged committed the offence. For example, you could report a bank robbery and say that "a" man had been arrested but not "the" man.

09–15   The publishers and editor of the *Milngavie and Bearsden Herald* were each fined £250 for contempt in 1977 over a report of two men who appeared on petition at Dumbarton Sheriff Court on charges of assault and robbery. The newspaper reported that the two men, whom they identified, had both been wearing masks when they had been caught. The Crown submitted that this was a "fair indication of their guilt" and the court accepted that there had been an interference with the administration of justice.

09–16   In the case of *Hall* v. *Associated Newspapers Ltd.*, 1978 S.L.T. 241, the High Court had also decided that the starting point for contempt was arrest or issue of a warrant for arrest. This confirmed the traditional view of the Scottish courts as set out in the case of *Smith* v. *Ritchie* in 1892 when it was stated: "A prisoner has the right to ask the court to secure him against anything which might prejudice the public mind so as to endanger his prospects of a fair trial". The court took the view that from the moment someone was a prisoner he was entitled to the protection of the court to safeguard a fair trial.

09–17   The law had been thrown into confusion by Lord Clyde in the case of *Stirling* v. *Associated Newspapers Ltd.*, in 1959, when he said that the risk of contempt began, not when someone was a prisoner, but as soon as a crime was suspected and being investigated by the criminal authorities. The media in Scotland rightly felt that this interpretation of the law made their legitimate role in the investigation and exposure of crime well-nigh impossible.

Detention powers

09–18   One complication for the media in Scotland is that since the Criminal Justice (Scotland) Act 1980 police have the power to detain a suspect for up to six hours. This is not an arrest and proceedings are not active under the Contempt Act, but any story at the detention stage would have to be written with extreme care. By the time the newspaper was published or the item broadcast the suspect might either have been released or arrested, which could lead to problems with defamation or contempt of court. The possibility of contempt at common law would also have to be considered. This covers conduct intended to prejudice the administration of justice.

Defences under Contempt Act

9–19 There are several sections of the 1981 Act which come under Lord Hailsham's definition of liberalising the law, at least in theory.

9–20 For the first time in Scotland the journalist is afforded a defence of innocent publication. The Act provides that the publisher of information will not be guilty of contempt if, having taken all reasonable care, he does not know and has no reason to suspect that proceedings are active. The burden of proving this defence lies on the publisher of the information and it will not be enough simply to say that he did not know the case was active. Some positive steps, such as checking with the police and the procurator fiscal or Crown Office, would be necessary.

9–21 Section 5 provides a public interest defence and was included in the Act following the judgment in the European Court in favour of the *Sunday Times* in the thalidomide case. A publication made as, or as part of, a discussion in good faith of public affairs or other matters of general public interest, is not to be treated as contempt if the risk of prejudice to legal proceedings is merely incidental to the discussion.

9–22 This has proved a useful defence on several occasions, notably for the *Daily Mail* in the case of *Dr Leonard Arthur*, a paediatrician charged with the attempted murder of a Down's Syndrome baby. During the trial, the *Daily Mail* published an article by Malcolm Muggeridge in support of a Pro-Life candidate in a forthcoming by-election. The House of Lords decided that although the article, which did not specifically mention the *Arthur* case, did create a substantial risk of serious prejudice to the trial, it was a discussion of public affairs written in good faith. Any prejudice was merely incidental. To decide otherwise would have meant that all media discussion of mercy killing would have been stifled from the time Dr Arthur was charged in February 1981 until his acquittal in November. The court also made it clear that the burden of proving a section 5 defence is firmly placed on the shoulders of the journalist.

9–23 The following year, the *Mail on Sunday* also successfully pleaded a public interest defence in the case of *Michael Fagan* the man who managed to get into the Queen's bedroom. Lord Lane described the references in the newspaper to the appalling state of security at Buckingham Palace as a matter of the gravest public concern and an excellent example of the kind of information section 5 was designed to cover.

09–24   The test seems to be how close a link can be established between the trial in question and the publication. In 1989, TVS Television was fined £25,000 and the publishers of the *Reading Standard* £5,000 after Lord Justice Lloyd rejected the argument that they were protected by section 5. The TV station broadcast a programme about sham bed and breakfast accommodation in Reading and the newspaper ran an article about the programme. As a result, a trial in Reading had to be aborted after nearly a month at a cost of £215,000. The case involved a local landlord who was charged with defrauding the DSS over bed and breakfast accommodation, and his picture featured in the TV programme. Lord Justice Lloyd said that the commonsense test was to look to see how closely the subject matter of the discussion related to the particular legal proceedings. In this case the relationship between the two was very close.

09–25   In a case at Durham Crown Court in April 1991 Judge Jowitt took the highly unusual step of warning a jury not to watch a "World in Action" programme. The jury had heard a week of evidence in the trial of three prison warders charged with beating up inmates at Armley Jail, Leeds, and the TV documentary highlighted alleged brutality throughout Britain's jails. Granada Television would no doubt have argued that they were covered by section 5, but the judge said that if any of the jury watched he might have to consider restarting the trial with a fresh jury.

Journalists' Sources

09–26   On the face of it section 10 of the Act protects the confidentiality of journalists' sources. It states that no court may require the disclosure, nor will a person be guilty of contempt for refusing to disclose the source of information contained in a publication, unless it is established to the satisfaction of the court that disclosure is necessary in the interests of justice, national security or for the prevention of disorder or crime.

09–27   Practical experience of the section so far suggests that the exception is wider than the rule. The English courts have interpreted the phrases national security, the interests of justice and the prevention of crime, none so far in favour of the media.

09–28   In 1983 the *Guardian* came into possession of a secret Government memorandum about publicity surrounding the arrival of cruise missiles in the U.K. The Government asked the courts to order the return of the memo so that they could examine markings on it to try to discover who had leaked it. The *Guardian* claimed protection under section 10, but this was rejected by the House of Lords.

09–29   The court said that although there was no threat to national security in this particular case, the leaker might strike again, this time with more serious consequences. The result was that Sarah Tisdale, a Foreign Office Clerk, was identified as the informant and jailed for six months under the Official Secrets Act. This could, of course, have been avoided had the newspaper destroyed the document before any order for its return was made (*Secretary of State for Defence* v. *Guardian Newspapers Ltd*).

09–30   In 1988 *The Independent* newspaper was fined £20,000 after financial journalist Mr Jeremy Warner refused to answer questions put to him by inspectors appointed under the Financial Services Act to identify the source of suspected leaks from Government departments. The inspectors claimed this information was necessary for the prevention of crime and that two articles written by Mr Warner suggested he was in possession of leaked information.

09–31   Lord Griffith said in the House of Lords that the word "necessary" in section 10 had a meaning somewhere between "indispensable" and "useful". The nearest paraphrase was "really needed". The court's view was that Mr Warner's evidence was really needed by the inspectors for the purpose of their inquiry, which was the prevention of crime. The judges also rejected the argument that the phrase "prevention of crime" was limited to the situation in which identification of the journalist's source would allow steps to be taken to stop a particular, future, identifiable crime from being committed (*Re an Inquiry under the Company Securities (Insider Dealing) Act 1985*).

09–32   In 1990 William Goodwin, a young trainee reporter on *The Engineer* magazine was fined £5,000 after refusing to hand over the notes of a telephone conversation with his source. After he received information about a private company's plans for refinancing, the company went to court to stop publication and compel disclosure of the source. At least one judge took the view that the phrase "interests of justice" did not necessarily have to refer to legal proceedings. Lord Bridge said that it might refer to a company's wish to discipline a disloyal employee, even although legal proceedings might not be needed to achieve that (*X Ltd. v. Morgan-Grampian (Publishers) Ltd.; Re Goodwin*). However, in May 1994, the European Commission of Human Rights ruled that fining Mr Goodwin and threatening to jail him for refusing to reveal his source was a breach of his rights.

09–33   There have as yet been no decisions by the Scottish courts on section 10 but in the case of *Daily Record* journalist Gordon Airs in 1975, the High Court took the view that a witness who refused to answer a competent and relevant question was guilty of contempt. Lord Emslie took the view that it was hard to imagine any circumstances in which a relevant question could be judged unneccessary.

09–34   The *Stair Memorial Encyclopaedia of the Laws of Scotland* states that it is difficult to see what difference section 10 has made to Scots law and practice. The authors add: "It is submitted that a Scottish court will rarely, if ever, hold that a competent and relevant question is unnecessary in the interests of justice if the answer to that question would consist of relevant, admissible evidence".

Reports of court proceedings

09–35   The Act states in section 4 that a fair and accurate report of legal proceedings, held in public, published contemporaneously and in good faith, will not be contempt of court.

09–36   In 1986 at the High Court in Edinburgh Lord Sutherland refused to hold the *Herald* in contempt over a story about Thomas Campbell, who was serving 20 years in Peterhead prison after being convicted of murder in the Glasgow "ice-cream war" trial. He was later charged with mobbing and rioting in the jail and the *Herald* carried a story of a preliminary court hearing before the trial. The story was headlined: "Killer accuses prison officers" and defence counsel objected in the strongest possible terms to jurors being told that his client was a killer. He described the report as grave contempt.

9–37   Lord Sutherland pointed out, however, that the references to Campbell's murder convictions had been made in open court at the preliminary hearing and what the *Herald* had done was to report the proceedings in court. Given the terms of section 4, there was no contempt.

Legal debate in jury's absence

9–38   The question of whether this defence would be available where a newspaper published, before the end of a trial, legal debate in the absence of a jury has not been conclusively decided in Scotland.

9–39   In February 1985, Mr Justice McCowan, the judge trying the case of civil servant Mr Clive Ponting, asked the Attorney-General to consider a prosecution for contempt against the *Observer* newspaper. During the trial of Mr Ponting, who was charged with a breach of the Official Secrets Act, the newspaper published the contents of a legal debate outwith the presence of the jury.

9–40   The judge said he had made no order banning publication, because: "I assumed that the greenest reporter on his first day on a provincial newspaper with a circulation of 1,000 would know that he should not report remarks made in the absence of the jury".

9–41   However, the Attorney-General later confirmed that he would not prosecute the newspaper.

9–42   In March 1991 the publishers of the *Evening Times* were fined £5,000 and the editor £500 at Paisley by Sheriff James Spy. The sheriff said the newspaper had given details "for all the world to see" of information which had been kept from a jury. The jury in the trial had been reduced to 14 after one of their number claimed to know one of the accused. This had been the subject of a legal debate outwith the presence of the jury where the accused's lawyer said his client did not know any of the jurors, and that if one of the jurors knew his client, it could only be "by reputation".

9–43   The *Evening Times* reported what had happened outwith the jury's presence and the sheriff halted the trial after ruling that the report had created a substantial risk that the two accused would not receive a fair hearing. This was disputed by the newspaper, which also argued that despite the absence of the jury the proceedings were in public.

09–44   On appeal, the findings of contempt and the fines were set aside after the Crown said it did not support them. Unfortunately, no reasons were given for the Crown's view and no written judgment was issued by the court and it is difficult for the journalist to obtain any guidance from the appeal. We would suggest that the practice of not reporting anything which takes place outwith the presence of the jury should still be followed and that the appeal court decision in the *Evening Times* case should not be taken as authority to the contrary.

Restrictions on court reports

09–45   Section 4(2) has proved troublesome, particularly in England, where it seems to have been used much more frequently than in Scotland to postpone the reporting of court cases, sometimes for many months. A court may order that a report of proceedings, or any part of them, should be postponed for as long as the court thinks necessary to avoid a substantial risk of prejudice to the administration of justice. The risk can involve the proceedings in question or any other proceedings, pending or imminent.

09–46   Postponements in Scotland are sometimes ordered when one accused pleads guilty to a charge and a co-accused is to stand trial in the near future. This happened in a case where a solicitor admitted charges of fraud and embezzlement in July 1986. Because of an order under the Contempt Act, this could not be reported until September. A co-accused had been due to stand trial on associated charges in August but after it became clear that the trial would not go ahead because he was ill the Scottish Daily Newspaper Society instructed counsel to appear in the High Court to apply, successfully, for reporting restrictions on the July hearing to be lifted.

09–47   Reporting was also postponed in a case at the Court of Criminal Appeal in Edinburgh in 1991 where the judges ordered a retrial after a successful appeal by a convicted murderer.

09–48   The Contempt of Court Act also provides (section 11) that where a court has the power to allow information to be withheld from the public in court proceedings, it may also ban the publication of the information. The thinking behind this section is to prevent the purpose of the court order being frustrated by the publication by the media of the names of, for example, blackmail victims.

When contempt risk ends

9–49 In criminal proceedings, the risk of contempt under the Act ends when the accused is acquitted or sentenced or with the return of any other verdict, finding, order or decision which puts an end to the proceedings. Proceedings may also cease to be active because of some other process causing them to be discontinued or by other "operation of law". Proceedings are discontinued when they are expressly abandoned by the prosecutor or deserted *simpliciter* (*i.e.* absolutely or without qualification).

9–50 An accused is sentenced when he or she is made subject to any order or decision following on conviction or finding of guilt which disposes of the case, either absolutely or subject to future events. Where a sentence is deferred for two or three weeks to enable the court, for example, to obtain background reports on the accused the proceedings remain active during that time.

9–51 Criminal proceedings are also no longer active if the accused is found to be under a disability rendering him or her unfit to be tried or to plead, is found insane in bar of trial and a hospital order is made under the Mental Health Act 1959 or a transfer order ceases to have effect under the Mental Health (Scotland) Act 1960.

Contempt and appeals

9–52 For reasons which are not entirely obvious, the Act extends the contempt law to cover cases at the appeal stage, as if judges were as susceptible as jurors to influence from what they may read in the Press or see on television.

9–53 This has made the media in Scotland more wary than before about the terms of background articles published at the end of criminal trials. It is worth remembering, however, that there has to be a substantial risk of serious prejudice and that three senior judges rather than a jury will be hearing any appeal. It was also made clear in Parliament during the debate on the Contempt Bill that there would normally be a "free for all period" for the media between the end of a case and an appeal being lodged.

09–54   A case does not become active for contempt purposes merely because a lawyer says at the end of a case that his client intends to appeal. There must be a definite starting process which, according to the Act, is when leave to appeal or to apply for review is applied for, notice of appeal or of application for review is given, or there is some other originating process. Appeal proceedings are active until disposed of, abandoned, discontinued or withdrawn. However, if the appeal court grants the Crown authority to bring a fresh prosecution, the risk of prejudicing the new proceedings begins from the end of the appeal.

09–55   All this is against a background where the High Court in Scotland has stated in the case of *Bernardi* in 1984 that lay magistrates, far less legally-trained sheriffs and High Court judges, cannot be influenced by the media. The English courts, however, seem to have found a different reason for extending contempt to appeals.

09–56   In 1987, Lord Chief Justice Lane banned the showing of a Channel 4 re-enactment of hearings in the the Birmingham pub bombings appeals. The programme was based on daily transcripts of what had already been said in court, but Lord Lane decided that showing it was likely to undermine public confidence in the legal system. With all due respect, this seems to show little faith in the robustness of the legal system or the commonsense of the public.

09–57   Criminal proceedings are no longer active 12 months after a warrant has been issued unless the person in question has been arrested within that period. If he or she is arrested after the expiry of the 12 months, the proceedings become active again. An illustration of this is the Lockerbie bombing case, where the Sheriff in Dumfries issued warrants for the arrest of two Libyans in December 1991. The strict liability rule ceased to operate in December 1992 as no arrests had been made. Since then the media have had only to fear the possibility of common law contempt.

09–58   Under the strict liability rule criminal proceedings before a court-martial or standing civilian court are not concluded until the completion of any review of finding or sentence.

Juries and Tape recorders

-59 Section 8 of the Act protects the confidentiality of the jury room and changes the law following the decision in England that it was not contempt for the *New Statesman* to interview a juror in the *Jeremy Thorpe* case. It is now contempt to obtain, disclose or solicit any particulars of statements made, opinions expressed, arguments advanced or votes cast by members of a jury in the course of their deliberations in any legal proceedings. A journalist who interviewed a juror about a particular case would be guilty of contempt even although nothing was ever published, but a general discussion about the merits or otherwise of the jury system would not be contempt.

-60 It seems clear that, at the very least, section 8 has not made it any easier to carry out genuine research into how juries approach their job. This is regrettable in an area like contempt where the whole approach of the courts hinges on how jurors are thought to be affected by publicity.

-61 Section 9 makes it contempt to use a tape recorder in court, or bring one into court for use, without the court's permission. It would also be contempt to publish a recording of legal proceedings by playing it in public or to dispose of a recording with a view to publication. The section gives courts a discretion to allow tape recording under such conditions as they think fit. The courts also have power to order forfeiture of a tape recorder and any recording.

Common Law contempt

-62 It is still possible to commit contempt of court at common law, outside the provisions of the 1981 Act, if the court decides that the conduct involved was intended to impede or prejudice the administration of justice. Section 6 of the Act specifically leaves that possibility open. The kind of behaviour that the courts might regard as serious enough to amount to deliberate contempt can be seen in a case in 1988 in which the publishers of the *Sun* newspaper were fined £75,000 in England.

09–63   The authorities had decided there was not enough evidence
to prosecute a doctor accused of raping an eight-year-old girl.
The *Sun* financed a private prosecution and published a
number of articles describing the doctor as a "beast" and a
"swine". They also published his name and his picture on the
front page. The doctor went to trial at Chelmsford Crown
Court and was acquitted.

09–64   In later proceedings taken against the publishers, Lord
Justice Watkins agreed with the Attorney General that the
Sun had been guilty of contempt, although not under the
1981 Act. The court said that where a newspaper gave
practical help to stage a private prosecution then published
a series of articles intended to prejudice a fair trial, it was
guilty of contempt at common law (*Attorney-General* v. *News
Group Newspapers* [1989] QB 110).

09–65   In May 1991 the editor of *The Sport* newspaper was cleared
of contempt after the Attorney-General brought proceedings
against him at common law. North Wales police had issued a
picture of David Evans, a man they wished to interview in
connection with the disappearance of a schoolgirl. They asked
that his previous convictions for rape and a history of sex
attacks should not be published. Two days before a warrant
was issued for Evans' arrest (which meant the case was not
active under the 1981 Act) *The Sport* published a story headlined "Evans was given ten years for rape".

09–66   Evans was jailed for life for the girl's murder, and in subsequent proceedings, the High Court decided that the Attorney-General had failed to show that the editor of *The Sport*
had intended to prejudice a fair trial. In court, the editor, Mr
Peter Grimsditch, defended the decision to publish Evans'
record because "he was on the run and a danger to other
women".

09–67   In the course of his decision, Mr Justice Hodgson was
strongly critical of the decision in the *Sun* case. He said the
decision was wrong and were it necessary to do so, he would
refuse to follow it. He warned that to find a newspaper guilty
of contempt in these circumstances could impede investigative journalism. He added: "Many of the targets of investigative journalism are rich and powerful and who is to say that
they, when attacked, will not respond by seeking leave to
move for contempt?"

Sunday Times case

–68 In a decision with wide-ranging implications for the media, the House of Lords decided in April 1991 that the *Sunday Times* had been guilty of contempt at common law by publishing extracts from the book *Spycatcher* while an injunction was in force banning publication by a number of other newspapers. There was no injunction restraining publication by the *Sunday Times* and the newspaper argued that it would be an unwarranted extension of the law to find it guilty of contempt. Although it knew of the existence of the orders against other papers it was not bound by them nor was it assisting a breach of the injunction by those newspapers which were caught by the injunction. The *Sunday Times* had received legal advice that to publish in these circumstances would not amount to contempt.

–69 The Attorney-General, who brought proceedings against the *Sunday Times*, accepted that the newspaper could not be bound by a court order to which it was not a party. His argument, which the court accepted, was that by publishing *Spycatcher* extracts, the paper had knowingly destroyed the whole point of the injunctions, and that was a deliberate interference with the course of justice. Lord Ackner pointed out that *Sunday Times* editor Mr Andrew Neil accepted that he knew of existing injunctions against the *Observer* and *Guardian* and regarded *Spycatcher* as "banned in Britain". To avoid the risk of an injunction against his own paper, Mr Neill kept the *Spycatcher* extracts out of the first edition.

–70 Lord Ackner said that since the whole point of contempt was to prevent interference with the course of justice, it would leave a remarkable gap in the law if it could not deal with a situation of this kind. "Whatever would be the point of a court making an order designed to preserve the confidentiality of material, the subject matter of a dispute between A and B, pending the trial of the action, if, at the whim of C, the protection afforded by the court by its order could be totally dissipated?"

–71 Lord Jauncey, one of the Scottish judges in the appeal, said he was quite satisfied that a person who knowingly acted to frustrate the operation of a court order could be guilty of contempt even though he was neither named in the order nor assisted anyone who was named to breach it. He did not accept that this necessarily converted every injunction from an order against a named person to one against the world. It was only in a limited type of case that independent action by a third party would interfere with a court order in which he was not named.

09–72   However, Lord Oliver recognised the wide-ranging implications of the decision and the potential for gagging the media for a lengthy period. He said he had reached his decision with "a measure of disquiet" not because he doubted its validity, but because of the possibilities that it opened up. He stressed the importance of the courts keeping a vigilant eye on the possibility of the law of contempt being invoked in support of claims which were, in truth, insupportable.

09–73   This was because a plaintiff seeking an injunction never had to show more than a fairly arguable case to succeed.

09–74   He added: "The effect in a contest between a would-be publisher and one seeking to restrain the publication of allegedly confidential information, is that the latter, by presenting an arguable case, can effectively through the invocation of the law of contempt, restrain until the trial of the action, which may be two or more years ahead, publication not only by the defendant by anyone else within the jurisdiction". By this means, what might turn out to be perfectly legitimate comment could be stifled until it was no longer important or had any public interest. (*Times Newspapers* v. *The Attorney-General* [1992] 1 A.C. 191. See also Chapter 30, "Official Secrets".)

Right of Appeal

09–75   Any doubt that existed about the right of a publisher to appeal against a finding of contempt in criminal proceedings was removed by a judgment of the High Court in 1982 setting aside convictions against *The Herald* and *The Scotsman* following reports of a High Court trial in Glasgow in July 1981. The case involved 11 accused charged with conspiring to further the aims of the Ulster Volunteer Force by illegal means.

09–76   The reports of the case included reference to a Mrs Gibson and her husband (witnesses at the trial) being surrounded by police as they left the building and taken in an unmarked police car to a secret address. Lord Ross, the trial judge, held there was a risk that jurors might be influenced in their consideration of the credibility of the two witnesses, and admonished both papers after finding them guilty of contempt.

–77 They appealed by way of a petition to the *nobile officium*, to a Bench chaired by Lord Emslie, the Lord Justice-General, which decided there had been no contempt. It was understood to be the first case of an appeal by any newspaper against a conviction for contempt in Scotland.

–78 The judgment stated that Gibson was a self-confessed accomplice in the crime, who admitted being a commander of the UVF and implicated several of the accused. The appeal judges agreed with the newspapers' submission that it was mere speculation to say the jury might be influenced by what the newspapers had said about the two witnesses. The reports had to be read in the context of the particular trial and of the extraordinary security precautions obviously being taken throughout its course, which were a matter of public knowledge (*Kemp Petitioners* 1982 SLT 357).

Background information

–79 Apart from establishing the procedure for appeal in a contempt case, *Gibson* provided some useful guidance for the media over the publication of outside information which is not part of the evidence in court. Although references to an unmarked police car and a secret address were not based on evidence that had come out in court, Lord Emslie was satisfied that their mention was not prejudicial.

–80 However, it would be highly dangerous to assume that it is always safe to include information from outside the courtroom in reports of criminal cases. As in *Gibson*, there will usually be no substantial risk where the information consists simply of facts which are already known to members of the jury and will not therefore influence their minds in reaching their verdict. And it should always be made clear that it is a statement of known fact and does not form part of the proceedings as such.

–81 The dangers of background knowledge were well illustrated by a case in 1989 in which the *Alloa Advertiser* admitted contempt. At the end of a report of a ongoing trial at Alloa Sheriff Court, the newspaper stated that all the accused were released on bail, except two (who were named), "who are serving sentences for drugs offences imposed at the High Court in Edinburgh". The result of revealing the previous convictions was that the Crown had to desert the case and serve a fresh indictment.

09–82　　It is also highly dangerous to mix together background with what is said in court. In December 1991 the BBC were fined £5,000 over a television news report on a drugs trial in Shrewsbury, a report described by Lord Justice Watkins in the High Court as "literally strewn with error". Counsel for the BBC told the court: "There was a series of mistakes, in no small measure due apparently to the inability of this reporter to distinguish what he had heard and seen in court on the one hand, and what he had been told some time before in briefings by Customs and Excise".

Courts' attitude to contempt

09–83　　In Scotland a complaint of contempt against the media in a criminal case can be brought from three separate sources—the Crown, the defence, and the judge who is hearing the case in question. It is also worth remembering that prejudice can affect the prosecution as well as the defence. In the case of *Michael Fagan*, the man who broke into the Queen's bedroom, the High Court in London took the view in 1983 that inaccurate statements in a newspaper story to the effect that certain charges against Fagan had either been withdrawn or dropped created a substantial risk of serious prejudice to the prosecution.

09–84　　The classic example of contempt proceedings being brought by the Crown is the case of *Stuurman* in 1979 which illustrates several important points—most importantly, that there can be contempt even although the court decides at the end of the day that there was no actual prejudice. The test is whether there was a substantial risk. *Stuurman* also makes clear that anyone who publishes prejudicial material cannot plead as a defence that the information came from police sources nor that the story was passed as safe by a lawyer.

09–85　　In *Stuurman*, the *Herald* was fined £20,000 and the then editor £750 for publishing a front-page story about a major drugs operation in the Scottish borders. The headline read:

"Armed raids smash big drugs ring in Scotland", and the accompanying story provided details of how a "huge illicit drugs operation" had been smashed by police. It also informed readers that three of the Dutch nationals who had been arrested were believed to have escaped from prison in Holland. A police spokesman said the four people under arrest had been operating the biggest laboratory ever found in Scotland.

9–86   The Lord Advocate presented a petition for contempt to the High Court and, given the tone of the story, *the Herald* had little option but to admit its guilt. Lord Justice General Emslie described the offence as being of the gravest character and well-nigh incomprehensible. The court was appalled to learn that publication had been checked by a legal advisor.

9–87   The court was also informed that the story had been sent out by the Press Association and was based on information released by police in England. Lord Emslie said: "There can surely be no lingering doubt that if information, even from police sources, about a person who has been charged with criminal offences and arrested, is such that, if published, it would constitute contempt of court, the source of the offending material cannot be relied upon in mitigation of the offence".

9–88   The defence then presented a petition to the High Court, arguing that since the pre-trial publicity was so blatantly prejudicial a fair hearing was now impossible. Having previously instituted the contempt proceedings against the *Herald* (and Radio Forth) the Lord Advocate now informed the court that in his opinion there was not such a risk of prejudice that the trial should be aborted and the court agreed.

9–89   Following their convictions, three of the accused appealed on the ground that their trial should not have been allowed to go ahead because of the prejudicial publicity. The Court of Criminal Appeal rejected this argument. Lord Emslie said the question for the court was whether the risk of prejudice was so grave that even the careful directions of the trial judge could not reasonably be expected to remove it:

9–90   "In our opinion, that question falls to be answered in the negative. The publications occurred almost four months before the trial diet was called. In considering the effect of these publications, the court was well entitled to bear in mind that the public memory of newspaper articles and news broadcasts and of their detailed contents is notoriously short. "That being so, the residual risk of prejudice to the prospects of a fair trial could reasonably be expected to be removed by careful directions such as those which were given by the trial judge".

09–91   In the light of Lord Emslie's remarks, the media could be forgiven for wondering why the contempt was treated so seriously in the first place if the public's memory is short and the problem could be cured by a careful direction by the trial judge. While one can appreciate the desire of the Crown Office and the courts not to see the prosecution of serious crime thwarted by pre-trial publicity, the *Stuurman* case leaves the distinct impression of the authorities having their cake and eating it. The approach of the English Courts appears to be different. In May 1994 the High Court in London regarded a lapse of 9 months between publication and trial as being of "over-riding importance" in rejecting contempt complaints against ITN and four newspapers. They had referred to a previous conviction of IRA terrorist Paul Magee—the murder of an SAS captain—when Magee was arrested in June 1992. Magee was later jailed for 30 years for the murder of special constable Glenn Goodman. Following the conviction, the Attorney General brought contempt proceedings, but his case was rejected by the High Court. Lord Justice Leggatt said the media organisations involved might be thought to be "extremely fortunate" but 9 months was a long time to retain a story in one's mind. The court could not say with certaintly that reports had created a substantial risk of prejudice to the trial.

Tom King case

09–92   There may be circumstances in which the courts will decide that the risk of prejudice is so great that no direction by the trial judge can remove it. In 1990 the Appeal Court in England quashed the convictions of three Irish people who had been jailed for 25 years on charges of conspiring to murder Home Secretary Mr Tom King. Less than 24 hours after the three declined to give evidence at their trial Mr King made a statement in the House of Commons declaring his intention to curb the right to silence because, in his view, too many guilty people were being acquitted. He repeated his views in a number of TV news bulletins.

-93 The following day, the trial judge rejected a defence plea for a retrial and went on to direct the jury about the inalienable right of the accused to remain silent. The Appeal Court took a different view. Lord Beldam said: "We are left with the definite impression that the impact the statements on television and in the press may have had on the fairness of the trial could not be overcome by the direction to the jury".

Joseph Trainer case

-94 The first modern case in which a Scottish court has accepted the logic of a finding of contempt by aborting a trial was that of Joseph Trainer at the High Court in Paisley in 1987. Trainer was on trial for the murder of his brother-in-law, his defence being that the fatal stabbing was an accident. After closing speeches, Radio Clyde reported that he had offered to plead guilty to a reduced charge of culpable homicide. This had not been said in open court and, in any case, was not consistent with a plea of accident.

-95 Lord Allanbridge took the exceptional step of polling the jury to see how many had heard the offending broadcast and it turned out that seven out of the 15 had. The judge fined Colin Adams, the news editor of Radio Clyde, £20,000 and Gavin Bell, the freelance who had sent out the story, £5,000. He also decided the prejudice was so great that the trial must be halted.

-96 The case had two interesting sequels. Mr Trainer was retried at the High Court in Edinburgh and acquitted. Mr Adams appealed against his fine which was quashed by three appeal court judges. Lord Emslie said that Mr Adams had relied on the expertise of a freelance journalist with 20 years' experience and it was difficult to attach any blame to him for what had happened. However, the court took the view that the culpability of Mr Bell, who did not appeal against his fine, was of a high order.

-97 The case is also interesting for anyone trying to answer the question of who is liable for contempt. In many cases it will be the publisher and editor, but *Trainer* illustrates that freelance reporters and news editors can also be found liable and fined heavily. It will depend on the particular circumstances of each case.

Mistakes in court reports

09–98   In a number of other recent cases, the Scottish courts have decided that the fact that a mistake has been made in a story will not necessarily lead to a finding of contempt. This should not however, be taken as a signal to relax standards of accuracy. As the *Trainer* case illustrates, mistakes can still be costly.

09–99   In a murder trial at the High Court in Kilmarnock in 1989, a reporter's story stated that the two victims had been "felled" by single blows. A sub-editor changed the word to "killed" and also used the word killed in the headline. Counsel for the editor of the *Daily Record* argued that any problem created by the story could be solved by a direction by the trial judge that the jury should concentrate solely on the evidence in court. Lord Kirkwood said that in the circumstances, he was not satisfied that the *Record* story had created a substantial risk of serious prejudice.

09–100   Lord Cameron reached a similar decision in a trial at the High Court in Glasgow in which the accused was alleged to have said: "I'll get life for it". The quote appeared in the *Herald* and *Evening Times* as: "I'll get life for what I've done". The second statement amounts to a confession, while the first need not.

09–101   The approach is perhaps best summed up by Lord Cowie in the case of Daniel Pollock at the High Court in Airdrie in 1984 where the BBC reported details of charges which were no longer on the indictment before the jury. Lord Cowie accepted the argument that the realistic view of what a juror would think if he had heard the BBC report was that the reporter had got it wrong because the story did not coincide with the indictment. Any risk of prejudice could be cured by a simple direction to the jury to ignore the BBC report and decide the case solely on the evidence. That case illustrates the importance of checking with the clerk of court that the indictment in the hands of the reporter is the same as the one in the hands of the jury.

09–102   A reporter would be unwise to believe, however, that all judges adopt this approach when a mistake has been made. In the case of Alistair Keating at the High Court in Edinburgh in 1987, the publishers of the Sun were fined £5,000 by Lord Mayfield. This was a case where a fireman was accused of trying to kill his wife by wiring explosives into her car. The *Sun* ran a story in the middle of the trial giving the impression, wrongly, that the accused had admitted putting the explosives in place.

-103   It is also possible to commit contempt through a simple misunderstanding of criminal procedure. In 1990 the *Aberdeen Press and Journal* was found guilty of contempt over a report of a murder trial which was headed: "Husband decides on no defence in wife-murder trial". This was based on the first paragraph of the story which stated that the accused had decided not to defend the charge. In fact all that had happened was that his defence counsel had decided not to call any witnesses in support of his not guilty plea. After an unqualified apology by the editor, Lord Cameron decided that the contempt had been purged.

    Journalists must also be wary of reporting trials at an early stage when all that has happened is that an indictment has been read to the jury. Scottish Judges do not approve of phrases such as "The court was told" or "The court heard" at this stage. They take the view that this gives the impression that evidence has been led, when in fact, it has not.

    If basing a story simply on allegations in the indictment it is safer to use a phrase such as "The Crown alleges" or "The indictment states". To a journalist the distinction may seem artificial, but the courts regard it as crucial and it could avoid a finding of contempt.

Penalties for contempt.

-104   Where a court imposes a prison sentence for contempt it must, under section 15 of the 1981 Act, be for a fixed term although the court retains its power to order discharge at an earlier date. The maximum prison sentence which may be imposed by the High Court or a sheriff court in cases taken on indictment is two years, but a fine (without statutory limit) may be imposed as well or as an alternative. Where the contempt is dealt with by a sheriff in summary or civil proceedings other than on indictment the maximum penalty is three months' imprisonment or a fine of £2,000 or both. In the district court the maximum is 60 days or £1,000 or both.

Civil proceedings

09–105   The Act also applies to civil proceedings which now become active either from the time arrangements for a hearing are made (in Scotland when the record is closed) or from the time the hearing begins, whichever happens first. This brought about an important change in the stage at which the contempt law began to operate under the strict liability rule in the Court of Session and civil cases in the sheriff court. Previously, it was possible to commit contempt from the much earlier stage of the case appearing in the Calling List of the Court of Session or in the official list of cases intimated in the sheriff court.

09–106   A hearing need not necessarily be the hearing of the case on its merits or for disposal of the main point. It can be a hearing to deal with an incidental or preliminary matter, such as interim interdict, interim custody or access, amendment of pleadings, appointment of curator, etc. As we have seen, a fair and accurate report of such a hearing would be protected under section 4 of the Contempt of Court Act.

09–107   The making of arrangements for a hearing is defined in the Act as meaning, in the case of an ordinary action in the Court of Session or sheriff court, when the record is closed; in the case of a motion or application, when it is enrolled or made; and in any other case, when the date for a hearing is fixed or a hearing is allowed. Again, it is the step which happens first that has the effect of deciding when the case becomes active.

09–108   Since some of the steps referred to—such as closing the record, enrolment of a motion or allowance of a hearing—take place usually in the offices of the appropriate court without public intimation, the journalist will have to check with either court staff or lawyers in the case as to whether any of the stages in question has been reached.

09–109   The changes made in the Act on contempt in civil cases have an important bearing on the summons as a possible source of information for journalists. Before the passing of the Act it was understood from the case of *Richardson* v. *Wilson* (1879) R. 237 that a summons was a private document. Publication of material from a summons in that case, which had only appeared on the Calling List, led to a newspaper being sued for slander. The First Division, in upholding a complaint against the paper, also ruled that it would be contempt for a lawyer to make the contents of a summons available to the press before the case had come into open court. Publication from a summons could therefore lead to a risk of contempt as well as proceedings for defamation. The 1981 Act appears to rule out the risk of contempt by the media by the publication of information from a summons. A summons will normally be issued before a date for a hearing has been fixed or any other relevant step under the Act has caused the case to become active.

-110   But the Act does not alter the pre-existing law that it is contempt to publish matter intended to prejudice the proceedings. So far as clerks of court and lawyers in possession of summonses are concerned, it may still be contempt at common law for them to disclose the contents at that early stage.

-111   There certainly have been cases since the Contempt Act was passed where stories have appeared in the media based almost entirely on summonses which have have been handed over either by lawyers or one of the parties involved in the case. This has happened, for example, in cases where prison officers have been suing the Secretary of State for Scotland over injuries received in prison riots. It has also happened in the case of haemophiliacs who have been diagnosed as suffering from the AIDS virus after receiving batches of contaminated blood. No objection was taken to these reports. Journalists should always bear in mind, however, that particularly where an individual is being sued rather than some public body such as a health board, the summons may include allegations which could lead to a defamation action, even although publication would not be contempt.

-112   Civil cases remain active until they are disposed of, discontinued or withdrawn. It is also worth noting that when an action is adjourned or interrupted so that negotiations can take place, the case remains active in terms of the Act and until the proceedings are settled, disposed of or withdrawn. But section 5 of the Act is designed to ensure that this fact does not preclude comment on a case while active, provided it is published "as part of a discussion in good faith of public affairs or other matters of general public interest'.

09–113   Some eminent judges have expressed the view that there is no need for contempt to protect civil cases, but it must be remembered that some civil cases are heard by juries. The editor and publishers of *Private Eye* were each ordered to to pay £10,000 by the Court of Appeal in England for their "serious contempt" in publishing two articles about the wife of the Yorkshire Ripper while her libel action against them was pending. The allegations—that Mrs Sonia Sutcliffe had provided her husband with a false alibi and defrauded the DSS— were published three months before the hearing of the libel action. The Appeal Court took the view that apart from the possibility of influencing potential jurors by blackening Mrs Sutcliffe's character, the articles were intended to deter her by what were tantamount to threats. They posed a threat to the administration of justice and clearly created a substantial risk of serious prejudice.

Tribunals and other bodies

09–114   Tribunals and "bodies exercising the judicial power of the State" are now treated as courts for the purpose of applying the law of contempt under the Act. This measure met strong opposition during passage of the measure through Parliament. The Government could not undertake to provide a list of the tribunals and other bodies which fitted the definition. If the Government with its resources found the task beyond it, it is not one this book can be confident of achieving, given the great number and variety of bodies possibly involved. (The provision is understood to have been included in the Act because of a controversial English decision arising from a BBC television discussion of a valuation tribunal case while it was *sub judice*.)

09–115   The problem may be simplified to some extent by leaving out of the definition all those tribunals set up to deal with disputes or complaints over the conduct of members of professions, trades or specialised bodies where no judicial power of the State is involved. In most of these cases the body in question is deciding questions of discipline, ethics or practice within the profession or trade in question. The definition does, however, cover a judicial appeal from a tribunal which is not itself within the category.

116 It also covers tribunals of inquiry set up under statute or by ministerial order, fatal accident inquiries, the Lands Tribunal for Scotland, industrial tribunals, rent tribunals, inquiries into deaths at sea, shipping casualties or railway accidents held under statutory provisions laid down for the purpose, local planning inquiries, inquiries into objections to Private Acts of Parliament, and inquiries held under statute dealing with safety in mines and collieries.

117 This list is not exhaustive, and in doubtful cases the journalist may have to inquire into the nature of the powers of the tribunal in question before deciding whether the contempt law applies. If in doubt, the journalist should ask the advice of the Crown Office in Edinburgh on whether a particular tribunal or other body comes within the definition given in the Contempt of Court Act. During Parliamentary debate on the Bill the Attorney-General gave assurances, so far as England was concerned, that assistance of this kind would be provided, where possible, by his office.

118 Where there is a tribunal to which the Tribunals of Inquiry (Evidence) Act 1921 applies, the risk of contempt runs from when the tribunal is appointed until its report is presented to Parliament. Such tribunals are extremely rare.

Fatal accident inquiries

119 There have been attempts to bring contempt proceedings against the media over the reporting of fatal accident inquiries, although these are held by a sheriff sitting alone without a jury.

120 In 1990 Sheriff Principal John Mowat, Q.C., ordered the editor of the *Sunday Telegraph* and the author of an article in the newspaper to appear before him in the inquiry into the Lockerbie disaster.

121 In an article headed "Lockerbie Whitewash Warning" the *Sunday Telegraph* suggested that lawyers acting for the bereaved families were trying to avoid bringing out evidence of security flaws at Heathrow airport so as not to damage a possible future compensation claim against Pan Am. Mr Brian Gill, Q.C., counsel for the relatives, complained that the article could influence the way in which legal representatives carried out their duties.

09–122   The sheriff principal said, however, that he was reasonably confident that the implication in the article that he was conducting a whitewash did not impede the course of justice. He added that Mr Gill had some grounds for suggesting that he had been defamed in the article, although that was not a matter for the court.

09–123   In 1991 there were contempt hearings at Dunoon Sheriff Court during an inquiry into the death of a Glasgow lawyer who had lost her life while hillwalking. There was a complaint by counsel for the dead woman's family that an article in the *Evening Times* previewing the inquiry had anticipated the outcome of proceedings by pointing out that the woman was an experienced hill walker who died in fair weather conditions. There was also a complaint that the *Herald* had committed contempt because inaccurate remarks had been attributed to a witness. Although it was accepted that the sheriff was an experienced professional who could dismiss the article from his mind, it was argued that witnesses could have their evidence influenced by what they had read.

09–124   Both newspapers submitted that there was no contempt since there was no jury to be influenced at a fatal accident inquiry. To decide that witnesses might be influenced by something they had read in a newspaper was to suggest that they were not going to fulfil their oath to tell the whole truth and that would be a dangerous extension of the law. It was also argued on behalf of the *Evening Times* that the pre-inquiry publicity might in fact have had the desirable effect of bringing witnesses forward.

09–125   Sheriff William Palmer said he was not satisfied that there had been a substantial risk of serious prejudice to the proceedings, but the question of influencing witnesses is an interesting one. It has been decided in at least one sheriff court case (*Tudhope* v. *Glass* in 1981) that witnesses will not be affected by pre-trial publicity. Also, in the *Stuurman* case Lord Emslie said: "We are not impressed by the supposed risk that the evidence of witnesses would or might be tainted by anything they had read or heard" (following the arrest of the accused). "The basis upon which any witness's evidence or opinion was given or expressed was open to the test of cross-examination."

126 While it would be going too far to say that publicity in advance of a fatal accident inquiry could never amount to contempt of court, it is clear that fatal accident inquiries are not in the same position as criminal trials. The crucial difference is the absence of a jury, but another important factor is that no one is on trial at a fatal accident inquiry. The authorities might, however, take a different view if the complaint was not merely that a witness had read something in a newspaper but that his evidence had been influenced by his being interviewed by a journalist shortly before the inquiry or trial. There could be an argument that this had changed the evidence the witness would otherwise have given.

Coroners' inquests

127 These are confined to England and Wales, but because the 1981 Act applies to the whole United Kingdom, it is important for journalists and publishers in Scotland, whose work may circulate elsewhere, to know the position of the inquest in the context of contempt law. In 1986 the English Court of Appeal upheld a ruling by a High Court judge that it would be contempt for London Weekend Television to screen a programme about the death of a man in police custody during an adjournment of an inquest into his death. The Police Federation and six policemen had successfully applied to the High Court of Justice to stop transmission of a TV programme dealing with events leading up to the death of John Mikkleson, aged 34, at Feltham police station. The inquest had been opened at Hammersmith and adjourned and police investigations were proceeding to discover whether there were grounds for criminal charges. Lord Justice Watkins said in the Appeal Court that there was a high probability that if the programme was shown there would be a substantial risk to the course of justice; proceedings which were "active" might well be prejudiced.

Contempt in court

128 If a party to a legal action or a witness or member of the public commits contempt by his behaviour in court or makes offensive remarks amounting to contempt, it will not normally be contempt for a report of the incident to be published, including quotations of what was said by the offender, provided his remarks can be treated as relevant to the proceedings before the court. It may be a matter of degree to decide when remarks not relevant to the case are safe to publish, but proceedings for contempt against the publisher are unlikely where the report is accurate. No action was taken, for instance, against newspapers which published accurate reports of a litigant in the First Division of the Court of Session who called the judges "Nazis".

Dignity of the court

09–129   The media would be failing to meet their responsibilities if they failed to criticise the judiciary and court decisions where criticism is deserved. A court would be extremely reluctant, unless in the most exceptional circumstances, to treat this as contempt of court. Outspoken attacks on the legal system and on individuals within it are now far more frequent than before.

09–130   Proceedings for contempt are rarely taken unless there is a clear infringement of the law and in the case of *Royle* v. *Grey* in 1973 the High Court made it clear that the power to punish for contempt should be exercised only with care and discretion. In their judgment the court quoted with approval what Lord President Normand had said in the earlier case of *Milburn* in 1946: "the greatest restraint and discretion should be used by the court in dealing with contempt of court, lest a process, the purpose of which is to prevent interference with the administration of justice, should degenerate into an oppressive or vindictive abuse of the court's powers".

09–131   Justified criticism of the system or individuals is one thing, but it would be highly dangerous to state or imply, for example, that a judge or sheriff had been guilty of of dishonest or criminal behaviour. The most likely result would be an action for defamation.

Escaped prisoners

09–132   Care must be taken in publishing reports about prisoners who have escaped from prison or from custody, in case what is said will prejudice their subsequent trial or proceedings taken against them for having escaped. (See the case of David Evans, paragraph 09–65.) It is by no means unknown for someone to plead not guilty to a charge of escaping from custody. An accused charged with attempting to defeat the ends of justice by escaping has the same basic right to protection from prejudice by publicity as any other person awaiting trial, but the extent of this right may be modified because of his own violent behaviour. Where the escaped prisoner has a record of violence he may be a danger to members of the public, and the media would feel entitled to publish details sufficient to warn them.

–133   In deciding how much to publish, journalists must be guided by official sources—the Scottish Information Office, the Crown Office or the procurator-fiscal—who may authorise publication of a fugitive's violent tendencies in appropriate cases. In certain instances, by authority of the Lord Advocate or Solicitor-General, the media may be allowed, or encouraged, to publish a photograph or photofit picture of a violent person at large.

–134   Normally, official statements will not contain reference to the crime of which the escaped prisoner has been convicted, or the charge for which he awaits trial, except where a departure is justified by considerations of public safety. The basic information—name, home area, date and place of sentence and term of sentence—will normally be issued for publication.

–135   In 1981 a man serving life for murder was allowed out of Saughton Prison to visit his family under escort, escaped and, while at large, raped a woman. At the time of his escape an official of the Scottish Prisons Department was quoted as saying he was not considered dangerous. Next day a public warning was issued through the media, along with his photograph, authorised by the Lord Advocate. After the man was caught and sentenced for the rape, the Scottish Home and Health Department stated that in future cases of the kind, their advice to the media would be that, although a person's behaviour in prison did not suggest he would be a danger to the public, his record involved violent crime.

KEY POINTS

–136   Contempt law tries to balance the often conflicting interests of freedom of speech with the right to a fair trial. The approach of Scots law is that pre-trial publicity should be kept to a minimum.

The Contempt of Court Act 1981 says that anything which creates a substantial risk of serious prejudice to legal proceedings is contempt, even although prejudice was not intended. Publication of previous convictions before a trial would amount to contempt, as would publication of the accused's picture if identification was in issue.

The risk of committing contempt starts when someone has been arrested, a warrant has been issued for his arrest, an indictment has been served or a summons issued, whichever comes first.

Bear in mind, however, the possibility of common law contempt which covers publication *intended* to prejudice legal proceedings.

The risk ends when the accused is acquitted or sentenced or with the return of any other verdict or decision which puts an end to proceedings.

The risk of contempt starts to run again when an appeal is lodged but publication must create a substantial risk of prejudice and the case will be heard by three judges rather than a jury.

In civil cases the risk of contempt normally runs from the moment the record is closed.

CHAPTER 10

PHOTOGRAPHY

10-01 The publication of a photograph is just as capable as a story or a headline of creating a substantial risk of serious prejudice in terms of the Contempt of Court Act. The Act makes no specific mention of pictures at all but lays down rules which apply to "publications", and goes on to explain that this includes "any speech, writing, broadcast or other communication in whatever form, which is addressed to the public at large or any section of the public". "Other communication in whatever form" must include photographs, as well as television pictures, videos, sketches, drawings or cartoons.

10-02 The Act does not, however, deal with the whole law of contempt as it affects photography, and it is still necessary to go back to the old common law for guidance, particularly over the restriction on taking or making pictures within court precincts.

10-03 It should certainly not be assumed that, although the Act is a United Kingdom statute, the Scottish courts will apply the same standards as the English in interpreting it. For example, English newspapers have always exercised much greater freedom than those in Scotland in publishing pictures of criminal suspects. Even since the passing of the 1981 Act they have continued publishing this kind of picture to an extent that would be inviting contempt proceedings in a Scottish case.

10-04 An outstanding instance was the case of *Dennis Nilsen* who, after the unearthing of parts of a number of human skeletons in London in 1983, appeared in pictures published in English newspapers handcuffed to two detectives. Lord McCluskey, former Solicitor-General for Scotland, asked the Lord Advocate in the House of Lords whether Scottish newspapers were free to follow the example of the English Press and to publish pictures of people accused of murder, allegedly committed in Scotland, without risk that the Lord Advocate would petition the High Court to treat publication as a contempt of court. Lord Mackay of Clashfern, the Lord Advocate, made it clear that they were not.

10–05   Lord McCluskey was also the judge who found the BBC guilty of contempt in March 1992 for broadcasting footage of Paul Ferris, a murder accused on trial at the High Court in Glasgow, being led from a police van to the court. The judge made it clear that the duty of the court was to ensure that those accused of serious crimes received a fair and impartial trial. He added: "It is clearly essential that witnesses are not materially influenced in any way. It follows that in any case where the question of identification may arise it is clear that the publication in the press or television of any film, photograph, or even an artist's likeness during a trial or after a warrant has been issued, causes a potential risk to the administration of justice". There might be circumstances where the risk was small, for example if the accused was well known to the public as a sports or showbusiness personality, but such cases would be rare.

10–06   "There is only one safe route for the media to follow and it is this—do not publish any picture of an accused person in Scotland until a trial is finished or the charge has been dropped by the Lord Advocate. It has been made clear in many cases that any breach of this rule is liable to be dealt with by this court as contempt".

10–07   The BBC submitted that viewers saw only a fleeting glimpse of Mr Ferris for two or three seconds and not at a peak viewing time, but Lord McCluskey said the accused had been clearly identified and there was a substantial risk that the course of justice might be seriously prejudiced.

10–08   The kind of picture that would invite trouble, even in England, can be illustrated by the case of *Peter Hain* in 1976. The *Evening Standard* was fined £1,000 for printing a picture of Mr Hain on its front page on the day he was due to attend an identification parade. Even although the caption read "Hain, he's no bank robber", the court ruled that the picture prejudiced his trial by making it more likely that someone would pick him out at the identification parade.

10–09   It would be wrong, however, to treat it as a total certainty in every case that the publication of a picture would bring contempt proceedings. As Lord McCluskey suggested in the

Ferris case, there will be circumstances in which the identification of the accused will not give rise to a risk of prejudice. To give one example, if a celebrated television chat show host appeared on a speeding charge there would be unlikely to be any objection to his picture being published. His identity would already be well-known and a speeding case would not be tried by a jury. Even in that kind of case, however, it would be sensible to take legal advice before publishing.

0–10   On the basis of several decisions by the Scottish courts before the 1981 Act, contempt could be committed by the publication of a picture of an accused person during his trial although there was no possibility of any issue of identification arising in the case and no question of prejudice.

0–11   Commonsense was restored to the law in the case of *Atkins v. London Weekend Television Ltd.* in 1978, when the High Court accepted that there was no hard and fast rule that the publication of a photograph of an accused person would always constitute contempt. The court added:''' We accept, too, the further proposition that the publication of a photograph of an accused person will constitute contempt only where a question of identification has arisen or may arise and where the publication is calculated to prejudice the prospect of fair trial''.

10–12   Pictures of witnesses who have completed their evidence are normally permissible, but the safest course is to check whether the identification of a witness is still relevant. In a case where there is a defence of incrimination (where the accused blames someone else for the crime), if the person being incriminated gives evidence his picture should not be used until the trial is complete.

Care with captions

10–13   Even although a picture is regarded as safe, great care has to be taken to avoid a substantial risk of serious prejudice in writing the caption. At the risk of stating the obvious, there must be a check that the caption matches the picture. In a libel case before the High Court in London in December 1986 Dr Abdel Yassine, director of research at the Arab Institute for Socio-Economic Studies in Jordan, won undisclosed damages after a picture identifying him as the notorious terrorist Abu

Nidal was published in *The Times* and the *Guardian*. Both newspapers and the Press Association, who distributed the picture, agreed to pay substantial damages and costs. The court was told the photograph had been distributed and published in good faith.

Civil cases

10–14   While contempt cases stemming from publicity in civil proceedings have been extremely rare, it should not be assumed that no risk exists. It is still possible, for example, for a jury to be involved in a damages action in the Court of Session.

Inside the court

10–15   The precise aim and scope of the law of contempt not covered by the 1981 Act, for example, where there has been no publication and possibly none is intended, are by no means clear. While it is easy to understand the desire to prevent prejudice by publicity, it is less obvious why, for example, it should be contempt merely to bring a camera into a courtroom without actually using it or possibly even intending to do so.

10–16   There is no statute specifically dealing with the taking of photographs, or having a camera in court. The Criminal Justice Act 1925, which bans the taking of photographs and the publication of photographs taken in court, applies only to England and Wales, although the attitude towards photography in and around the courts in Scotland was similar. Photographing court proceedings in the Supreme Courts was permitted only with the permission of the Lord President and permission was always refused.

10–17   However, as we shall see, this policy was reversed in 1992 when Lord President Hope paved the way for court proceedings in Scotland to be televised.

English Act

10–18   The 1925 Act provides that no-one shall take or attempt to take in any court any photograph or, with a view to publication, make or attempt to make in any court any portrait or sketch of any person, either a judge or a juror or witness or a party to any proceedings, civil or criminal. The Act also bans the publication of any photograph, portrait or sketch taken or made in contravention of the Act. The Act covers a photograph, portrait or sketch taken or made in the courtroom or in the building or in the precincts of the building in which a court is held.

9–19 There were two examples in 1986 of how the English and Welsh courts deal with this situation. One involved a member of the public who took a flash photograph of Judge Malcolm Ward during a sitting of Wolverhampton Crown Court. Mrs Joan Maynard, recently married to a solicitor, had been taken to the court by her husband to see justice being administered and gain experience before starting work in her husband's office. Mrs Maynard, who said later she had no idea she was breaking the law, was detained in the cells until the judge later dealt with her, fining her £500 (later reduced to £100 on appeal) and confiscating her camera.

0–20 The publishers of the *Merthyr Express* were fined £200 for contempt when a staff artist was discovered sketching during a trial after permission to do so had been refused by Judge Lewis Bowen. The editor, Graham Jones, who was ordered to appear, told the judge he had sent the artist to sketch from memory and not during the case. Judge Bowen said he had refused permission to sketch in court because he felt it might make the jury uncomfortable and because it was unfair to the defendant (a hospital consultant) who had already had widespread publicity. He conceded the editor acted in good faith.

0–21 In a case in Glasgow Sheriff Court in 1975 a Mr Peter Sweeney admitted being in contempt of court in that, during the proceedings in a criminal case in the court, he was in possession of a camera and took photographs in the court. His solicitor said Mr Sweeney had wanted a souvenir of his first visit to a courtroom, but, after being told by an attendant to leave, which he did, he had been pursued by a detective, apprehended and detained in custody overnight. The following day the photographs he took were produced in court and Sheriff Archibald Bell, Q.C., admonished Mr Sweeney for contempt of court and confiscated the camera. He stated: "Proceedings in court cannot and should not be subject to any interruption", although Mr Sweeney's solicitor had said what his client had done was so quiet and unobtrusive that even the sheriff was "unaware and not troubled by the matter".

10–22   It is difficult to see why the taking of a photograph should amount to contempt when it does not interfere with the proceedings before the court. It would be a different matter if the photography disturbed the judge or counsel or a witness or jurors. Obviously, the taking of a photograph with flash equipment in a courtroom during the hearing of a case would invite swift retribution. At the other end of the scale—without implying that such conduct would be approved by the court—there can be no doubt that tourists visiting our courts have taken photographs with miniature cameras and the court has been none the wiser nor the worse for it.

10–23   The Criminal Procedure (Scotland) Act 1975 (which came into operation after the *Sweeney* case) provides, that "any person who interrupts or disturbs the court (in solemn procedure) shall be liable to imprisonment or a fine or both as the judge thinks fit" and no maximum is specified. In light of the decision in *Sweeney*, it would appear that a photographer might be held in contempt of court even though the judge was unaware that the camera had been used in court, or even that there was one in the courtroom at all, and there could therefore have been no actual interference with the progress of proceedings as a result.

Precincts of the court

10–24   In a case in which official guidance was sought in 1964, the then Lord President issued a ruling which stated: "No photographing is permitted within the precincts of the Law Courts. The precincts of the Law Courts are defined as the areas occupied by the car park and the piazza". The reference was to the portion of Parliament Square, Edinburgh, lying between St Giles' Cathedral and Parliament House, and offered no guidance as to the precincts of any other law court in Scotland. Neither did it define the extent of the precincts at other exits from Parliament House which have been used in some cases to help parties escape the attentions of the Press.

10–25   It was probably the first formal attempt to define the precincts of any Scottish court over restrictions on photography. When invited to supply a definition of precincts of the court in an earlier case, the Lord Advocate of the day, Lord Wheatley, stated that a definition was not possible because the extent of the precincts must vary with the circumstances and requirements of each case.

10–26 Over the years the precincts rule was relaxed to the extent that cameras (including television cameras) were allowed into Parliament House to take pictures or film of, for example, a judge who is to appear in some future programme or feature article. The inside of Parliament House was also filmed to provide background shots for a TV series about lawyers. This was, of course, always done after asking the permission of the Lord President.

Televising the courts

10–27 A significant breakthrough came in the summer of 1992 when Lord President Hope announced that he no longer thought it in the public interest that there should be an absolute ban on televising court proceedings. He stated:

10–28 "The rule hitherto has been that television cameras are not allowed within the precincts of the court. While the absolute nature of the rule makes it easy to apply it is an impediment to the making of programmes of an educational or documentary nature and to the use of television in other cases where there would be no risk to the administration of justice. In future the criterion will be whether the presence of television cameras in the court would be without risk to the administration of justice".

10–29 Lord Hope felt that technology had now reached such an advanced stage that certain court cases could probably be televised without undue interference with the proceedings, much as had happened in Parliament. He felt that there was sufficient support for the change within the judiciary and the Scottish legal profession in general. He added:

10–30 "It is also in the public interest that people in Scotland should become more aware of the way in which justice is being administered in their own courts. There is a risk that the showing on television of proceedings in the courts of other countries will lead to misunderstandings about the way in which court proceeedings are conducted in our own country".

10–31 The Lord President issued a series of guidelines under which requests by broadcasting organisations to televise proceedings in the Court of Session and High Court would be dealt. The televising of current proceedings in criminal cases at first instance, for example trials or preliminary hearings, were not be to be permitted under any circumstances "in view of the risks to the administration of justice." The same rule was to apply to civil cases at first instance. Although juries are not normally involved, Lord Hope felt there were risks in televising civil cases while witnesses were still giving their evidence.

10–32   However, cameras are to be allowed into the courtroom to televise appeal cases, both civil and criminal, subject to satisfactory arrangements being made about the placing of cameras and provided there is no additional lighting which would make courtroom conditions intolerable. The cameras will be allowed in subject to the approval of the presiding judge and under such conditions as he chooses to impose. Subject to the same conditions ceremonial occasions may be televised in the courtroom for use in a news bulletin. The taking of television pictures (without sound) of judges on the Bench, as a replacement for still pictures, will be allowed with the permission of the judge concerned. Requests by television companies to film proceedings, including proceedings at first instance, for later showing in educational or documentary programmes, will be given favourable consideration. However, the consent of all parties involved in the proceedings will be needed as will the approval of the presiding judge before the final product is screened. Similar guidelines were introduced by the Sheriffs Principal for Sheriff Courts as from November 1992. The first ever broadcast of a Scottish criminal trial was seen in April 1994 when BBC Scotland screened "Focal Point—The Trial" a case in Glasgow before Sheriff Brian Lockhart and a jury. In November 1994 BBC2 began showing a six-part series filmed in the Scottish Courts. The first programme featured a murder trial. The programme was broadcast only after the accused's trial and appeal had been completed and there was no risk of prejudice to the proceedings.

10–33   The attitude of the court to pictures being taken of people arriving at and leaving court may depend on the particular circumstances of the case. A picture of a convicted murderer being led away to begin his sentence might be treated completely differently from a photograph of a witness in a custody case who later complained of press harassment.

In the open

-34   When the judge, jury, clerk and counsel leave the courtroom, for example to go outside to inspect a piece of evidence such as a car, the place where the inspection takes place becomes, for the time being, the equivalent of the courtroom.

-35   Parties or witnesses or counsel walking along the street, either going to or leaving the court buildings, are in a different position and there is no danger in taking pictures provided nothing is done that would amount to obstructing or molesting them. Any conduct by photographers which discouraged a witness from coming voluntarily to court to give evidence might be regarded as an interference with the course of justice and punishable as common law contempt.

"Assault by photography"

-36   In 1975 proceedings were begun, but later abandoned, against two Press photographers who took pictures of a solicitor in the street outside the sheriff court at Dunfermline. The solicitor was appearing on behalf of a client at an inquiry into a suspicious death and the picture was taken during an adjournment. The solicitor complained to the procurator-fiscal, on whose authority the photographers were later charged with assault and had their films confiscated. The case was unprecedented.

-37   Researches could produce only a civil case in 1916 in which a boy aged 17, charged with a minor offence, had his fingerprints and photograph taken by the police without his parents' consent. He brought proceedings against the chief constable for defamation, claiming that his reputation had been damaged by having his fingerprints and photograph filed by the police along with those of notorious criminals.

-38   In the Dunfermline case, the Crown Office intervened and instructed the procurator-fiscal not to proceed with the case against the photographers, whose films were returned to them. The case establishes only that there has been no instance in Scotland of a successful prosecution for assault by photography. It is possible, however, that a photographer could be charged with breach of the peace—the scope of which has been gradually extended over the years—if he persisted in photographing someone in public against his wishes with results which led to a complaint by them or some kind of disturbance.

10–39   In March 1992 at Kilmarnock Sheriff Court a photographer was warned by police that if he tried to take a picture of a witness at a fatal accident inquiry he could be charged with breach of the peace. The case concerned the death of the witness's five children in a house fire, and he had made it clear to police that he did not wish to be photographed.

Children

10–40   There are special provisions to protect children under 16 involved in court proceedings from publicity. This is an area of particular importance to photographers and anyone involved in television journalism. The law is contained in section 22 of the Criminal Justice (Scotland) Act 1980, and a full account of the section is contained in Chapter 12.

10–41   An important point to remember is that the ban on identifying a child will also mean that the picture of an adult involved in the case cannot be used if this would lead to the identification of the child. The ban could also extend to pictures of a school or any other area that could lead to the child's identification.

10–42   There is an automatic ban on publishing anything that could lead to the identification of any child concerned in a children's hearing, or an appeal in such a case before the sheriff or Court of Session, under the terms of the Social Work (Scotland) Act 1968 (see paragraph 12–25).

Fatal accident inquiries

10–43   The sheriff presiding at a fatal accident inquiry has power to order non-publication of a picture of any person under 17 in any way involved in the inquiry (see Chapter 12).

10–44   The Civic Government (Scotland) Act 1982 makes it an offence to take any indecent photograph of a child under 16, to distribute or show such a photograph, or to possess one with a view to its distribution. The prohibition covers also video-recordings and films (see also paragraph 25–08). Contravention can result in a fine of up to £2,000 or a jail sentence of not more than two years, or both. It is a defence to prove there was a legitimate reason for distribution or possession of the item in question or that there was no knowledge or suspicion it was indecent.

Official secrets

-45 There is a voluntary system administered by a joint comittee representing the media and civil service to restrict publication of sensitive material, and matters which are subject to restriction are listed under a series of "D-A Notices". These are dealt with in more detail in Chapter 30; the aspect most likely to concern photographers covers pictures of defence establishments, installations, dockyards and factories.

KEY POINTS

Publication of the picture of an accused person before or during a criminal trial will almost certainly be treated as contempt of court if identification is in issue. Cases where identification is not in issue will be rare. Pictures of witnesses are normally permissible after their evidence is complete, but take legal advice before publishing. The taking of pictures in court is not banned by statute in Scotland but has been held to be contempt even although the proceedings were not disrupted. In 1964 Lord Clyde ruled that no pictures should be taken within the precints of the law courts. In 1992 Lord President Hope announced that the absolute ban on pictures within the precincts was to end. Televising of appeal court cases, under strict rules, was to be allowed.

CHAPTER 11

MATRIMONIAL PROCEEDINGS

11–01 There appears to be a widespread impression in some quarters, including the legal profession, that divorce actions in Scotland are conducted in the glare of publicity. That was the phrase used in the Report of the Royal Commission on Legal Services which was published in 1980. It was also one of the reasons put forward by the Faculty of Advocates for keeping divorces exclusively in the Court of Session. The Faculty talked about the glare of publicity that would probably be focused on an examination of private lives in the local sheriff courts. This was contrasted with the "relative anonymity" of the Court of Session, an observation much nearer the mark.

11–02 The fact is that reports of divorce proceedings are and have been rare in Scottish newspapers, and there are several reasons for this. Firstly, because of the Judicial Proceedings (Regulation of Reports) Act 1926, the media are extremely limited as to what they can publish about divorce, nullity and separation actions. Secondly, the overwhelming majority of divorces in Scotland are undefended and since 1978 are not normally heard in open court at all. It is also undoubtedly the case that the breakdown of marriage is so commonplace in Scotland these days—about one marriage in four fails—that the average case is not newsworthy.

11–03 The general situation has not changed with the passing of the Divorce Jurisdiction, Court Fees and Legal Aid (Scotland) Act 1983, which gave power to sheriff courts as well as the Court of Session to deal with divorces. There has been no explosion of publicity for divorce cases from sheriff courts around Scotland. Indeed, reports of sheriff court divorces have been almost non-existent and local newspapers have not followed the practice of some of their English counterparts of publishing weekly lists of names of people who have been divorced in undefended cases. There have also been very few reports of judgments of the courts in defended cases. However, now that divorce is competent in the sheriff court it is important that journalists should be familiar with the terms of the 1926 Act.

-04   The Act is unusual because, rather than banning the publication of specific details of matrimonial cases, it says that reports are prohibited altogether except for four limited categories of information. Section 1(i)(a) is not restricted to divorce cases and applies to judicial proceedings of any kind. It bans the publication of any indecent material or any indecent medical, surgical or physiological details, publication of which would be calculated to injure public morals.

-05   It is clear from evidence which was led at public inquiries before Parliament passed the 1926 Act that much concern was being voiced at the time about the effects on public morals of unrestricted reporting of full details of some scandalous divorce cases. The Act was passed following publicity about intimate medical evidence in a divorce involving a member of the Royal household. However, there has obviously been a shift in attitudes on the question of public decency and morals since then, and much of what would have been prohibited in the 1930s would pass without comment today.

-06   The part of the 1926 Act which has most relevance to the working journalist is section 1(i)(b) which affects reports of any judicial proceedings for dissolution of marriage, nullity of marriage or judicial separation. Nothing may be published about these types of case except: (a) the names, addresses and occupations of the parties to the action and of witnesses; (b) a concise statement of the charges, defences and counter-charges in support of which evidence has been given; (c) submissions on any point of law arising during the proceedings and the court's decision on that and (d) the judgment of the court and any observations made by the judge in giving judgment.

-07   The maximum penalty for each contravention of the Act is four months' imprisonment or a £500 fine or both, liability lying with the proprietor, editor, and printer or publisher.

-08   The Act applies to both defended and undefended divorces and undefended cases are by far the more frequent.

-09   In undefended cases an important change in procedure affecting the working practice of journalists was introduced in 1978. Anyone seeking a divorce in an undefended case no longer has to attend court personally with his or her witnesses. Written evidence in the form of sworn statements or affidavits has replaced evidence in court, and these cases are now normally dealt with by a judge in chambers.

11–10 A list of the divorces granted in undefended cases in the Court of Session is published in the court rolls once a week. A similar list is published in at least some sheriff courts. These lists do not contain enough information in themselves to provide the reporter with a story and a check to confirm details would have to be carried out with the relevant court department.

11–11 But only the brief details permitted by the 1926 Act should be used from the court documents. The few reports published in newspapers of affidavit divorces have run to only a few paragraphs setting out who has been divorced, on what ground and which judge granted decree.

11–12 As far as defended cases are concerned the normal practice in the Court of Session has been to wait until the judge issues his decision in a case before carrying a report. This is likely to be several weeks after he has heard evidence. The decision is normally given in writing and a copy is made available to journalists. Divorce judgments are normally in very full terms and provide the journalist with more than enough information to present a complete picture of a case while keeping within the terms of the 1926 Act.

11–13 There may of course be defended cases which are seen as so interesting and important that a decision is made to report them before the judgment stage. Again, this can be done only within the terms of the 1926 Act. The basic point to remember is that unlike most other cases, a detailed account of the evidence as it unfolds cannot be given in a divorce, nullity or separation action. The Act talks about a "concise" report of claims on both sides "in support of which evidence has been given". In other words, the journalist must wait until he has heard enough of the evidence to produce a "concise" summary of the case.

11–14 The word "concise" could present some difficulty, since its exact interpretation will vary with the circumstances of each individual case. A recital of alleged incidents or allegations based on the evidence given in court would not come within the definition of "concise". Where there is doubt, or the case is complicated, the safest course is to err on the side of brevity and keep the summary to a single sentence for the charges and another for replies and countercharges.

-15   The restrictions in the Act apply to reports "in relation to court proceedings". In any follow-up story, such as an interview with one of the parties, it would be sensible to avoid a mere rehashing of any evidence given in court, as this could arguably be caught by the terms of the Act. The dangers of defamation should also be kept in mind.

-16   Submissions on a point of law which crop up during the proceedings can provide a good source of copy. There have been several outstanding instances, for example the question of whether artificial insemination by a donor (AID) was a good defence to an action of divorce for adultery. In the *Argyll* divorce case the issue arose as to whether a wife could be compelled to surrender as evidence passages in her diary containing references to her alleged association with men other than her husband.

-17   In reporting this kind of submission the reporter must be careful that what he is publishing is not in essence an argument on the facts but truly deals with a question of law. A legal argument must of course be based on a certain minimum amount of fact, but any report, to come within the Act, should contain no more factual information than necessary for a proper report of the legal submissions.

-18   The next permissible category is "decision of the court" on the submissions on any point of law. This brings in the judgment given by the court at certain preliminary stages in a case where the issue is a legal one, but the judge is not necessarily being asked to give a final decision on the case. In the AID case referred to above Lord Wheatley heard preliminary debate on issues of great legal interest and public importance. The arguments contained a great deal of reportable and permissible material although very few newspapers took advantage of the opportunity, and of course the judgment was publishable.

-19   In another case a wife made a preliminary application to the court for an advance of a very large sum of interim expenses to enable her to bring witnesses from various countries to Scotland to help her defend a divorce action. The judge, Lord Guthrie, gave his view that under the 1926 Act his judgment on the point could be legally reported provided that the only other matters published were the parties' names and addresses as they appeared on the calling list.

11–20　　In reporting such preliminary matters, as well as the judgment, the provisions of section 1(i)(a) mentioned earlier in the chapter should not be forgotten. This prohibits the publication of any material calculated to injure public morals.

11–21　　The Act does not say that the media are allowed to publish in matrimonial cases the name of the judge or the court in which he is sitting or description of the parties or witnesses. But it seems a matter of commonsense that the Act cannot have been intended to ban the publication of details of this kind provided any descriptive material does not amount to evidence.

11–22　　The term "decree nisi" applies only in English law where, in divorce actions, decree becomes effective only after a certain period of time during which the authorities must be satisfied that no reason has arisen why decree should not be granted. Decree in Scotland becomes absolute when it is granted subject to a 21-day period to allow for any appeal to be lodged.

11–23　　The granting of a decree is, however, delayed in certain cases where the court has to be satisfied about the circumstances in which the children of the marriage are being cared for before issuing decree.

11–24　　The restrictions imposed by the 1926 Act upon the reporting of matrimonial cases apply to the appeal stages as well as in the court which first hears the case.

11–25　　No proceedings appear to have been taken against the media under the Act. In 1956, however, a newspaper published material from a petition for dissolution of marriage on the ground of presumed death at the stage when the document was displayed on the wall of Parliament House. The editor was required by the Lord Advocate to give a written undertaking that he would not allow a repetition, although the offence was a purely technical one.

11–26　　The case was not a matrimonial one in the usual sense and publicity of this kind would more likely help than hinder the ends of justice being achieved. Parliament has since rectified the situation, however: section 14 of the Presumption of Death

(Scotland) Act 1977 states that, for the avoidance of doubt, section 1(i)(b) of the 1926 Act does not apply to an action of declarator of death under the Act.

–27   The 1926 mechanism may be a trifle rusty through lack of use, but it would be dangerous to ignore the Act at a time when there is a growing feeling in some quarters that reporting of divorces is an intrusion into private lives. There was a threat to invoke the Act in a case in 1983 involving the Scottish entertainer Billy Connolly. His lawyers claimed that a custody hearing in the Court of Session was part of the Connollys' divorce action and that reports in several newspapers had gone far beyond the scope of the Act. The threat was never carried out, so that the question remains unanswered. The case does, however, illustrate the care reporters must exercise in distinguishing between a custody hearing pure and simple (where there are normally no reporting restrictions under the 1926 Act) and divorce proceedings where custody is in dispute.

KEY POINTS

–28   The Judicial Proceedings (Regulation of Reports) Act places strict limits on what can be reported in divorce and related cases. Detailed reporting of evidence is not allowed. Legal argument can be reported. The safest way to report defended divorces is to wait for a written judgment. There is no decreee nisi in Scotland.

CHAPTER 12

CHILDREN

12–01 The law provides the protection of anonymity for children involved in legal proceedings on the basis that they may be harmed by publicity. The protection is provided in various ways in criminal and civil cases, children's hearings and fatal accident inquiries.

12–02 The law on identifying children in criminal cases is contained in section 22 of the Criminal Justice (Scotland) Act 1980.

12–03 Section 22 applies to any criminal court in Scotland and forbids disclosure in court reports of a name, address or school, or any information calculated to lead to the identification of "any person under 16 years concerned in the proceedings". The section is intended to protect a child against or in respect of whom the proceedings are taken—an accused or victim—or who is appearing as a witness. The ban on identification applies to pictures as well as to newspaper, radio and television reports of cases. But see 12–25 below as to whether even "non identifiable" pictures are allowed. Where the person under 16 is involved as a witness only and no one against whom the proceedings are taken is under 16, there is no bar on identification unless the court makes a direction to that effect.

12–04 A court may at any stage of the proceedings dispense with the ban on identification if satisfied that this is in the public interest. The Secretary of State for Scotland is also given power, after a case has been dealt with, to make an order lifting the prohibition or to overrule an order made by the court.

12–05 In a case before the High Court in Edinburgh in 1983 (*H.M. Advocate* v. *George Aitken*), in which the Crown asked for a ruling, Lord Brand held that section 22 does not apply to dead children. He ruled that a "person" within the meaning of the section was a live person and someone who was dead could not be "concerned" in the proceedings. The judge added that, if he had decided the section did apply, he would have allowed identification in the particular case in the public interest. Had the defence submission that the section did apply to the child in the case been upheld, reports of the case could not have identified the father, who was charged with culpable homicide of the child, since this would have been "calculated" to identify the child.

–06   In deciding whether or not to allow identification, the court must bear in mind the public interest and the decision will depend very much on the view of the individual judge. In a case in 1991 at the High Court in Edinburgh, Lord Sutherland decided that it would not be in the public interest to lift reporting restrictions in the case of a 12-year-old boy who had been convicted of culpable homicide.

–07   The maximum penalty for contravening the section is a fine of £1,000.

–08   The journalist must look at the child's age when the case is in court. If the child becomes 16 on the day the case is before the court, the automatic ban on identification no longer applies. It is now the practice of the Crown Office in framing indictments to include the age of accused and victims under 16.

–09   There may be a question about exactly when the section 22 restriction takes effect. The section has to be read subject to its opening words—"No newspaper report of any proceedings in a court shall reveal. . ." On a strict reading, this means that the ban on identification operates only when the proceedings are in a court and not, for example, at preliminary stages of a case before a hearing takes place.

–10   This has led to some rather strange results. Cases have been reported including the name of a child victim one day, only to be published anonymously the next, after someone has been arrested and appeared in court.

–11   The Act makes no express provision for appeal against a court's direction either allowing or banning publication in terms of section 22, but the power given to the Secretary of State to make an order dispensing with the requirements of the section may provide a means for the media to ask in individual cases for the automatic bar to be lifted in the public interest. This, however, would not be possible until the end of the case.

12–12   Some unforeseen results of section 22 have become apparent only with experience. For example, in a child custody case, if either parent was charged with an offence connected with the dispute, such as assault or abduction, the reporting of these criminal proceedings might become subject to reporting restrictions to prevent identification of the child. Disclosure of the child's identity in the civil action would have to be withheld, since to disclose it would defeat the purpose of section 22 in requiring anonymity in the criminal case.

12–13   A case at the High Court in Edinburgh in 1990 illustrated the unexpected problems the section can cause. A man was charged with murdering his wife, and the only person under 16 involved in the case was the wife's son by a previous marriage, who was an eye-witness to the fatal attack. The Crown asked for an order to prohibit the child's identification in media reports on the basis that he was now living with relatives at a new address and attending a new school where no one knew of his tragic background.

12–14   Lord Milligan acknowledged the wide public interest in the free reporting of our criminal courts, but decided that in this case the boy's identity should be protected by banning publication of his name, address, or school. Reporters present in court pointed out, through the clerk, that it would be difficult, if not impossible to report the names of the accused and the victim of the alleged murder without revealing the boy's identity. They argued that it was highly undesirable to report a murder trial anonymously.

12–15   Lord Milligan stressed that his intention was that there should be no publicity only as to the fact that the boy had given evidence, the content of the evidence or that he was present when the alleged murder took place. The compromise was reached that the trial was reported with the names of the accused and the deceased but no mention whatsoever was made of the boy or his evidence, although from the media's point of view, it would have been of great news value.

12–16   When Parliament bans publication of information "calculated" to lead to identification, that does not mean that the journalist will be excused if he did not actually "calculate" that identification would take place as a result of what he had written. The journalist must decide whether identification of the child would follow as a natural and likely result of

publication. In 1982 the *Lothian Courier*, Bathgate, was fined
£75 at Linlithgow Sheriff Court for naming a man in a report
it carried of his conviction for assault on his 18-month-old
daughter. The newspaper admitted a charge under section 22,
that publication of the man's name was "calculated" to lead
to the identification of the child, although that was not the
paper's intention.

Incest cases

-17   In reporting cases of incest or other sexual offences, the media
in Scotland have followed the practice of not identifying
young people who are innocently involved. Where the person
in question is under 16 it is an offence to publish his or her
identity under section 22, but over that age there is no statutory protection. Incest cases often come to light after many
years when the victim has grown up although only a child at
the time of the offences.

-18   In 1966 the Press Council recommended a course which has
been widely followed. The object is to avoid "jigsaw identification" where two or more reports, each protecting the
anonymity of a child, may disclose his identity when read
together. This could happen where one report names the
accused but does not disclose his relationship to the victim,
while another publishes an anonymous report indicating the
accused's relationship to the victim. The Press Council proposed that editors should adopt a formula by which the
accused is named (if an adult) but the relationship to the child
involved is not specified.

-19   In 1980 Scottish newspaper editors agreed that in such a
situation they would apply a formula on the following lines:—
Where a case of incest is reported the adult is identified but
the word "incest" is not used, the offence being described as
"a serious offence against a young child" or the like; the child
is not identified and the report excludes anything implying
the relationship between the accused and the child.

Children's hearings

-20   The Social Work (Scotland) Act 1968 abolished juvenile courts
and brought about important changes in the methods of
dealing with children. It laid down that a child could be

prosecuted for an offence only on the instructions of the Lord Advocate, and that no court, other than the High Court of Justiciary and the sheriff court, had jurisdiction over a child for an offence.

12–21 It requires every local authority to set up a children's panel—a pool of suitably qualified citizens to hear cases involving children who may need compulsory measures of care, including children who have committed offences.

12–22 The Act also requires each local authority to appoint an officer, known as a Reporter (who must be legally qualified) to arrange children's hearings. The hearings have, in effect, taken over from the old juvenile courts. Where the Reporter considers that a child may be in need of compulsory measures of care, it is his duty to arrange a children's hearing.

12–23 Cases of the kind are heard by three members of the appropriate panel. This tribunal of three, consisting of a chairman and two other members, must include at least one woman. It is properly referred to in media reports as a children's hearing and not as a children's panel, which, as already explained, refers to the complete list of people from whom the members of any particular children's hearing are selected.

12–24 There is a right of appeal by a child or his parent, or both, to the sheriff against a decision of a children's hearing, and the appeal is heard in chambers. The media can be present at such appeals, although attendance is rare. The sheriff has a discretion to exclude reporters, and, of course, the child cannot be identified in any report. Where the sheriff is not satisfied that the decision was justified he may send the case back to the children's hearing for reconsideration, and the normal rules then apply to reports of the proceedings.

12–25 The 1968 Act provides that these hearings take place in private but allows *bona fide* representatives of a newspaper or news agency to attend. It prohibits any newspaper, radio or television report of any children's hearing, or of any hearing before a sheriff or appeal before the Court of Session in such a case, to reveal the name, address or school, or include any particulars calculated to lead to the identification of any child concerned. The maximum penalty for a breach of the ban is a fine of £500 for each offence. The provisions apply also to pictures. The restrictions may be dispensed with wholly or partly by order of the Secretary of State in any case if he is satisfied this would be in the interests of justice; they apply also to reports of children's hearings published in England, Wales and Northern Ireland. The part of the section which prohibits the use of pictures of the child should be noted. The media have interpreted that provision for 25 years as meaning that only a picture which identified the child was prohibited. A rear view (for example) was thought to be permissible. Such pictures were used extensively by all newspapers and television broadcasters when reporting the proceedings before the children's hearing and the referral hearing before the Sheriff in the Orkney case. Their use of such pictures was never challenged in the courts until February 1993 when in the case of Bette McArdle, the Editor of the *Highland News*, the Justiciary Appeal Court appeared to take the view that *all* pictures of children are prohibited by the 1968 Act—irrespective of whether the child could be identified from the picture or not.

In this case the newspaper had published photographs of the children with their faces 'blanked out'.

If that is the correct interpretation of S58 of the Social Work (Scotland) Act 1968, presumably a similar interpretation must be put on S22 of the Criminal Justice (Scotland) Act which relates to reporting of criminal cases involving children under 16 as accused, victims or witnesses.

-26   It was decided in 1991 in a case in which it was alleged that nine children in Orkney had been sexually abused, that when a case is referred from a children's hearing to a sheriff to determine whether the grounds of referral are established, a sheriff has the discretion to allow the Press into chambers to report the proceedings. Of course reports must not contain any information which would identify any child involved.

-27   In cases coming before children's hearings, "child" means a person under 18 years, where a supervision requirement of a hearing is in force, and in other cases a person under 16 years.

-28   List D Schools provide residential education and care for children referred to them by children's hearings or sheriff courts. They are administered by local authority social work departments. Since June 1985 a person known as a safeguarder or curator may be appointed in certain cases where there appears to be a conflict of interest between parent and child in a children's hearing. He or she is usually a person, not necessarily a lawyer, qualified by knowledge of and interest in problems of children who can safeguard the interests of the child involved. This practice is becoming increasingly common in children's hearings, particularly in the situation where the case is referred to the sheriff for a proof hearing.

12–29   The Criminal Procedure (Scotland) Act 1975 states that no child under 14, other than an infant-in-arms, can be in court during the trial of any other person charged with an offence, or during any preliminary proceedings, except when required as a witness or otherwise for the purposes of justice.

12–30   The Act provides that in any proceedings involving an offence against or conduct contrary to decency or morality, where a person who, in the opinion of the court, is a child, is called as a witness, the court may direct that the courtroom be cleared. *Bona fide* reporters will be allowed to remain. This section does not affect the courts' ordinary powers to hear a case *in camera*.

12–31   Disclosure of the sex and age of a child in a named village or small community or, for example that he is the son of a policeman or teacher, could well lead to his or her identity being disclosed. In cases of that kind it may be necessary to leave out a local name and give instead only the name of the county or region so that the child's identity is protected. The aim of the legislation is to prevent anyone being able to identify the child and it will not be a defence to say that the public at large without any special knowledge could not make an identification. The law will be breached if, for example, neighbours could identify the child from what is disclosed in the media.

Custody cases

12–32   Where a custody dispute is part of divorce proceedings, reporting will be restricted under the Judicial Proceedings (Regulation of Reports) Act 1926 (see Chapter 11). After many years of confusion about the legal position, it has now also been decided by the Court of Session that the media may be banned from identifying children in any custody hearing even although it is not part of a divorce action.

12–33   In an international custody dispute in 1988, Lord Murray agreed that publicity would be harmful to the child involved and made an order directing the media not to publish anything calculated to lead to the child being identified. He made the order under section 46 of the Children and Young Persons (Scotland) Act 1937 (as amended).

2–34   The judge referred the case to three judges in the First Division of the Court of Session because of the doubts which had existed for many years as to whether this section applied to civil cases. Lord Emslie, the Lord President, said the court had not the slightest doubt that Lord Murray's order was competent.

2–35   Section 46 states that in relation to any proceedings in any court, the court may direct that no newspaper report shall reveal the name, address or school, or include any particulars calculated to lead to the identification of a person under the age of 17 concerned in the proceedings. It applies to a person by or against or in respect of whom the proceedings are taken, or who is a witness. The prohibition applies to pictures and would also now cover radio and television.

2–36   The long-standing doubt over whether section 46 applied to civil cases came about because it was originally included in a section of the 1937 Act which referred expressly to criminal proceedings. However, in the 1988 case, the judges accepted the argument that, following a series of amendments to the 1937 Act, it now had a wider scope. Since the 1988 decision judges in the Court of Session have made orders banning the identification of children in custody cases on a number of occasions. The effect is that if the case is reported at all, it has to be done anonymously. Note, however, that it is only where the judge makes an order that the media are prevented from identifying the child involved. In criminal cases, identification is banned unless the judge makes a specific order to the contrary.

Adoption procedure

2–37   Under the Rules of the Court of Session, adoption proceedings are normally heard *in camera*, unless the court directs otherwise. Likewise, all documents lodged in court in adoption proceedings are treated as confidential. The reporting of adoption proceedings is therefore extremely difficult, if not impossible, except where the court permits the hearing to take place in public. This rarely happens in practice, but occasionally, the proceedings may be reported, provided, of course, the identities of the parties are not disclosed and no information is published from any of the documents regarded as confidential by the Rule of Court.

12–38   An example of this was a case in 1973 where an important point affecting procedure to be followed in adoption cases in general was debated in the First Division. The proceedings were of sufficient importance to be reported in some newspapers, without names and addresses. Judgments of the court may sometimes be made available for publication by authority of the court, again subject to non-identification of the parties.

12–39   The anonymity rule applying to wardship cases in English courts may sometimes apply in Scotland. In a case before the English High Court Family Division in 1984, Mr Justice Balcombe ruled that he had power to make an anonymity order "against the world at large"—*i.e.* the entire media. He was dealing with the case of a Scotswoman aged 27, who had been convicted of the culpable homicide of two boys, aged four and three, when she was 11 years old and living in Scotland. She was released on licence in 1980, moved to England, made a new life for herself under a different name, and had a baby daughter who had been made a ward of court. The judge issued an injunction to stop the *News of the World* revealing the woman's identity, that of her child or of the child's father, and extending his order to apply to all the media in the interests of the ward.

Fatal accident inquiries

12–40   The Fatal Accidents and Sudden Deaths Inquiry (Scotland) Act 1976 states that inquiries under its terms should be held in public unless a person under the age of 17 is in any way involved (a provision open to wide interpretation). The sheriff may at his own hand, or on an application by a party, order that no report in any publication or broadcast shall reveal the name, address or school of that person or otherwise identify him.

12–41   The sheriff also has power to order that no picture of the person under 17 may be published "in any manner", which must be taken to cover television as well as newspapers.

-42   The wide scope of the Act can be seen from a fatal accident inquiry at Dumbarton Sheriff Court in 1984 into the death of a six-week old baby boy. Sheriff Principal Philip Caplan, Q.C., agreed to a motion by counsel for the boy's parents that there should be reporting restrictions in the case. The result was that no one was named in reports of the inquiry, although the names had already been published in a statutory advertisement published in the *Herald*. The reason given in court for applying reporting restrictions was to protect the three-year-old sister of the dead infant. She was said to be involved in the case because of the father's evidence that he had dropped his baby son after the little girl pulled his arm.

-43   At Forfar Sheriff Court in 1992, during a fatal accident inquiry into the death of a 14-year-old girl from inhaling solvent, Sheriff Stewart Kermack made an order purporting to ban the media from naming everyone involved in the inquiry under the age of 17, including the dead girl. It is difficult to see how this order could properly be made insofar as it related to the dead girl. On the analogy of Lord Brand's decision in the *Aitken* case (see paragraph 12–05) the dead girl was not legally a person.

KEY POINTS

-44   Section 22 of the Criminal Justice (Scotland) Act bans the identification of an accused, victim or witness aged under 16 in criminal cases. The ban can be lifted by the court and does not apply where the child victim is dead. Unless the court directs otherwise, identification is allowed where the child is a witness only and no one against whom proceedings are taken is under 16.

The ban relates to court proceedings and does not come into effect at an earlier stage. It may sometimes result in a guilty adult being protected. To protect children in incest cases, the general practice is to say that a named accused has been guilty of a serious sexual offence. The term incest is not used.

Children's hearings are in private but the media can attend as long as they do not identify the child (Social Work (Scotland) Act 1968).

In custody cases the court can make an order banning the identification of a child under the age of 17 involved in the proceedings. (Children and Young Persons (Scotland) Act 1937, s. 46).

In fatal accident inquiries a sheriff can ban the identification of a child under the age of 17 in any way involved in the proceedings (Fatal Accidents and Sudden Deaths Inquiry (Scotland) Act 1976).

CHAPTER 13

SPECIAL PROBLEMS

Civil juries

–01 Although civil jury trials have virtually disappeared in England, it is still a statutory right in certain important cases in Scotland. In 1988 the Lord Advocate of the day issued a discussion paper on whether civil juries should be abolished in the Court of Session, but they survived despite opposition from some judges and from lawyers acting for defenders, who felt that juries were expensive, unpredictable and made awards which were too high.

–02 Until recently the number of cases dealt with each year by civil juries had greatly diminished, but a jury award of £50,000 to a woman clerical officer who sued the *Sun* newspaper following an allegation that she had sex with a prison inmate looked likely to lead to a revival for juries. The action by Mrs Lilian Winter was said to be the first dealt with by civil jury in a defamation case in Scotland in living memory and the award was by far the highest won by an individual in a case of its kind. Three Court of Session judges refused to interfere with the award after an appeal by the newspaper that the jury award was too high.

–03 The right to jury trial in Scotland in both criminal and civil cases appears to date from the 14th century, but it fell into disuse in civil cases during the 17th century and was not reintroduced until the passing of the Jury Trials (Scotland) Act 1815. It was already in operation in England and was brought to Scotland experimentally and, at first, for a limited period only. The Scottish civil jury in modern times is based on the English model, which explains why there are 12 jurors and not the traditional Scottish figure of 15. The Law Reform (Miscellaneous Provisions) (Scotland) Act 1980 abolished civil jury trial in the sheriff court.

13–04   Meanwhile in England it was eventually decided by the courts themselves that jury trial in civil cases would not in future be permitted except by specific authority of the court. In Scotland, on the other hand, the position remains that, if a party with a statutory right to jury trial insists on this form of procedure, unless there is some "special cause" why it should not be allowed, there must be a jury trial.

13–05   "Special cause" usually consists of difficult questions of law or mixed fact and law which would be difficult for a jury to deal with, or undue delay in raising the action, resulting in special problems in assessing the reliability of evidence given by witnesses whose recollection is dimmed by the passage of time.

13–06   For example, in the case of *Shanks* v. *BBC*, a defamation action arising out of a TV programme, the BBC successfully asked the Court of Session to have the case conducted before a judge sitting alone without a jury. The case involved allegations about share dealings, which, the court felt, a jury would have difficulty in understanding.

13–07   A virtue of the old Scottish jury was that it had (and still has in criminal cases) 15 members, and it was thus possible to achieve a majority verdict. (The traditional Scottish attitude, in favour of majority verdicts, has been based on the concept of deciding the "sense of the meeting" rather than—according to the English approach—coercing every member of a jury to reach the same result.) In civil cases, because of the even number, derived from the English model, there is always the risk of a jury being equally divided—the "hung" jury. This occurred in a Court of Session case in 1973, when, after expiry of the statutory time of three hours, the jury, in an action of damages for personal injuries, failed to produce a verdict, and were discharged.

13–08   In practice, civil juries are most often used to deal with claims for damages for injuries caused by accidents of various kinds, at work, on the roads and so on. As the *Winter* case shows, juries are also eminently suited to deal with defamation actions.

13–09   Since the Interest on Damages (Scotland) Act 1971, juries' verdicts in civil actions are easier to understand than they used to be. Juries are now required to return a verdict which (if any award is made at all) is divided into separate sums for each element of damages, such as past and future loss of earnings and pain and suffering. The result not only produces a verdict which is subject to closer examination if an appeal is being considered, it also provides more detailed information for journalists at the end of the trial.

–10 The procedure at jury trials in the Court of Session differs in certain important respects from cases dealt with by a judge sitting alone. The hearing is opened by an address to the jury by junior counsel for the pursuer who outlines the circumstances of the case and summarises the basis of his client's claim. After the jury have heard the evidence for the pursuer, they are addressed by junior counsel for the defender, who, in his turn, introduces the evidence for his client.

–11 At the end of all the evidence senior counsel for each side sum up the case to the jury, and the hearing is completed with the judge's charge. The judge, who is responsible for seeing that the whole proceedings are kept on a proper and competent basis, guides the jury on any question of law arising in the case, and may also express to them his own opinion on the evidence while making it clear to them that they are judges of the facts in the case.

–12 Sometimes during a trial the jury are taken from the courtroom while counsel make legal submissions to the judge on some point of procedure. These may result in the case being withdrawn from the jury but, if not, care must be taken not to publish reports of statements made by counsel (although in open court) which could be read by the jurors before the case is finished. This could be said to be an interference with the course of justice or to prejudice the case of one party or the other, and to amount to contempt of court. In terms of the Contempt of Court Act 1981, s. 4(2) the responsibility for preventing such interference with the course of justice now lies with the judge, but if the judge forgets or is not asked for an order under the Act, the reporter would be well advised to exercise his own judgment.

–13 Appeal against a civil jury verdict is taken by way of a motion for a new trial. This is heard in the Inner House and may be on any of a variety of grounds, such as misdirection by the presiding judge at the trial, insufficiency of evidence, lack of corroboration or perverseness on the part of the jury. The appeal may be directed against the amount of damages awarded, either as too high or too low. The appeal judges, if satisfied that the verdict cannot stand, may order a re-trial before a new jury, or, in certain circumstances, where the judges unanimously agree that the jury were not entitled to find for the pursuer and that there is no fresh evidence available to bring before a new jury, they can find in favour of the defender.

Proof before judge

13–14   The hearing of evidence before a judge in civil proceedings is called a proof—in other words, the judge hears evidence to ascertain the proof of the case one way or the other. There are no opening speeches by counsel; at the end of the evidence the judge hears counsel's submissions upon the evidence. The judge may give an immediate decision or he may make avizandum, that is reserve his judgment.

13–15   In reporting cases decided by a judge, it is important to distinguish between those in which the action is dismissed and those where the defender is absolved. Absolvitor is a higher degree of success for a defender than dismissal, since a decree of absolvitor precludes the pursuer from suing the same defender again over the same matter. In the case of dismissal, however, the pursuer may find another remedy against the same defender in a different action. It is important to the successful defender to see whether he is reported as having won absolvitor or merely dismissal.

13–16   Apart from damages for financial loss or loss of property, the court, whether in cases tried by jury or by proof, may in appropriate circumstances make an award for pain and suffering incurred by an injured pursuer (solatium), or award a sum to compensate, as far as possible, a bereaved relative of a person who has died as the result of the defender's negligence (loss of society). A loss of society award is intended to cover a variety of kinds of loss, such as companionship and guidance besides the element of grief and sorrow.

Judicial review

13–17   A simplified procedure for dealing with petitions for judicial review of administrative decisions came into operation in the Court of Session in June 1985. The first case under the new procedure, dealt with by Lord Ross in July 1985, concerned a girl aged 16, who left home as a result of being assaulted by her father, and applied successfully to the court for reversal of a decision of Monklands District Council rejecting her claim for accommodation as a person with a priority need under the Housing (Homeless Persons) Act 1977. She had no assets and no income, had nowhere to go and had attempted suicide. The judge held that no reasonable authority could fail to conclude she was vulnerable, and ordered that she be given accommodation under the Act. She was also awarded damages against the council.

3–18   Judicial review has proved a frequent source of copy. It has been used to test such diverse questions as the ownership of assets of the Trustee Savings Bank in Scotland, the nature and extent of Crown immunity in building a fence at a submarine base and the policy of the D.S.S. on the payment of special cold-weather allowances.

3–19   Judicial review was described by Lord McCluskey in the Reith Lectures in 1986 as one of the old forms of remedy now rediscovered by the judges to enable citizens to challenge infringements of their rights, especially infringements by public officials—a process by which, he said, the judges had armed the citizen with rights he did not know he had. If so, then clearly such cases deserve close attention from the journalist for their potential news value.

Standard of proof

3–20   There is an important distinction between the standards of proof demanded by the law in criminal and in civil cases. In criminal proceedings generally proof must be beyond reasonable doubt. In civil cases the court has to be satisfied merely on a balance of probabilities—in other words, the judge or jury has to decide which of two conflicting stories is more probable.

3–21   An important change in the legal requirement of corroboration in civil actions for personal injuries was brought about by the Law Reform (Miscellaneous Provisions) (Scotland) Act 1968. The Act provides that, if the court is satisfied that any fact has been established by evidence given in the case, it may hold that fact proved even in the absence of corroboration.

The requirement for corroboration in other civil cases was abolished by S1 of the Civil Evidence (Scotland) Act 1988. There is then, now no need for corroboration in any Scottish civil proceedings.

Trust variation

13–22   The Trusts (Scotland) Act 1961 gave the Court of Session the power to vary or "break" trusts which formerly were inflexible. It also resulted in a departure from the accepted rule applied to the reporting of court proceedings generally: that the Press was entitled to have access to, and to publish fair and accurate excerpts from, the pleadings put before the court.

13–23   To take an example, the most usual kind of petition brought before the court under the Act is aimed at getting round a provision in a trust which restricts a beneficiary to the income and puts the capital of the trust beyond his reach. The court may under the Act, where satisfied as to the interests of other beneficiaries, authorise payment of the capital of a trust to a person who previously was entitled only to the income. A variation of this kind will usually be designed to enable the interested parties to save tax. This is legitimate tax avoidance, and must not be referred to as tax evasion. The court has taken the view that the figures contained in this type of case must not be made public. For this reason reporters are not usually allowed access to documents containing figures.

13–24   The only means of reporting such cases—which from time to time produce copy of considerable interest, especially where the estates of well-known public figures are concerned—is to sit through the proceedings, and obtain the names and addresses of the parties from the clerk of court or solicitors.

13–25   In some cases solicitors for the petitioner will allow the Press to see the petition, and this happened in a case in 1963 in which the petitioner, Lord Sorn, was a judge. But, in the first case under the 1961 Act to be reported in the media, the parties complained to the court about publication of figures not actually disclosed in court. The then Lord President (Lord Clyde) took the view that, since the court in such cases was performing what was in effect an administrative act on behalf of the parties, the figures should not be published. This is still the attitude of the court, except where the particulars in question actually emerge in court.

Petition in chambers

3–26   Special care has to be taken in the handling of reports of criminal proceedings in their early stages. Where an accused appears on petition before a sheriff in chambers, the reporter's scope for coverage is strictly limited and, in the matter of deciding how much he may safely publish, he must be guided by the procurator-fiscal, who will usually provide the name and, where available, the address of the accused (except where he or she is under 16) and the gist of the charge. Special caution is necessary at this preliminary stage of a case, since proceedings could still be dropped or the terms of the charge(s) altered before the case is called in open court.

The grant or refusal of bail can be reported, but the reasons for the court's decision on bail are confidential. Refusal could, for example, be based on the accused's previous convictions or suspicion that he might intimidate witnesses. Such information would be highly prejudicial and so cannot be published (see 8–78).

Fitness to plead

3–27   When someone charged with a criminal offence suffers from such degree of unsoundness of mind as to render it doubtful whether he is capable of instructing his defence or of pleading to the charge, he appears before a judge of the High Court of Justiciary, who hears the evidence of two or more medical experts on the accused person's mental condition. Upon the evidence the court decides whether or not the accused is fit to plead. If he is, a diet for trial is fixed; if not, the judge will make the appropriate order for the detention of the accused in a state hospital or other suitable institution.

Nobile officium

3–28   The *nobile officium* of the High Court and the Court of Session has been used in a variety of cases in recent years to seek a remedy where none was provided by statute or precedent. A bench of at least three judges is normally required, although certain matters may be dealt with by a single judge. For many years it was almost entirely in civil cases that this special power of the court was exercised, but its use in criminal cases has become increasingly frequent. The *nobile officium* is a valuable power inherent in the supreme courts in Scotland to provide a solution and achieve a just result within certain strict bounds where Parliament—as is by no means unknown or even unusual—has omitted to legislate for Scotland. It is of more than terminological importance that reports of such a case should not treat it as just another appeal.

Rape cases

13–29   Judges of the High Court of Justiciary normally "close the doors" while the evidence of an alleged victim of rape or attempted rape is being heard, the object being to protect the witness from anything which might inhibit her in giving evidence. It has also become the practice of the judges to allow reporters covering the proceedings to remain in court provided they do not identify the witness in their reports.

13–30   This practice was judicially recognised in a case in 1983 in which Lord Avonside said: "In our courts a victim alleged to have been raped almost invariably gives evidence behind closed doors. In such a situation the public is not permitted to hear her evidence. It has been the practice, particularly in Glasgow, to allow the Press reporters to remain. They are asked to exercise a wise discretion, and, in my experience, this they do admirably. The trial judge could, of course, if he thought it desirable, exclude the Press and clear the court completely".

13–31   Besides the powers the judges have under statutes of the Scottish Parliament, under the Criminal Procedure (Scotland) Act 1975 they may, from the opening of the evidence in a rape trial "or the like", clear the court of all persons except those actually involved in the proceedings. Judges can now also give directions to prohibit publication of "a name or other matter" where they were already able merely to prohibit disclosure of it in open court.

13–32   The law in England on rape reporting has a much more chequered history, perhaps illustrating the wisdom of a voluntary code.

3–33   In England identification in court reports of the alleged victim of rape or attempted rape was banned by the Sexual Offences (Amendment) Act 1976, which also made it an offence to identify the accused in such cases unless and until he was convicted. The absurd consequences emerged in a number of cases, in particular in a case in 1986 when a man charged and named by the police in connection with a series of murders became anonymous when he was charged also with rape. Apart from the difficulties this created for the media, the police were hampered in circulating details of the man wanted for the crimes. It became clear also that a man acquitted of rape and convicted of murdering his victim could be jailed for life but not identified by the media, which, however, would be free in law to name the victim.

3–34   Following the Ealing Vicarage rape case in London in which the victim was identified in a number of reports, major changes were made in England under the Criminal Justice Act 1988. The Act did away with the anonymity of rape accused and increased restrictions on identifying the victim.

3–35   The position in England now is that after an allegation of a rape offence, the name, address, or picture of the woman cannot be published in her lifetime if this is likely to lead to her being identified by members of the public as an alleged victim. Also, after a person is accused of rape, or information is laid before a magistrate accusing him of rape, nothing may be published in the woman's lifetime to identify her as an alleged victim.

3–36   The restrictions apply in cases of rape, attempted rape, aiding, abetting, counselling or procuring rape or attempted rape, incitement to rape, conspiracy to rape and burglary with intent to rape. They also apply in civil cases, for example if the woman claims damages for rape.

3–37   The restrictions may be lifted in certain circumstances, for example if the woman was charged with a criminal offence arising from the rape allegation, such as wasting police time because of a false allegation.

3–38   The woman may also be named if, before trial, the accused satisfies a Crown Court judge that this is necessary to bring witnesses forward and the defence will be prejudiced if the restriction is not lifted; the court is satisfied that anonymity places an unreasonable restriction on reporting the trial; or the alleged victim gives her written consent to what is published.

KEY POINTS

13–39 Trial by a jury of 12 is still possible in the Court of Session, but not in the sheriff court. A hearing of evidence by a judge is known as a proof. In both, the case must be proved on a balance of probabilities.

The media in Scotland do not name rape victims, although there is no statutory ban against identification. There has never been a ban in Scotland on naming a rape accused. In England the Criminal Justice Act 1988 removed the anonymity previously enjoyed by rape accused.

CHAPTER 14

TITLES AND TERMINOLOGY

4-01 The principal judge in Scotland holds the dual office of Lord Justice-General (in which capacity he is president of the High Court of Justiciary) and Lord President of the Court of Session. The Lord Justice-Clerk, who is next in order of precedence, holds office in both courts and carries the same title in each. In the Court of Session the Lord President presides over the First Division as well as over sittings of the full bench (which are not common); the Lord Justice-Clerk presides over the Second Division. He also deputises for the Lord President in his absence as head of the courts.

4-02 There are 24 other judges (including the Chairman of the Scottish Law Commission, who may perform his judicial function also from time to time). Each bears the title of Lord Commissioner of Justiciary when sitting in the High Court and Senator of the College of Justice when performing the functions of a Court of Session judge. In either capacity he is entitled to the courtesy title "Lord", but he is not a peer, unless he is one of the few judges who have been made Life Peers. There is no objection to the forms "Lord President Smith" or "Lord Justice-Clerk Black", styles which are in use in the legal textbooks. The term Lord Ordinary is used frequently in court with reference to a judge of first instance; the reporter will usually have to inquire or search in the documents of the case for the particular judge's name. The Court of Session sits only in Edinburgh, the High Court of Justiciary deals with criminal business in Edinburgh and on circuit in various parts of Scotland.

Sheriff court

4-03 When a sheriff principal or sheriff is a Q.C., this designation should not be omitted from the first mention of his name in a report. Sheriffs principal and sheriffs in court or when discharging their shrieval functions are addressed as "My Lord" or "My Lady". They should be given their judicial titles only in reports of matters concerning their discharge of these duties. When a sheriff is reported as speaking or participating in any activity as a private individual, his shrieval title should be omitted. (This practice may be reversed in local papers, where "the Sheriff" tends to carry this style with him wherever he goes and whatever he does in the public eye.)

Faculty of Advocates

14–04 From the point of view of etiquette, to which the law attaches much importance, it may be as offensive to describe an advocate as a Q.C. as to call a Q.C. an advocate. This can be understood if it is realised that when an advocate takes silk his junior practice comes to an end. There have been instances of juniors losing briefs because they were prematurely described in the Press as Q.C.s—and, of course, members of the Faculty of Advocates may not advertise themselves, even in order to rectify such inaccuracies. The former rule by which a Q.C. could not normally appear without a junior was rescinded in 1977. In the High Court an advocate-depute who is a Q.C. may appear alone. The title advocate-depute belongs to several members of the Bar who assist in the preparation and conduct of criminal prosecutions. They are deputies to the Lord Advocate, and not advocates' deputies (as the title might suggest).

Law officers

14–05 The Lord Advocate holds one of the most ancient offices in the Scottish legal system. Besides having the supreme authority over all prosecutions conducted on behalf of the Sovereign in Scotland, he represents various government departments where these are involved in civil litigations in the Court of Session. He does not often appear personally to represent the Crown, although he will do so in important cases. He is more often represented by his senior deputy, the Solicitor-General for Scotland. These two law officers are allocated special places in court—the Lord Advocate at the clerk's table on the right of the chair, and the Solicitor-General in the corresponding place on the left. It is usual for at least one of them to be a Member of Parliament, where he answers Scottish questions on legal subjects and advises the government on the conduct of Scottish Bills, but there have been occasions when this has not been possible. Both appointments are made on a political basis, and when a government goes out of office, so do the law officers. When a vacancy occurs on the High Court and Court of Session Bench the Lord Advocate recommends a successor who may be himself. The Lord Advocate is in charge of the Crown Office in Edinburgh (where criminal prosecutions are prepared) as well as the Lord Advocate's Department in London (where Scottish legislation is largely drafted).

–06 Members of the Society of Advocates in Aberdeen, who are solicitors, are not to be confused with members of the Faculty of Advocates. Unless they have qualified as solicitor-advocates, Aberdeen advocates do not share the right to plead before the supreme courts.

–07 The term "counsel" applies only to members of the Faculty and is not accurately used in reference to solicitors appearing in court.

–08 It is necessary in the reporting of Scottish court cases to avoid the use of English court terms. We use pursuer, not plaintiff; defender, not defendant. In England divorce proceedings are taken by way of a petition; in Scotland, by way of a summons in the Court of Session and by way of an Initial Writ in the Sheriff Court. The distinction results in quite separate terms being used for the parties concerned in the proceedings. Thus, while in England the person who institutes divorce proceedings is the petitioner and the opposing party the respondent, these in Scotland are respectively pursuer and defender. The term respondent is used in Scotland in reference to a party contesting a petition as well as to one resisting an appeal. A third party who comes into divorce proceedings to deny allegations implicating him or her may do so by lodging a minute and is known as a party-minuter.

–09 A number of Scottish and English court terms are interchangeable according to the particular requirements of the newspaper, having regard to its readership. For example, although in Scotland a court order prohibiting some act which is the subject of complaint is properly called an interdict, the reporter writing for an English paper might find it desirable to call such an order an injunction, the equivalent English term which would be more readily understood by his readers and is at the same time not entirely unknown in Scotland. The same might be said of such terms as aliment (English maintenance or alimony), arbiter (arbitrator) and expenses (costs).

CHAPTER 15

ESSENTIALS OF DEFAMATION

–01 "I do not for my part, consider that any privilege whatever attaches to a newspaper report as such. If a newspaper gives circulation to a slander, it is simply in the position of any other party circulating a slander and the general rule is that a person circulating a slander is answerable equally with the author of the slander". (Lord Kyllachy in *Wright & Greig* v. *Outram* (1890) 17 R. 596 at p. 599.) The law has changed slightly since Lord Kyllachy said this at the end of the last century and newspaper reports of certain matters are now privileged by statute. But apart from these special cases the principle remains the same. The law of defamation applies to journalists as to ordinary mortals. There is no general privilege of journalism. "It would be a total mistake to suppose that the editor of a newspaper, who sits behind a curtain like another veiled prophet, is entitled to vote himself public accuser, to the effect of calling every member of society to account for his misdeeds and to confer upon every anonymous contributor whom he admits into his columns, the same privilege". (Lord Deas in *Drew* v. *Mackenzie* (1862) 24 D. 649 at p. 662.)

–02 The second part of Lord Kyllachy's remark should also be noted. "A person circulating a slander is answerable equally with the author of the slander". This means that the author, publisher and printer of a book can be, and frequently are, all sued for the one slander. It means that both the writer of a defamatory article, report or letter and the proprietor of the newspaper in which it is published may be liable for damages and it means that the newspaper which merely repeats a defamatory statement already published in the columns of another is as liable to be sued as if it originated the slander. (By the Defamation Act 1952, s.12, however, a newspaper owner can prove in *mitigation of damages* that other newspaper proprietors have already paid damages in respect of the statement in question.) It would seem, however, that people such as newsagents and librarians who merely disseminate a defamatory publication are not liable if they have no reason to think that what they are circulating is slanderous (*Morrison v. Ritchie* (1902) 4 F. 645). It should be noted however that in the various actions raised in England by Sir James Goldsmith in connection with libellous material printed by the magazine *Private Eye* he successfully obtained injunctions against newsagents from distributing the offending copies of the magazine.

15–03   It is sometimes thought that it is safe to publish a statement if it is stated clearly that it is merely being repeated for what it is worth. Nothing could be further from the truth. A newspaper is as legally responsible in these circumstances as when a statement is printed and endorsed by the newspapers. The good journalist should always try to have a balancing comment to a potentially defamatory statement. It is important to note that if the opportunity to comment is given but not taken, this is no defence whatsoever to an action of defamation.

Civil wrong

15–04   In Scotland defamation is a civil wrong giving rise to an action for damages and not a criminal prosecution. However, the Representation of the People Act 1983 makes it a criminal offence for any person before or during a Parliamentary election to make or publish for the purpose of affecting the return of any candidate any false statement of fact in relation to the personal character or conduct of such candidate. In theory, too, a publication tending to cause a breach of the peace might render the publisher liable to prosecution for this common law offence. In England and many other countries defamation can be a criminal offence.

Publication

15–05   You can shout a slander to the waves and write reams of libellous invective. If nobody hears or reads there will be no defamation. Publication of some sort is essential. In this respect there is a difference between Scots law and English law. Scots law allows an action for injury to the feelings caused by an insulting and defamatory statement even if it is not made known to any third party. English law requires communication to a third party before there will be civil liability. From the journalist's point of view the difference is not important. In his case there can seldom be any doubt about publication. There is no technical distinction in Scots law between words published in writing and words spoken. The terms libel and slander are often used interchangeably.

Falsity

-06 Only false statements are actionable. Truth, or *veritas*, is a complete defence. But defamatory statements are presumed to be false and, if the defender relies on *veritas*, the burden of proving the truth of his statements rests on him. If he makes one allegation, he must prove that it is true and not merely that it is partly true or that something less is true. If a man has been called a liar, it is not enough to prove that he lied on one occasion (*Milne* v. *Walker* (1893) 21 R. 155) and if a man has been called a thief it is no defence to prove that long ago, as a boy, he had two convictions for petty theft (*Fletcher* v. *Wilson* (1885) 12 R. 683).

-07 On the other hand, if the pursuer founds upon two separate allegations, the defender can always prove the truth of one of them even although he may not also be able to prove the truth of the other (*O'Callaghan* v. *Thomson & Co.*, 1928 S.C. 532). Before 1952 this had the effect of diminishing the damages. Under section 5 of the Defamation Act 1952, it may absolve the defender from liability altogether. The section provides that: "In an action for defamation in respect of words containing two or more distinct charges against the pursuer, a defence of veritas shall not fail by reason only that the truth of every charge is not proved if the words not proved to be true do not materially injure the pursuer's reputation having regard to the truth of the remaining charges". It should be noted that, under the present law, a pursuer can choose to base his action on only one allegation out of several. If he does this, the defender has no opportunity to prove the truth of the remaining allegations so as to take advantage of section 5.

-08 It was formerly the law, at least in England, that if a man was said to have committed a crime it was not a defence to a defamation action to prove merely that he had been convicted of that crime. It had to be proved that he had *in fact* committed the crime. However, in a defamation action proof that a person stands convicted of an offence by a United Kingdom court or British court-martial is now conclusive evidence that he committed the offence (Law Reform (Miscellaneous Provisions) (Scotland) Act 1968, section 12; Civil Evidence Act 1968, section 13). As we shall see later, the Rehabilitation of Offenders Act 1974 adds a new complication to *veritas* in relation to criminal offences. If the offence in question is the subject of a "spent conviction" the defender in an action of defamation by the rehabilitated person cannot rely on *veritas* if the publication is proved to have been made with malice.

15–09   The defence of *veritas* can be a very difficult one. Even where charges seem justified, they may not be easy to prove. It can also be an unwise defence if there is serious risk of failure as it means that the defamation is persisted in and this is a factor which can aggravate damages.

Defamatory

15–10   There is no clear rule on what is and what is not defamatory. Generally speaking, however, a defamatory statement involves some imputation against character or reputation, including business or financial reputation. The best way of answering the question "What is defamatory?" is to set out by way of example various types of statement which the courts have regarded as actionable. It must be emphasised, however, that this is only a guide. The fact that a statement has been regarded as defamatory in the past, does not necessarily mean that it will be regarded as defamatory now. Fashions in defamation change. Accusations of Sabbath breaking are less likely to be held defamatory today than they were in the last century, but in particular local communities such accusations might well still be considered defamatory. An example of this arose in 1990 when the *Stornoway Gazette* published a reader's letter which criticised the local M.P., Calum MacDonald, for not voting in favour of legislation intended to prevent the promotion of homosexuality. While this incorrect allegation might well not have been considered defamatory in most parts of Scotland, in the Western Isles it was seen as a slur on the MP's reputation. Mr MacDonald successfully claimed against the newspaper.

-11   To call a man a criminal in general terms is clearly defamatory. To call him a thief or accuse him of some other serious crime is also defamatory. The *Sunday Mail* once made an unfortunate mistake. In reporting a murder of which William Harkness and his wife had been found guilty, it said beside a photograph of the two murderers, "John Harkness and his wife, both of whom were condemned to die but the man alone paid the extreme penalty. The woman is serving a life sentence". John Harkness and his wife were allowed an action for defamation (*Harkness* v. *The Daily Record Ltd.*, 1924 S.L.T. 759). It would not normally be actionable for example to say that a man had exceeded the speed limit. Probably the majority of drivers do so and it is not generally regarded as reprehensible. But to say this of someone who makes their living from driving and so should observe the Road Traffic Act carefully as part of their job, might give rise to an action. As stated above it is simply impossible to draw up a definitive list of what is defamatory and what is not. It all depends on the circumstances.

-12   An interesting case was that of *Leon* v. *Edinburgh Evening News*, 1909 S.C. 1014. The *Evening News* reported a police court case under the headline "The Edinburgh Licensing Prosecution: Prisoners Acquitted". One of the accused referred to, who had in fact never been in custody but had simply appeared in court in answer to a citation, sued for defamation, pointing out, quite correctly, that he had never been a prisoner. It was held that in the circumstances of the case the statement was not defamatory. Lord Kinnear observed that "the description was not technically exact. But a newspaper in a paragraph of this kind does not necessarily use technical language: and in ordinary language an accused person at the Bar of a court may not improperly be described as a prisoner. To an ordinary reader, the paragraph with its heading, would not in my opinion convey any more injurious meaning than that the pursuer had been accused and had been acquitted." There were also observations that it would not necessarily be defamatory to refer to a man as a prisoner in any event as a person may be a prisoner quite innocently. But clearly the word "prisoner" is not one to be recklessly bandied about.

-13   Imputations of sexual immorality are clearly actionable. There can be no doubt about accusations of adultery or prostitution but, depending on the standards of the time and the views of reasonable people generally, very much less may suffice. Accusations of want of womanly delicacy have been held actionable. *Blackwood's Magazine* carried a story describing life in a Fife mining village. The author said that in the course of a social evening in one house, a girl of seventeen grew tired and in the presence of more than a dozen people of both sexes prepared herself for bed and got into it. She showed no embarrassment and the company took no notice. "Now this", said the author, "might be called 'indelicate'. Delicacy, however, is a standard of the more complex world, and this girl knew nought of it". The girl in question thought differently and brought an action against the publishers. It was held that the passage was actionable. (*A.B.* v. *Blackwood & Sons* (1902) 5 F. 25).

15–14   A recent cause celebre arose out of an allegation of sexual immorality in *The Sun* newspaper concerning a female employee at Glenochil Prison in Tullibody. The newspaper alleged that the lady, a Mrs Winter, had an affair with a prisoner and that she had sexual relations with him while she was on duty. *The Sun* was duly sued in respect of these untrue allegations and the pursuer was awarded £50,000 by the jury in the Court of Session. An appeal by the defenders on the amount of damages awarded was unsuccessful. This case was important for two reasons. Firstly, it shows that Scottish juries are willing to award damages not too far removed from the awards made by their counterparts in England. Secondly, it shows that in defamation cases normally the pursuer can insist on a jury trial. It is only if the court feels the case is too technical and would not be suitable for consideration by a jury that the defender can avoid having the case decided in this way. An example of a court rejecting a jury trial was the case of *Shanks* v. *BBC* where in 1991 at the interlocutory stage the court felt that as the matters involved related to company frauds it would be best if the case were to be considered by a judge rather than a jury.

15–15   Actions have often been based on imputations of drunkenness or dishonesty—the latter covering anything from appropriating public funds to evading payment of rent. In one case two political lecturers engaged a hall. A newspaper commented later, "Now one of them has left the town. Any information as to his whereabouts will be thankfully received by a sorrowing landlord, the proprietor of the hall, who now concludes that a Tory Cleon is no more profitable as a tenant than a Socialist Boanerges" (*Godfrey* v. *W. & D. C. Thomson* (1890) 17 R. 1108). An action was allowed.

-16   To sum up, any charge of conduct which is usually regarded as discreditable or dishonourable may be defamatory.

-17   It has been held defamatory to call a man debauched, corrupt, two-faced, a blackguard, a low dirty scum, a coward, a calumniator, a scoundrel, a disquieting brute, a mansworn rogue, an infidel, a hypocrite, an informer, a glutton or a plagiarist, but it would be very much a question of circumstances whether any of these expressions standing alone would be regarded as defamatory today. The leaning of the law is now against actions based on words of mere general abuse.

-18   Imputations on solvency are clearly actionable. They need not go as far as to allege bankruptcy. It is enough if they imply financial embarrassment. Indeed, it is possible to imagine enormous damages being paid by a newspaper which makes unfounded or unapprovable allegations against a firm or company. If the pursuer can demonstrate that losses occurred as a direct result of these allegations (*e.g.* cancellation of contracts by customers), then such losses would be recoverable. Further, it is vital to remember that the companies are often quoted on the public Stock Exchange and the value of their shares is dependent on the confidence in which they are held in the financial community. If a company could prove that its share value had plummeted as a result of an erroneous story in a newspaper it might well be able to recover substantial damages from the newspaper.

5-19   Numerous defamation cases have been concerned with imputations on a man's fitness for his occupation or profession. To give only a few examples, it is dangerous to accuse a minister of brawling with his parishioners (*Mackellar* v. *Duke of Sutherland* (1859) 21 D. 222), a Christian missionary of being a Mohammedan (*Davis* v. *Miller* (1855) 17 D. 1050, 1166), a teacher of ignorance of his subject (*McKerchar* v. *Cameron* (1892) 19 R. 383), a medical practitioner of cruelty to a patient (*Bruce* v. *Ross & Co.* (1901) 4 F. 171), an accountant of being unfit to be a trustee in bankruptcy (*Oliver* v. *Barnet* (1895) 3 S.L.T. 163) or a solicitor of conducting cases for his own advantage and without regard to the interests of his clients (*McRostie* v. *Ironside* (1849) 12 D. 74).

15–20   False allegations of insanity are actionable. There is more doubt about physical disease but it would probably be defamatory to say that a person suffered from some obnoxious disease which rendered him repulsive in the eyes of his fellows. AIDS is perhaps the most obvious example as it carries with it in the public mind the suspicion of homosexuality or drug abuse. In this connection journalists should remember that the test in defamation cases is what is perceived by the public as being derogatory. So while homosexuality for people over a certain age is perfectly legal it is still regarded by many members of the public as unacceptable and so such an allegation may give rise to a right of action. Jason Donovan the TV soap star successfully sued over statements in a magazine to the effect that he was homosexual. The damages awarded by the English jury in the High Court in London were £250,000.

Innuendo

15–21   Journalists must be aware of the legal concept of a defamatory innuendo. This arises in two situations. Firstly, it can arise where words are innocent on their face but, in reality, carry a defamatory meaning. It is a question of fact in each case as to what meaning a reasonable right thinking person would take from the article or broadcast.

The most extreme example of this is where the words are conveyed in such a way as to mean precisely the opposite of their ordinary meaning. An example will illustrate the point. In 1993, on the BBC programme "Have I Got News for You", the panellists repeatedly made reference to the sexuality of a pop star who had successfully sued in the High Court in London over a magazine article which claimed he was gay. In the broadcast it was repeatedly stated for a number of weeks "X is certainly not a homosexual". It is suggested it would have been possible for that individual to plead that these words were conveyed in such a sarcastic manner as to bear the opposite meaning.

It will be seen then that the concept of innuendo can be very problematical for journalists, particularly those working in television and radio. An innuendo can arise from a wink, a nudge, a facial expression or intonation of voice. It is, of course, necessary for the pursuer to plead very precisely what innuendo he is setting out to prove. The defender has to be given proper notice of the charge of innuendo against him.

Secondly, a defamatory innuendo can be plead by the pursuer if the words have a special (derogatory) meaning for certain people. For example, to say that a Scottish solicitor paid promptly for office furniture by a cheque from his client's account might seem unremarkable to the general public. To other solicitors, however, it would mean that, at best, he was guilty of professional misconduct and, at worst, was a thief.

'Private Eye' phraseology it is suggested would, as a matter of law, be held to carry defamatory innuendos. Thus 'tired and emotional' means drunk, 'Ugandan discussions' means sexual intercourse and so on.

It must be understood that a defamatory innuendo, like defamation itself, can arise unintentionally. That is no defence. If the court is satisfied that an ordinary right thinking person would draw a defamatory meaning from the words (and possibly pictures) used, then the test for defamation is satisfied.

16–22   It is not enough that the words *could* bear the meaning alleged. It must be shown that they probably *would* bear that meaning when heard or read by a reasonable man. The innuendo must represent what is a reasonable, natural or necessary inference from the words used, regard being had to the occasion and the circumstances of their publication (*Russell* v. *Stubbs*, 1913 S.C. (H.L.) 14). With regard to newspaper articles, it has been said that the court must consider the meaning which the words used would convey to an ordinary reader reading them as newspaper articles are usually read (*Hunter* v. *Ferguson & Co.* (1906) 8 F. 574; *Stein* v. *Beaverbrook Newspapers Ltd.*, 1968 S.L.T. 401, 409). If they would not appear defamatory to such an ordinary reader, no action will lie. This, however, is subject to the qualification that the reader may have knowledge of special facts making an apparently innocent statement defamatory. It seems harmless to say that Mrs M gave birth to twins on a certain date but this becomes defamatory when read by those knowing that she had been married for only a month (*Morrison* v. *Ritchie* (1902) 4 F. 645, and see 16–31, below).

Statement

15–23   There must be a statement. It need not, however, be in words. It may be inferred from acts, as where a waxwork effigy of the pursuer was placed in a waxworks among the effigies of notorious criminals (*Monson v. Tussauds* [1894] 1 Q.B. 671) or where a boy's photograph was placed by the police in their "rogues' gallery" (*Adamson v. Martin*, 1916 S.C. 319). Of more importance for the journalist is the possibility of inferring a defamatory statement from drawings and photographs. An issue of the magazine *Lilliput* contained on a left-hand page a photograph of an outdoor photographer called Sydney Garbett with his camera. On the opposite page was a photograph of a naked woman. Under Mr Garbett's photograph were the words, "Of course for another shilling, Madam" and under the other photograph, the words, "You can have something like this". Mr Garbett alleged that after these photographs appeared, his friends stopped calling him "Sydney" and began to call him "Smutty". The court held that the arrangement of the photographs and captions was quite clearly libellous (*Garbett v. Hazel Watson & Viney Ltd.* [1943] 2 All E.R. 359). More recently in the High Court in London in 1994 the Chancellor of Glasgow University, Sir Alex Cairncross, successfully sued the London Evening Standard over the juxtaposition of his photograph and an article on the Blunt/Philby/McLean spy ring. This clearly gives rise to a duty by the sub-editor to take care when laying out his pages. It is wise for the sub-editor to look over the whole page to see if any defamatory innuendo might arise from the juxtaposition of photographs and stories.

About a person

15–24   The statement must be of and concerning the pursuer. He must show that reasonable persons would take the words to refer to him but need not prove that they were intended to refer to him (see 16–31 to 39, below).

15–25   Difficulties arise where a class of persons is defamed. The general rule is that members of the class can sue if and only if the class is sufficiently well defined for the defamation to be applicable to them individually. A particular minister could not sue on an attack against ministers generally but could sue on a charge of drunkenness against the ministers of his particular presbytery (*Macphail* v. *Macleod* (1896) 3 S.L.T. 91). Only a person in life can sue; *Broom* v. *Ritchie & Co.* (1904) 6 F. 942. It is often said, quite rightly 'you cannot defame the dead'. The death of Robert Maxwell in 1992 was followed by a spate of articles, books, programmes and even plays about him which would never have seen the light of day had he been alive for fear of receipt of a defamation action—a technique used successfully by Maxwell to stifle much criticism of him.

If, however, a defamation action is raised and the pursuer dies when the case is in court, it is perfectly competent for his trustees to carry on the proceedings; Section 3 of the Damages (Scotland) Act 1993. In this respect defamation and verbal injury actions are distinct from all other damages actions for personal injury. In all other cases it has been possible since the Damages (Scotland) Act 1993 for trustees/executors to raise proceedings for both solatium and patrimonial loss even if the deceased had not raised the action during his lifetime.

26   A company can sue for defamation relating to its business interests but cannot, of course, recover damages for injury to feelings. As previously indicated above (at paragraph 15–18) the damages recoverable by a company could be substantial if it can prove loss of revenue caused by the defamatory statement. In the *Capital Life* v. *Sunday Mail* case the damages awarded in 1978 were a then record £327,000 (excluding interest and expenses!) where the newspaper had unjustly accused an insurance company of unlawful business practices. At the time although this was a Scots case this was the highest libel award in Great Britain. The main element in the award of damages in the Capital Life case was the substantial loss of business the pursuers could prove to have resulted from the articles.

27   As a general rule only the person defamed can sue and hence no action will lie for defamation of somebody already dead. When a widow brought an action based on a newspaper statement that her late husband had attempted suicide, her action was dismissed on this ground (*Broom* v. *Ritchie* (1904) 6 F. 942). But if aspersions on the deceased cause actual patrimonial loss to a pursuer, he may establish a title to sue the person who cast them.

Key Points

A statement about a person which lowers his reputation in the eyes of the general public is defamatory. A statement can be plainly defamatory on its face or defamatory only by reason of the innuendo which it carries. A statement which is defamatory is presumed in law to be untrue. The burden of proving the defence of truth (veritas) rests on the (journalist) defender.

A corporate body such as a firm or a company can sue for defamation. If they can prove that they have lost business as a result of the defamatory statement such a corporate pursuer could be entitled to very substantial damages.

Chapter 16

DEFENCES

01 In defence to an action for defamation the defender may claim that one of the essentials of defamation is lacking—for example, that no statement was made, or that, if made, it is true, or is not defamatory or would not be taken by a reasonable man to refer to the pursuer. These points were considered in the last chapter. We must now deal with various other defences.

Rixa

02 Words spoken in *rixa* are words uttered in the heat of a quarrel. Even if apparently defamatory they will not be actionable, unless it would appear to third parties that a specific charge was being seriously made. This defence is properly applicable only to spoken words and is hence of little importance for the journalist.

Fair comment

03 The defence of fair comment is of great importance to newspapers and broadcasters but its limitations should be understood by journalists. The press is perfectly entitled to comment on matters of public interest but the comment must both be fair and be based on fact not supposition. The defence is much more likely to succeed in features work rather than in news stories. Journalists regularly misunderstand this defence saying for example to call someone "a rogue" or "a thief" is fair comment. Such an approach shows a complete misunderstanding of this defence.

04 Fair comment is a particularly relevant defence when dealing with stories on public figures. There is a belief amongst many journalists that people in public life must accept that they will be criticised in the media. To a degree

this is true but the law of defamation applies to public figures such as politicians as well as to the man in the street. There is no equivalent in Great Britain to the *Sullivan* v. *New York Times* case where the American Supreme Court decided that public figures had to accept a substantial degree of criticism in the media in the interests of freedom of speech as enshrined in the American constitution. The most recent committee on Defamation (The Lord Chancellor's Supreme Court Procedure Committee) specifically recommended that *Sullivan* v. *New York Times* should not become a part of the law of defamation in this country (The Neill Report, July 1991). It is perfectly clear from the experience of the English courts over the past 10 years that politicians will now sue regularly over defamatory statements. Journalists should take great care that their facts are both accurate and provable.

16–05   Certain conditions must be present before the defence of fair comment will succeed. First, the matter complained of must be comment: the defence does not protect defamatory statements of fact (*cf. Waddell* v. *BBC*, 1973 S.L.T. 246). Secondly, the comment must be such as an honest man could have made. Comment, however, does not cease to be fair merely because it represents a stupid, partisan or eccentric point of view. Fools and cranks can have their say. Nor does comment become actionable merely because it is couched in strong or vituperative language (*Archer* v. *Ritchie & Co.* (1891) 18 R. 719). Thirdly, the comment must be based on facts and, if these are set out, they must be set out accurately. Under the Defamation Act 1952, section 6, however, a defence of fair comment will not fail only because the truth of every allegation of fact is not proved, if the expression of opinion is fair comment in view of such facts as are proved. Fourthly, the comment must be on a matter of public interest. This gives plenty of scope. It clearly covers comment on affairs of central and local government, the administration of justice and the conduct of those holding or seeking public office. It also covers comment on sport and criticism of books, and of films, plays and other public entertainments. It does not, however, cover observations on matters regarded by the law as lying outside the legitimate sphere of journalism such as the private lives of private citizens. "While it is in the public interest that the Press should exercise freely its right of criticism in regard to public affairs, it is equally important that the right of a private individual to have his character respected should be maintained, and that people should not as private persons be exposed to unjustifiable and arbitrary comment" (*per* Viscount Haldane in *Langlands* v. *Leng*, 1916 S.C. (H.L.) 102 at p. 106).

06 It seems that proof of malice may vitiate a defence of fair comment (*Brims* v. *Reid* (1885) 12 R. 1016; *McKerchar* v. *Cameron* (1892) 19 R. 383). If this is so, then possibly a newspaper could not plead fair comment in respect of remarks contained in an anonymous letter the writer of which was not disclosed. The newspaper would be putting forward a defence and at the same time depriving the pursuer of an opportunity of overcoming it. "How can anyone prove malice on the part of a person of whom he knows nothing at all?" (*Brims* v. *Reid*, above at page 1021). On the other hand, it is arguable that in this sort of case it is only the newspaper's malice which is relevant. It is the publication which is complained of, not the writing of the letter. If the newspaper has published without malice on its part, or on the part of its agent or employees, then it should be entitled to the defence of fair comment. The Scottish cases on this point (*Brims* v. *Reid*, and *McKerchar* v. *Cameron*, above) are old and unsatisfactory and reveal so much confusion between fair comment and privilege that it is difficult to interpret them with confidence.

Fair retort

07 A certain latitude is allowed to the man who denies charges made publicly against him. Even if his denial is not entirely true and is in strong terms it will not be actionable. But he must not pass from repudiation to the making of separate defamatory allegations against his accuser. The retort must be a shield and not a spear. The defence of fair retort is thus of very narrow scope. Its main practical effect is to prevent a man being sued for saying his accuser lied.

Privilege

08 There are two types of privilege—absolute and qualified. If a statement has absolute privilege, no action can be based on it, however false, defamatory or malicious it may be. If a statement has qualified privilege an action can be based on it but

the pursuer must prove that it was made with malice. The theory behind both types of privilege is that in some circumstances the public interest demands freedom to speak without fear of an action for defamation.

Absolute privilege

16–09   Absolute privilege applies to statements made in Parliament, reports authorised by Parliament and statements made in court with reference to the case in progress by judge, advocate, solicitor or witness. The litigant, however, has only qualified privilege: he cannot indulge with impunity in malicious defamation simply by raising an action. In contrast, in England a litigant enjoys absolute privilege. By statute, absolute privilege attaches to certain communications by, or to, or arising out of an investigation by the Parliamentary Commissioner (see Chapter 6) commonly known as the Ombudsman, the local authority Ombudsman, the National Health Service Ombudsman and the Pensions' Ombudsman. Of most importance for journalists is the privilege accorded to a fair and accurate report of proceedings in a public court of justice. In England by statute (the Law of Libel Amendment Act 1888 S3) absolute privilege is conferred on fair and accurate reports of public proceedings before any court exercising judicial authority if published contemporaneously with the proceedings. There is no equivalent statutory provision in Scotland and it is now the generally accepted view that the Scots journalist has only the protection of qualified privilege (see below 16–22 *et seq.*).

The absolute privilege enjoyed by most participants in the judicial process extends to quasi judicial proceedings before tribunals, public inquiries, Children's Hearings and arbitrations. The journalist must be clear that the absolute privilege attaches only to the statements made by the judge (in the case of the tribunals, the Panel), Advocates, solicitors, or witnesses. It does not extend to his reports of these proceedings. Reports enjoy only qualified privilege.

Qualified privilege—court reports

16–10   For the working journalist the most important form of qualified privilege is that which attaches to fair and accurate reports of judicial proceedings which take place in public. This form of privilege affords protection to the report unless and until the pursuer can show that it was malicious (for example, omitting the challenges made to evidence in cross-examination thereby giving a one-sided report, could be evidence of malice). The watch words *fairness and accuracy* are not merely professionally desirable, they are legal requirements. If they are not observed the protection of qualified privilege flies off. We will now consider reports of judicial proceedings in detail.

-11 The report must be both accurate and fair. It need not be verbatim or even complete. Where a newspaper merely purports to report the result of a case and does so accurately it cannot be liable in damages because it fails to narrate the steps leading up to judgment. "There is no duty on a reporter in a report of a law suit to make his report exhaustive. It is ... sufficient if the reporter gives the result of the litigation truly and correctly" (*per* Lord Anderson in *Duncan* v. *Associated Newspapers*, 1929 S.C. 14). When more than the result is reported, however, great care must be taken to see that the report is not one-sided. If one party's allegations are mentioned, the other party's replies should be given equal prominence (*Wright and Greig* v. *Outram* (1890) 17 R. 596). If reported allegations are found unproved this must always be clearly stated as soon as possible. There is no objection to publishing daily accounts of a case lasting several days but the reports should be kept up to date. If both allegations and refutations are available there will be no privilege if the allegations are published one day and the refutations held over till the next. The burden of proving that a report is fair and accurate lies on the newspaper (*Pope* v. *Outram*, 1909 S.C. 230).

-12 Care should be taken with headlines in reports of judicial proceedings. If these take the form of comment on the case, they cannot be regarded as part of the report and will not be privileged. They should therefore always be fair and justified by the facts reported so as to be protected by the defence of fair comment. Sub-editors should be mindful of this. They may have to sacrifice clever or amusing headlines in the interests of observing the law. The courts take the view that a reader's approach to a story can be very much affected by the headline on it so a defamatory innuendo could be created in a story by the terms of the headline.

-13 It has never been expressly decided in Scotland that a report must be contemporaneous in order to have privilege, (*Buchan v. N.B. Ry. Co.* (1894) 21 R. 379, indicates that a report need not be contemporaneous but the grounds of the decision are not clear; see also Contempt of Court Act 1981, section 4), but it might well be that the law would look less favourably on the exhumation of old cases than it does on the publication of current reports. Public policy demands freedom in the one case but not in the other. In England only contemporaneous reports have absolute privilege and if a Scottish paper circulates in England, there is always the possibility of an action being brought under English law. For these reasons it is prudent to publish only contemporaneous reports. In practice this means that a report should be published as soon after the proceedings as is reasonably possible. A report in the next edition of a daily paper would be contemporaneous and so too would a report in the next issue of a weekly or fortnightly paper although appearing some days after the proceedings.

16–14   A fair and accurate report of statements made in open court is protected by qualified privilege. It is often impossible, however, to understand a case completely without reference to the various documents connected with it. How far are statements derived from this source protected? The answer varies with the circumstances. In civil cases a report of statements made in an open record is completely unprivileged and the same would seem to apply to reports derived from a closed record which has not yet been referred to in open court. In practice, of course, there are many circumstances where it may be judged safe to publish information from a closed record at this stage but the law seems clear. A litigant is not privileged if he sends his pleadings (whether the record is closed or not) to a newspaper for publication. "If the pleadings so published are slanderous, then the paper publishing them, and the person sending them for publication, are liable in damages for slander" (*per* Lord Young in *Macleod* v. *J.P.s of Lewis* (1892) 20 R. 218 at p. 221). The same principles would apply to the indictment or complaint in criminal cases. Once the case comes up in open court the position is different. Publication of a document actually read out in open court is, of course, privileged and privilege may also protect statements derived from documents which are merely referred to expressly or impliedly in open court. The test here would seem to be whether the information in the documents is an essential part of the case and is merely referred to for the sake of convenience. The point arose in *Harper* v. *Provincial Newspapers*, 1937 S.L.T. 462. A man called James Harper appeared in the Edinburgh Burgh Court. The clerk of court read out his name but not his address. He was found guilty of a fairly minor offence. A reporter verified the name and took down the address from the complaint, which was shown to him for that purpose by the clerk of court. In fact the address given in the complaint was not that of the accused but that of his father who was also called James Harper. When the report appeared the father sued the newspaper and the question then arose whether the statement derived from the complaint was privileged. It was held that it was. The address was an essential part of the case which was omitted from the proceedings in open court simply for reasons of speed and convenience. But it was observed that different considerations might apply to information taken from documents which were merely productions in a case.

-15   In the case of *Cunningham* v. *Scotsman Publications Ltd.*, 1987 S.L.T. 698, Lord Clyde held that privilege applies to a document which "is referred to and founded upon before the court with a view to advancing a submission which is being made", even if not read out in open court (see Chapter 8, paragraphs 08–15 to 08–26, above).

-16   No privilege attaches to reports of proceedings held in private. It is a question of circumstances in each case whether proceedings are in private or in public. In *Thomson* v. *Munro and Jamieson* (1900) 8 S.L.T. 327, it was held that when a statutory examination of a bankrupt took place in public in the sheriff-clerk's room this "was for the occasion a public court". An interesting question arises regarding children's hearings. They are not, strictly speaking, courts. They are not open to the public, but *bona fide* journalists are admitted. Do fair and accurate reports of their proceedings have privilege? The point has not been decided but it can hardly be doubted that such reports would enjoy qualified privilege. The journalists are there to represent the public. There would seem to be the strongest reasons for according privilege to the only source of information on the proceedings available to the public.

-17   Situations may arise where there is doubt whether remarks form part of the proceedings. Thus in one English case (*Hope*

v. *Leng Ltd.* (1907) T.L.R. 243) a witness shouted from the well of the court that the plaintiff's evidence was "a pack of lies". It was held in this case that a report containing this statement was none the less privileged. It is clear, on the other hand, that a report of a conversation between two spectators at the back of the court would not be privileged. The journalist must exercise his discretion in deciding whether or not the interruptions can properly be regarded as part of the proceedings (see paragraph 09–128, above).

16–18   What is meant by a public court of justice? The term certainly covers the ordinary civil and criminal courts in the United Kingdom and it can safely be assumed that it covers special courts such as the Lands Valuation Appeal Court, the Restrictive Practices Court, Election Courts, the Registration Appeal Court, the Scottish Land Court, the Lyon Court, and Licensing Boards. It also seems safe to assume that reports of proceedings before Courts-Martial sitting in the United Kingdom will be privileged. The courts of the Church of Scotland have a special kind of qualified privilege under the Defamation Act 1952. This will be dealt with later.

16–19   The position with regard to foreign courts is interesting. In two Scottish cases (*Pope* v. *Outram*, 1909 S.C. 230; *Riddell* v. *Clydesdale Horse Society* (1885) 12 R. 976) the Court of Session treated reports of proceedings in foreign courts on the same footing as reports of proceedings in United Kingdom courts and assumed that privilege would apply. The point, however, was neither expressly argued nor expressly decided. The question arose in England in connection with reports of the trial of Donald Hume in Switzerland in 1960 (*Webb* v. *Times Publishing Co. Ltd.* [1960] 2 Q.B. 535). It was held that there was not the same close public concern with the administration of justice abroad and no reason for allowing privilege to reports of foreign judicial proceedings unless there was "a legitimate and proper interest" in the proceedings "as contrasted with an interest which is due to idle curiosity or the desire for gossip". Even where there is a legitimate interest it should be noted that, in England, reports of foreign court proceedings have only qualified privilege. As the case in question involved a British subject who had confessed during the Swiss trial that he had committed a murder of which he had been previously acquitted in an English court, it was held that

there was a "legitimate interest" and that the report had qualified privilege. This decision is not, of course, authoritative in
Scots law but the possibility of its reasoning being applied by
a Scottish court and the possibility of an action being brought
under English law in respect of circulation in England would
both indicate prudence with regard to reports of foreign court
proceedings. One final complication with regard to foreign
courts is that some reports of foreign cases are protected by
statute. Under the Defamation Act of 1952 fair and accurate
reports of proceedings in Dominions outside the United Kingdom have qualified privilege.

-20   There is one more counsel of prudence. The privilege
enjoyed in Scotland by fair and accurate reports of proceedings in a public court is only qualified privilege. If the report
is proved to be malicious the pursuer can still succeed.

-21   To sum up, a report of judicial proceedings should always
be fair and accurate. It is advisable, in view of the English
law, that it should also be contemporaneous and that care
should be taken with reports of foreign judicial proceedings.

Other forms of qualified privilege

-22   Qualified privilege applies generally to statements made by a
person in the discharge of some public or private duty or in
matters where his own interests are involved. It applies, for
example, to statements made by an employer in giving his
employee a reference. No action of defamation can be founded
on such statements unless there is proof of malice (but see
19–08). This type of privilege may be relevant for newspapers.
If a person has a duty to make a statement and can only make
it adequately in a newspaper, then it seems that qualified
privilege will protect not only him but also the paper (*Brims* v.
Reid (1885) 12 R. 1016; *Waddell* v. *BBC*, 1973 S.L.T. 246). A recent
case which shows the limitations of qualified privilege is *Fraser*
v. *Mirza* 1993 S.L.T. 527. In that case a Glasgow Asian JP had
written to the Chief Constable of Strathclyde, complaining of
his treatment by Constable Fraser, whom he accused of being
motivated by racial prejudice when he arrested the JP for reset.
The House of Lords decided in March 1993 that although, normally a citizen writing to complain about a police officer would
be protected by qualified privilege, Mr. Mirza had misused the

occasion and so no privilege applied. The court awarded the constable £5,000 damages.

16–23   Of more interest to journalists, however, is the qualified privilege conferred on certain types of reports. Fair and accurate reports of proceedings in either House of Parliament are privileged in the absence of malice (*Cook* v. *Alexander* [1974] 1 Q.B. 279). Extracts from and abstracts of Parliamentary Papers, such as the Reports of Select Committees have also a qualified privilege, but they must not be made into a story. If meat is put on their bones they lose all privilege (*Dingle* v. *Associated Newspapers Ltd.* [1962] 3 W.L.R. 229).

16–24   The Defamation Act 1952 confers qualified privilege on certain types of newspaper reports, a newspaper being defined as "any paper containing public news or observations thereon, or consisting wholly or mainly of advertisements, which is printed for sale and is published in the United Kingdom either periodically or in parts or numbers at *intervals not exceeding thirty-six days*". The Act also applies to broadcasts. The reports having qualified privilege (*i.e.* privilege unless the publication is proved to be with malice) are as follows:

(1) A fair and accurate report of any proceedings in public of the legislature of any part of Her Majesty's dominions outside Great Britain.

(2) A fair and accurate report of any proceedings in public of an international organisation of which the United Kingdom or Her Majesty's Government in the United Kingdom is a member, or of any international conference to which that government sends a representative.

(3) A fair and accurate report of any proceedings in public of an international court.

(4) A fair and accurate report of any proceedings before a court exercising jurisdiction throughout any part of Her Majesty's dominions outside the United Kingdom or of any proceedings before a court-martial held outside the United Kingdom under the Naval Discipline Act, the Army Act or the Air Force Act.

(5) A fair and accurate report of any proceedings in public of a body or person appointed to hold a

public inquiry by the government or legislature of any part of Her Majesty's dominions outside the United Kingdom.

(6) A fair and accurate copy of or extract from any register kept in pursuance of any Act of Parliament which is open to inspection by the public, or of any other document which is required by the law of any part of the United Kingdom to be open to inspection by the public.

(7) A notice or advertisement published by or on the authority of any court within the United Kingdom or any judge or officer of such a court.

-25 The Defamation Act also provides that certain reports will have qualified privilege "subject to explanation or contradiction". Even if published without malice, these reports are not privileged if it is proved that the defender has been requested by the pursuer to publish a reasonable letter or statement by way of explanation or contradiction and has not done so or has done so "in a manner not adequate or not reasonable having regard to all the circumstances". These last words mean in practice that the letter or statement should be inserted in the same part of the newspaper as that in which the original report appeared. It should not be inserted in small type in a part less likely to be read by the general public. The reports having this lesser degree of qualified privilege are, to quote Part II of the Schedule to the Act:

(8) A fair and accurate report of the findings or decision of any of the following associations or of any committee or governing body thereof, that is to say—

(a) an association formed in the United Kingdom for the purpose of promoting or encouraging the exercise of or interest in any art, science, religion or learning, and empowered by its constitution to exercise control over or adjudicate upon matters of interest or concern to the association, or the actions or conduct of any persons subject to such control or adjudication;

(b) an association formed in the United Kingdom
for the purpose of promoting or safeguarding
the interests of any trade, business, industry
or profession, or of the persons carrying on or
engaged in any trade, business, industry or
profession and empowered by its constitution
to exercise control over or adjudicate upon
matters connected with the trade, business,
industry or profession or the actions or conduct of those persons;

(c) an association formed in the United Kingdom
for the purpose of promoting or safeguarding
the interests of any game, sport or pastime to
the playing or exercise of which members of
the public are invited or admitted, and
empowered by its constitution to exercise control over or adjudicate upon persons connected with or taking part in the game, sport
or pastime;

being a finding or decision relating to a person
who is a member of or is subject by virtue of any
contract to the control of the association.

(9) A fair and accurate report of the proceedings at
any public meeting held in the United Kingdom,
that is to say a meeting bona fide and lawfully
held for a lawful purpose and for the furtherance
or discussion of any matter of public concern,
whether the admission to the meeting is general
or restricted.

(10) A fair and accurate report of the proceedings at
any meeting or sitting in any part of the United
Kingdom of:

(a) any local authority or committee (including
sub-committee) of a local authority or authorities;

(b) any justice or justices of the peace acting otherwise than as a court exercising judicial authority;

(c) any commission, tribunal, committee or
person appointed for the purpose of any

inquiry by Act of Parliament, by Her Majesty or by a Minister of the Crown;

(d) any person appointed by a local authority to hold a local inquiry in pursuance of any Act of Parliament;

(e) any other tribunal, board, committee or body constituted by or under, and exercising functions under an Act of Parliament, not being a meeting or sitting admission to which is denied to representatives of newspapers and other members of the public.

(11) A fair and accurate report of the proceedings at a general meeting of any company or association constituted, registered or certified by or under any Act of Parliament or incorporated by Royal Charter, not being a private company within the meaning of the Companies Act 1948.

(12) A copy or fair and accurate report or summary of any notice or other matter issued for the information of the public by or on behalf of any government department, office of state, local authority or chief officer of police.

6–26   These provisions are complicated but they should be read, digested and understood. They form part of the journalist's Magna Carta.

6–27   Paragraph (8) above covers among other things the various professional disciplinary bodies and church courts. Note that it applies only to reports of *findings* and *decisions* and not to reports of *proceedings*. It would seem, however, that reports of public proceedings of the professional disciplinary bodies mentioned earlier in this book will have qualified privilege subject to explanation or contradiction by virtue of paragraph (10)(e) above. They are all constituted and exercise functions under Acts of Parliament. Similarly, reports of proceedings at licensing boards would be protected by paragraph (10)(e) even if not already protected by the common law privilege attaching to reports of judicial proceedings.

6–28   The definition of a public meeting in paragraph (9) may cause difficulty. The mere fact that admission is restricted to those who buy a ticket does not prevent a meeting being a public meeting. But a meeting restricted to members of a particular group or sect will generally not be a public meeting. A church service has been held not to be a public meeting; so a report of a sermon would not be privileged.

16–29   The term "local authority" in England and Scotland means any body to which the Public Bodies (Admission to Meetings) Act 1960 applies. This Act is considered later (see Chapter 23–21. It is to be noted that a report of a meeting of a *private company* is not privileged under paragraph (11).

16–30   There is one final provision of great importance in the Defamation Act. The statutory privilege conferred on the reports set out above does not extend to the publication of any matter which it is unlawful to publish or *"of any matter which is not of public concern and the publication of which is not for the public benefit"* (section 7(3)).

Unintentional defamation

16–31   As we have seen, a person can recover damages for defamation even if the statement complained of was not intended to refer to him or was not intended to be defamatory. This has given rise to some hard cases.

16–32   In *Morrison* v. *Ritchie* (1902) 4 F. 645, *The Scotsman* printed "birth notices" in August saying that Mrs Morrison had given birth to twins. This statement was false but was printed by the newspaper in good faith. It had no way of knowing that Mrs Morrison had been married for only a month. The cruel joker who inserted the notice could not be traced and an action was raised against the proprietors of *The Scotsman*. They maintained that they were not liable because the notices sent to them for publication were not defamatory on their face and they had no reason to suppose that they concealed a libel. The court rejected this defence. The defenders could not escape liability by saying that the slander was unintentional. In 1989 a spoof advertisement was sent to and then appeared in the *Herald* newspaper intimating that the company C. R. Smith had gone into liquidation. This was quite untrue and the newspaper quickly corrected the inaccuracy. But had any business losses been suffered by C. R. Smith they may well have been able to sue the newspaper for recovery. It follows that, in so far as possible, a newspaper should insitute a system of checking that the person inserting any advertisement is *bona fide*.

-33   The famous case of *Hulton* v. *Jones* [1910] A.C. 20, illustrates another type of unintentional defamation. The *Sunday Chronicle* published an article describing recent motor races at Dieppe. The article contained this passage: " 'There is Artemus Jones with a woman who is not his wife. Who must be—you know—the other thing!' whispered a fair neighbour of mine excitedly into her bosom-friend's ear.

-34   "Really, is it not surprising how certain of our fellow countrymen behave when they come abroad? Who would suppose, by his goings-on, that he was a churchwarden at Peckham? No one, indeed, would assume that Jones in the atmosphere of London would have taken on so austere a job as the duties of a churchwarden. Here, in the atmosphere of Dieppe, he is the life and soul of a gay little band that haunts the Casino and turns night into day, besides betraying a most unholy delight in the society of female butterflies."

-35   Artemus Jones was a product of the writer's imagination. He thought that nobody could have such a name. Unfortunately for his paper, he was wrong. There was a barrister known as Artemus Jones who read the article, brought a libel action and recovered £1,750 damages. This was in spite of the fact that he had no connection with Peckham and was not a churchwarden. More recently in 1994, Mr. Alex Wilbraham, an Old Etonian, won substantial libel damages from the publishers Faber & Faber in the High Court in London. His name (which had been selected at random from a New York telephone directory) had been used in a work of fiction about Eton School. The fictional character took drugs and indulged in homosexual activity. Not only did Faber & Faber have to pay damages to Mr. Wilbraham, but they also had to reprint the book using a different name for that particular fictional character.

-36   In other cases of unintentional defamation, statements referring truthfully to one existing person were held to be defamatory of another existing person. As a result of all these cases, the law placed writers and journalists in an intolerable position and encouraged "gold digging" actions. Section 4 of the

Defamation Act of 1952 was intended to alleviate injustice in
the case of innocent publication. Its provisions are, however,
limited and it is doubtful if it has achieved its aims.

16–37   To establish that words were published innocently the publisher must prove (a) that he did not intend them to refer to
the person complaining and did not know of circumstances
by virtue of which they might be understood to refer to him
or (b) that the words were not defamatory on their face, and
that he did not know of circumstances by virtue of which they
might be understood to be defamatory of the person complaining. The publisher must also prove in all cases that he
exercised reasonable care in relation to the publication and,
where he is not the author, that the words were written by
the author without malice.

16–38   If the publisher can satisfy these conditions, he can escape
liability by making an "offer of amends", under the Act. This
means an offer to publish a correction and apology and where
documents or records containing the words complained of
have been distributed, to take reasonable steps to notify the
recipients that the words are alleged to be defamatory of the
person concerned. There are technical rules as to the form of
the offer. These are the concern of the lawyer and as the offer
must be made as soon as practicable, it is important that he
should be informed as soon as it is known that the words give
rise to complaint.

16–39   The effect of these provisions is that if a case like Artemus
Jones's arose today the newspaper could escape liability by
making an offer of amends under the statute. The position is
not so clear with regard to the birth notices case or the liquidation notice case. The newspaper might find it difficult to prove
that it had exercised all reasonable care and impossible to
prove that the words were written by the author without
malice.

Lapse of time

16–40   Under the Prescription and Limitation (Scotland) Act 1973, as
amended in 1985, no action for defamation may be brought
unless it is begun within three years from the date when the
publication or communication first came to the notice of the

pursuer. The court has, however, power to extend this period
if it seems to it equitable to do so.

Possible future defences

-41   The report to the Lord Chancellor by the Supreme Court Procedure Committee (the Neill Committee) in July 1991 recommended a number of changes to the procedure in practice
presently used in defamation cases in England. Most important of these is the possible new defence of innocent defamation which would allow a publisher to escape liability if he
made an offer of amends. This would involve the enactment
of a new section 4 of the Defamation Act 1952. It is difficult
to believe that if such a new defence is created it would not
apply to Scotland as well as England as the Defamation Act
is a UK statute.

-42   The main proposal is that it would no longer be necessary
for the publisher to prove his innocence. The defence of innocence should be available unless the pursuer/plaintiff can
prove that the defender/defendant published the words
either knowing them to be false and defamatory or that he
published recklessly.

-43   There may be the beginnings of the recognition of a "public
figure" defence in UK defamation law along similar lines to
the American approach set out in *Sullivan* v. *New York Times*.
Apart from the European decision in *Lingens* v. *Austria* 1986
there is the House of Lords approach in *Derbyshire County
Council* v. *Times Newspapers* 1993 1 A.E.R. (HL) 1011. As far as
Scotland is concerned, it is at least arguable that there has
always been a public figure defence recognised in our law.
Langlands v. *Leng* in the House of Lords in 1916, *Waddell* v.
BBC in the Court of Session in 1973 and most recently *Mutch*
v. *Robertson* in the Court of Session in 1981 all give journalists
cause for optimism that the Scottish courts may be more willing to accept that public officials and public figures can be
fairly vigorously criticised in the media without having a right
to raise defamation proceedings. It must be emphasised that
this a grey area of law in which European considerations are
likely to play an increasingly large part. It will be of considerable importance and interest to Scots journalists if at some

stage an adequately funded media organisation sees fit to run a public figure defence through the Scottish courts and perhaps beyond.

16–44   It is interesting to note that these proposals were made by the Neill Committee against the background that the present section 4 defence set up by the Defamation Act is in practice unused. The Committee noted that their membership who had over one hundred years of specialised experience of libel law amongst them did not know of one single instance where the present section 4 defence had been successfully advanced.

KEY POINTS

If a defamatory statement is complained of the journalist may rely on the defences of a) veritas b) fair comment c) absolute privilege or d) qualified privilege. Very rarely the defence of unintentional defamation may be of assistance.

The defence of qualified privilege can be argued to apply in a good number of situations. In addition to the common law occasions of qualified privilege there are the occasions of qualified privilege set out in Schedule 2 to the Defamation Act 1952. Care should be taken to ascertain into which part of the Schedule the occasion falls.

A defence of qualified privilege if applicable can, however, be rebutted by proof of malice.

A defamation action has to be raised within three years or else it will be time barred.

CHAPTER 17

DAMAGES AND OTHER REMEDIES

-01   Having considered defences to an action for defamation, we now turn to the position where there is no defence. Here there will be either a settlement or an award of damages. The question of settlement will usually be in the hands of the newspaper's legal advisers but prompt action by the journalist or editor in publishing an apology may facilitate their task.

-02   Scots law, as we have seen (paragraph 15-05), allows damages for injury to feelings alone. Substantial awards may thus be made even although the pursuer has suffered no financial loss. A recent example of this was Sam McCluskey the leader of the National Union of Seamen obtaining an award of damages of £7,500 in respect of a defamation in a letter.

-03   In recent years the damages awarded by English juries have become the subject of much public interest and are naturally of concern to journalists. Examples are the award of half a million pounds obtained by Jeffrey Archer against the Star newspaper over allegations that he had consorted with a prostitute and the award of £400,000 pounds obtained by Koo Stark against a tabloid in respect of allegations concerning Prince Andrew and her private life. More recently Lord Aldington obtained an award of over £1m against Count Leo Tolstoy in respect of allegations made by the Count concerning the Lord's behaviour whilst a Commanding Officer during the last war. In Scotland due to the fact that recently judges have decided most defamation cases damages have been relatively low. But since the case of *Winter* v. *News International* there has been a growing fear amongst the Scottish media that substantial awards may become the norm north of the border as well as south. In *Winter* the jury's award of £50,000 was unanimously upheld on appeal. So the case could be the beginning of an escalating spiral of damages awards by juries. In the twentieth century jury trials in defamation cases have been rare. Increasingly however pursuers have seen the advantage of obtaining trial by jury and so have raised proceedings in the Court of Session where jury trial is available. The onus is very much on the defender to demonstrate to the court why a jury trial should not be allowed. It would appear from recent decisions that it will be necessary for the defender to demonstrate that there is some particular technical matter which the jury could not understand before he would succeed in his plea. Although it should be remembered that exemplary damages which are available to a plaintiff in England are not competent in Scotland a jury will always take a somewhat subjective view of the amount of damages to be awarded. It is clear from Winter that on appeal the judges are unlikely to interfere with substantial awards.

Aggravation

17–04 The general rule is that anything which increases the loss or injury to the pursuer will aggravate damages. In *Stein* v. *Beaverbrook Newspapers Ltd.*, (1968 S.L.T. 401) it was held that if a libel were actuated by malice, this fact would not by itself entitle a pursuer to greater damages. The court stressed that damages are intended to compensate the pursuer, not punish the defender (cf. *Cunningham* v. *Duncan & Jamieson* (1889) 16 R. 383, 388; *Fielding* v. *Variety Inc.* [1967] 2 Q.B. 841, 851). It is highly doubtful if juries heed the directions of judges on this point. An examination of the high awards in English cases suggests that juries are at least on occasion perfectly happy to ignore the directions of judges on the size of damages.

17–05 Persistence in, or repetition of, a defamatory allegation, will aggravate damages. If a defamation in one edition comes to light immediate steps should be taken to ensure that it is expunged from later editions.

17–06 The extent of publication is a relevant factor in assessing damages and a pursuer can bring evidence of a newspaper's circulation in order to aggravate damages. Boasts about big circulations may backfire. Remember that mass circulation may not be necessary for the law to regard the publication as particularly damaging. A leaflet distributed to a few well chosen individuals could ruin for example the reputation of a village minister. He would be entitled to substantial damages if the contents of such a pamphlet were held to be defamatory. An example of this kind of situation was seen in England in 1982 where a Greek ship captain obtained damages of £400,000 in respect of a defamation contained in a Greek newspaper which had a circulation of only 30 copies in London.

Mitigation

7–07 A prompt apology or explanation will tend to mitigate damages (*Morrison* v. *Ritchie* (1902) 4 F. 645). It was formerly thought that evidence of the defender's innocence or good faith in publishing the statement would also be admissible to mitigate damages (*Cunningham* v. *Duncan & Jamieson* (1889) 16 R. 383, 387, 390), but the case of *Stein* (above) throws doubt on this view and suggests that the defender's lack of fault will be relevant to damages only if and in so far as it affects the extent of the pursuer's injury.

7–08 It will, however, be competent to lead evidence of the pursuer's bad reputation in mitigation of damages on the theory that if the pursuer has a bad reputation already, the defamation makes little difference. Evidence of this sort must probably be limited to the particular aspect of character involved in the defamation. Where a woman was said to have had an illegitimate child it was held to be relevant to prove in mitigation of damages that she was well known in the neighbourhood as a person of loose and immoral character. Proof of specific acts of adultery was, however, not allowed. As Lord President Clyde said, "The point of such a defence is not that she is a bad character, but that she has a bad character" (*C.* v. *M.*, 1923 S.C. 1). This neatly summarises the maxim that the law of defamation protects the pursuer's reputation (whether deserved or not) and not his (true) character.

7–09 The Defamation Act 1952, s.12 provides that a defender may prove in mitigation of damages that the pursuer has already recovered damages or raised an action or settled or agreed to settle in respect of publication of words similar to those on which the action is founded. This is clearly of great importance for newspapers. It discourages "gold digging" actions against a series of papers in respect of one defamatory allegation. If libelled in a number of newspapers the wise pursuer will sue in respect of the most virulent article. On being successful he will then usually be able to settle out of court with the publishers of the less libellous material (this is what happened in the Jeffrey Archer case).

Interdict

17–10 Instead of seeking damages the person complaining of defamation may seek an interdict or interim interdict to prevent publication of the defamatory matter. These are perfectly competent remedies in relation to defamation. Scottish journalists do not enjoy the same degree of support from the courts as their colleagues south of the Border who on the basis of the case *Bonnard* v. *Perryman* (1891) can virtually ensure publication by telling the court at the injunction hearing that their facts are correct and that they will prove their facts correct if called upon to do so. Although they risk exemplary damages if proved wrong, an English Judge will allow journalists to publish in such circumstances. In contrast there is no absolute "right of unrestrained publication" in Scots law (see *Boyd* v. *BBC*, 1969 S.L.T. (Sh.Ct.) 17; *Waddell* v. *BBC*, 1973 S.L.T. 246). Nevertheless in deciding whether the balance of convenience lies in favour of granting an interim interdict the court will take into account the fact that the pursuer has the right to seek damages for defamation in a later action and that to this extent any harm resulting from the publication would not be irreparable (*Waddell* v. *BBC*, supra). However in the Sheriff Ewan Stewart case Lord Penrose stated *obiter* that he did not think that damages were invariably sufficient remedy for defamation. In November 1990 Sheriff Stewart presented a petition to the Court of Session craving interdict against the broadcast by BBC Scotland of the programme "Focal Point". The case was completed only five minutes before the programme was due to be broadcast. Sheriff Stewart obtained interim interdict but this was recalled a few days later at a further hearing in the Court of Session. Similarly in 1991 the Chartered Accountants Touche Ross applied for an interdict against the Focal Point programme concerning Glasgow's Glasgow Exhibition during the year of culture. Touche Ross claimed that the programme defamed them in respect of their actings as auditors to the limited company which ran the Glasgow's Glasgow

Exhibition. Their application for interdict was also heard just a few minutes before the programme was due to be broadcast. In this case the application failed. In these two cases as the BBC had lodged a caveat in court they were notified of the interdict application and were given the opportunity to oppose it.

–11   It is clear from the above that the media, particularly television broadcasters are in danger of being the recipients of interim interdict applications. The lodging of *caveats* each year in the Court of Session and the local Sheriff Court for the area of publication or broadcast is clearly a necessary precaution. The lodging of a *caveat* means that the court will give the *caveator* the chance to be heard before an interim interdict is pronounced.

KEY POINTS

Damages can be awarded for hurt to feelings alone. Such *general* damages are not likely to be as high as the *special* damages awarded when actual loss, such as business loss, can be proved. A jury trial in the Court of Session is much more likely to result in a higher award of damages than a case before a Court of Session Judge or a Sheriff. Exemplary damages are not competent in Scotland as they are in England.

A journalist who finds he has defamed someone can reduce his liability for damages by publishing an immediate apology.

As an alternative to claiming damages a pursuer can try to prevent publication by seeking an interim interdict. In Scotland it is much easier for a pursuer to obtain an interim interdict than it is for a plaintiff to obtain a similar order in England. All newspapers and broadcasters should lodge caveats annually in the Court of Session and in the case of local newspapers at the local Sheriff Court.

CHAPTER 18

LETTERS, ARTICLES AND ADVERTISEMENTS

18–01   A defamation can be contained in any part of a newspaper. It can lurk in a news item or editorial or it can be blazoned forth in a headline or even on a billboard. In these last two cases, however, the words in the headline or on the poster are regarded as simply drawing attention to a specific article and they will not usually be held to be defamatory if not so when read fairly along with the article (*Leon* v. *Edinburgh Evening News*, 1909 S.C. 1014; *Archer* v. *Ritchie & Co.* (1891) 18 R. 719). It is clear and just that a newspaper should be responsible for material produced in its own offices. It may seem less clear and less just that it should be responsible for material such as letters, articles or advertisements contributed by outsiders. This chapter deals with these matters. It is largely an application of the principles already explained.

An example of a dangerous advertisement was a "spoof" inserted in the *Herald* purporting to announce the liquidation of double-glazing company C R Smith.

Letters to the editor

18–02   A newspaper is liable for a defamation contained in letters to the editor and the person defamed can sue both it and the writer. In the case of a hidden libel, the newspaper may well be able to rely on the defence of innocent publication and an offer of amends but as we have seen it must be able to prove that the words were not written with malice.

18–03   Anonymous letters give rise to further difficulties. The general rule is that a paper will not be forced to disclose the name of the writer but this is a rule of practice not of law, and if the court orders disclosure, the newspaper must comply. Disclosure has been ordered when the pursuer alleged that a series of letters to the editor were in fact written by the newspaper itself as part of a systematic plan to ruin his reputation (*Cunningham* v. *Duncan & Jamieson* (1889) 16 R. 383), and a disclosure has also been ordered when a newspaper put forward a defence which the pursuer could only meet by finding out the names of the writers of the letters in question (*Ogston & Tennant* v. *Daily Record, Glasgow*, 1909 S.C. 1000). While the courts are unwilling to compel disclosure there are strong reasons why a newspaper should reveal the names of contributors of defamatory articles. If it does not, it may find itself cut off from a number of important defences.

3–04 It may, for example, lose the defence of qualified privilege. If the name of the writer is not disclosed it cannot be known whether he had a duty to make the statement complained of or whether he was actuated by malice (*Brims* v. *Reid* (1885) 12 R. 1016; *McKerchar* v. *Cameron* (1892) 19 R. 383; contrast *Egger* v. *Viscount Chelmsford* [1965] 1 Q.B. 248).

3–05 Although the law on the point is neither clear nor entirely satisfactory it seems that a newspaper may also in some circumstances lose the defence of fair comment if it will not or cannot disclose the name of the writer of a letter. This has been discussed in the previous chapter. And a newspaper will probably be cut off from the defence of innocent publication and an offer of amends if it does not disclose the author's name. It would obviously be very difficult or impossible in this case to supply the necessary proof that the words complained of were written without malice.

3–06 To sum up, the newspaper is in a much stronger position if it can reveal the name of the writer of letters appearing anonymously in its columns but it will not normally be compelled to make a disclosure.

3–07 Forged letters are a particularly insidious danger as so little can be done to guard against them. In 1963 the editor and proprietors of the *Daily Express* were sued for libel by the Orchestral Director of the Royal Opera House. The letter was a forgery. The defendants admitted that it was defamatory in that it suggested that the plaintiff was disloyal to his employers. They published a full explanation and apology, paid an agreed sum in damages and indemnified the plaintiff against his legal costs (*Smith* v. *Wood, The Times*, April 10, 1963).

3–08 Exactly the same considerations apply to articles contributed by a correspondent and published anonymously.

Advertisements

18–09   In the case of advertisements and notices of births, marriages and deaths, the newspaper will again be in a weak position if it cannot disclose the name of the contributor and the rules discussed above apply. As advertisements are not usually associated with defamation it may be of value to mention two cases where they did lead to litigation.

18–10   In the first case a newspaper published an advertisement which read:

> "A criminal information for conspiracy to defraud is being prepared re the estate of B. Malyon (deceased) 74 Argyle Street. All persons having made payments at the above address since September ... should send immediate information to T. Bernstein, private detective, 84 St. John Street."

18–11   The pursuer was B. Malyon's trustee and executor and had succeeded to his business which he carried on at 74 Argyle Street. He was allowed to bring an action against the newspaper as well as the private detective on the ground that the advertisement represented that he had been engaged in a fraudulent conspiracy in regard to B. Malyon's estate (*McLean* v. *Bernstein* (1900) 8 S.L.T. 42).

18–12   In the second case a herbalist inserted an advertisement in a newspaper disclaiming any connection with another herbalist's business and stating that he would not be responsible for any medicines sold at its address "or by any so-called herbalist". The pursuer was the herbalist at the address mentioned, and raised an action against the newspaper, claiming that the advertisement represented that her medicines were dangerous, that she was not a competent herbalist and that she falsely represented herself to be a herbalist. Her action was dismissed on the ground that the advertisement would not reasonably bear this meaning in the circumstances of the case (*Thompson* v. *Fifeshire Advertiser*, 1936 S.N. 56).

18–13   Advertisements are sometimes seen which state that somebody will no longer be responsible for another's debts or which warn the public against imitation goods. Such advertisements can be dangerous (see, *e.g. Grainger* v. *Stirling* (1898) 5 S.L.T. 272; *Webster* v. *Paterson & Sons*, 1910 S.C. 459) and should be accepted with caution. Care should be taken to ensure that they are genuine and phrased so as to avoid unnecessary aspersions. In the second type of case, for example, statements which would identify particular traders should be excluded.

CHAPTER 19

ACTIONABLE NON-DEFAMATORY STATEMENTS
VERBAL INJURY

19–01 Not only defamatory statements give rise to exposure to actions for damages in the courts. Statements which are not themselves defamatory may allow a right of action on the ground of either a) verbal injury or b) negligence. It is hoped that the possibility of journalists and their employers being sued for negligence are remote. There is, however, a worrying decision on negligent statements by the House of Lords on 7th July, 1994, in the case of *Spring* v. *Guardian Assurance plc*, which is discussed below.

Convicium

19–02 The most extreme form of verbal injury which was at one time recognised by Scots law is the old Roman law remedy of convicium. The essence of convicium was that the pursuer had been held up to ridicule by the defender. Perhaps the best modern day example of such lampooning is found in the television programme "Spitting Image". To succeed in a claim for convicium it was necessary for the pursuer to show that the defender had made the statement maliciously and that he had intended to bring the pursuer into public hatred, contempt or ridicule. It was also necessary to show that the pursuer had suffered some form of loss or injury (injury to feelings might be sufficient). For the journalist the most frightening aspect of the remedy of convicium was that truth was no defence.

It is submitted that if the remedy of convicium was ever one of the forms of verbal injury recognised by Scots law that this is no longer so. In modern times there have been no Scottish proceedings based on the remedy of convicium. It is suggested that journalists should proceed on the basis that such a remedy is no longer open to pursuers in Scotland.

Malicious Falsehood

9–03 Another form of non defamatory verbal injury is malicious falsehood. The pursuer will have a right of action if he can prove three things:
1. that the statement about him was untrue;
2. that it was made spitefully, dishonestly or recklessly; and
3. it caused him financial loss.

An example from the English courts illustrates the point. Stefan Grappelli, the jazz violinist, was due to appear at certain concerts in England. Due to illness he had to cancel these concerts. His agents put out a statement explaining to the public not only that he was ill but saying further that the illness was serious and that "it is likely Mr. Grappelli will never tour again". To say that someone is seriously ill is clearly not defamatory—it evokes sympathy rather than lowers his standing in the eyes of right thinking people. But, clearly, such a statement could affect the individual's business. Mr. Grappelli was allowed an action for malicious falsehood; *Grappelli v. Derek Block Holdings Limited* 1981 2 AER 272.

Slander of Goods

9–04 Scots law will allow an action to a pursuer if the defender has unjustifiably criticised the pursuer's goods or property. Perhaps the simplest example is criticism of a product which the pursuer is producing commercially. Again, as in the case of malicious falsehoods it is necessary for the pursuer to be successful that he show:
1. the statement was untrue;
2. it was made maliciously or recklessly; and
3. it caused him actual damage

This form of action should give particular concern to journalists working in the area of consumer affairs. Criticism of particular brand names is an exceptionally risky area.

Onus of Proof

9–05 As will have already emerged, the comfort for the journalist is that these actions for verbal injury are the reverse of defamation actions in that the onus of proving falsity lies firmly on the pursuer's shoulders. It is not, as in defamation, necessary for the defender to prove his statements to be true. It is also necessary for the pursuer to show that the statements were made either maliciously or recklessly. He must then go on to show some loss or injury. It might, however, be easy in the case of an individual pursuer to prove some form of injury in the form of hurt feelings. It should also be remembered that in terms of Section 3 of the Defamation Act 1952 if an action is raised for verbal injury it is not necessary for the pursuer to prove special damage, (i.e., actual pecuniary loss) if the words on which the action is founded are calculated to cause pecuniary damage to the pursuer.

Legal Aid

19–06   Legal aid is not available for actions based on defamation. But it may be available for actions based on malicious falsehood or slander of goods. The availability of Legal aid increases the journalist's exposure to action for the simple reason that more people have the ability to sue.

Negligent Statements

19–07   Since the case of *Hedley Byrne and Co. Limited* v. *Heller and Partners Limited* (1964) AC 465 it has been accepted in both Scots and English law that a statement made negligently which causes the pursuer loss is actionable. From the journalist's viewpoint the problems are obvious. The journalist does not enjoy the possibility of the defences of fair comment or privilege which he can use in cases based on defamation. On the other hand, it is necessary for the pursuer to show that the statement was firstly, false and that it was communicated negligently.

The legal principles involved in the Hedley Byrne case are complex. It will suffice for present purposes to summarise the law in the following simplified form:

a). A person making a statement on which others may reasonably be expected to rely has a duty to take care that the statement is accurate.

b). If he ignores his duty by making the statement negligently or recklessly then he can be liable in damages.

c). For the pursuer to succeed he must show that he relied on the statement and that he suffered loss as a direct consequence.

The defender can, however, exempt himself from liability by issuing a disclaimer—which is precisely what had happened in the Hedley Byrne case itself. This is why it is good practice for editors in the likes of financial advice columns in newspapers to include a footnote stating that the editor, his staff and the publishing company are not liable for the advice given.

–08   As stated at the beginning of this chapter, the House of Lords have recently (July 1994) dealt with the question of liability for statements made negligently in the case of *Spring* v. *Guardian Assurance*. In this case the House of Lords decided that the terms of an employment reference were actionable under the law of negligence. As was observed above, normally an employment reference is protected by the law of qualified privilege. Accordingly, unless it were made maliciously, it would not give ground to an action in defamation. The Lords in the Spring case, however, were willing to accept the plaintiff's contention that he had a good ground of action on negligence. At the time of writing, it is unclear as to how far the principles set out in Spring will apply. It is, however, an area of law which journalists would be well advised to monitor closely. If pursuers in Scotland could proceed regularly by way of the law of negligence, journalists might find themselves unable to plead the usual defamation defences of privilege and fair comment.

KEY POINTS

Some statements which are not defamatory are nevertheless actionable. In such an action it is necessary for the pursuer to prove that the statement made by the defender has been made with malice. In addition to proving malice, the pursuer must also prove that the statements were false. Finally, in most cases, the pursuer must also prove that actual pecuniary damage was caused to the pursuer. Remember, however, the terms of Section 3 of the Defamation Act 1952 in terms of which the pursuer may be relieved of the obligation of proving pecuniary loss. Statements made by a journalist negligently which are relied upon by others causing them financial loss can be actionable.

CHAPTER 20

DIFFERENCES IN ENGLISH LAW

20–01 The broad principles of the law of defamation are the same in England as in Scotland but there are several differences on particular points. The more important of these will now be briefly considered.

Distinction between libel and slander

20–02 Roughly speaking, a defamation which is written, or expressed in permanent form is a libel in English law, while a defamation which is spoken or communicated in some other transitory form is slander. Under the Defamation Act 1952, however, a statement which is broadcast by wireless telegraphy is treated as libel.

20–03 The importance of the distinction is that, with some exceptions, no action will lie for slander unless the plaintiff proves that the words complained of have caused him actual pecuniary damage. The exceptional cases where an action for slander will be allowed without such proof are those involving imputations (a) of a crime punishable by death or imprisonment, (b) of having a contagious or infectious disease, (c) of unchastity in a woman or (d) calculated to disparage the plaintiff in any office, profession, calling, trade or business held or carried on by him at the time of publication.

Criminal libel

20–04 In English law, libel is a crime punishable by fine or imprisonment as well as a civil wrong giving rise to a claim for damages. A criminal prosecution is rare, however, and tends to be discouraged if the civil remedy is available. It should be noted that while in England there must be publication to a third party before a civil action will lie, this does not apply to a criminal prosecution. It can be brought if the statement has been made to the defamed person alone and is of a type calculated to provoke a breach of the peace. The Supreme Court Procedure Committee reporting to the Lord Chancellor in England in July 1991 recommended that Parliament should consider whether the public interest required the retention of criminal libel in English law. Their recommendation was that if it was to be retained as a legal concept at all proceedings of criminal libel should only be launched with the approval of the Attorney General (the equivalent of the Scottish Lord Advocate).

Defences

-05   Justification is the English term for *veritas*. The same principles apply as in Scotland.

-06   As we saw, only contemporaneous reports of judicial proceedings have absolute privilege in English law. Noncontemporaneous reports, however, have qualified privilege provided they are fair and accurate. Reports of foreign proceedings (not coming under the Defamation Act) do not even have qualified privilege under English law unless they are of legitimate interest to the British public.

-07   In England a litigant has absolute privilege with regard to statements he makes in written pleadings or instructs his counsel to make in court. In Scotland he has only qualified privilege (*M. v. H.*, 1908 S.C. 1130).

-08   Formerly the period within which an action for defamation had to be brought was six years in England. It is now three years.

Injurious falsehoods

-09   The statements referred to in Chapter 19 as actionable nondefamatory statements are generally known in English law as injurious falsehoods. Before 1952 the plaintiff had to prove falsity, malice and actual financial damage in each case. Since the Defamation Act of that year he need not prove actual financial damage in many cases where the words are calculated to cause him financial damage.

Frequency of actions/exemplary punitive damages

20–10 Until comparatively recently defamation cases were rare in Scotland. The high awards given in the past 10 years by English juries, however, have encouraged Scots to feel that it is at least worthwhile intimating a claim though not carrying out the threat to raise proceedings. Undoubtedly the high award in the *Winter* case will encourage Scots pursuers to go into court. It is interesting to note that the *Winter* case was a 'speculative action' whereby the solicitors and counsel acting for Mrs Winter would have obtained no fee at all had they not succeeded. If more solicitors and counsellors were willing to approach defamation cases in this fashion it would undoubtedly be the case that there will be many more Scots defamation actions in the Court of Session in the future particularly if jury trial continues to be readily available. It has often been stated by Scots lawyers that the ability of the English jury to award exemplary and/or punitive damages in defamation cases may have made libel a much more popular form of action in England than in Scotland. In view however of the subjective nature of the jury's deliberations on the question of damages the distinction is probably not as important as is often claimed. Indeed the Supreme Court Procedure Committee when reporting to the Lord Chancellor recommended that English law should be brought into line with Scots law by removing the right the English jury presently holds to award exemplary or punitive damages.

CHAPTER 21

COPYRIGHT

-01 The idea behind copyright is that people should be able to enjoy the benefits of their own original work, in the knowledge that it will not be pirated or exploited by others. Copyright is in essence a right to prevent copying. It does not give a monopoly. If two people by some remarkable coincidence were to write two identical books and it could be proved that they were in fact completely independent, the one who got into print first could not prevent the other from publishing his book. There would be no copying.

-02 The law of copyright is the same throughout the United Kingdom and is now contained in the Copyright, Designs and Patents Act 1988 which made significant changes in the law. It is a lengthy and complex Act and there are several sections which are important to staff journalists, freelances and photographers in guiding them as to the use they may make of someone else's work.

-03 The Act describes copyright as a property right which covers original literary, dramatic, musical or artistic works, sound recordings, films, broadcasts or cable programmes and typographical arrangements.

-04 It is a person's work that is protected, not his ideas. This is an important distinction. Whatever the ethical questions, it is no infringement of copyright to lift the idea of another person's story and use it in a story of your own expressed in your own words.

-05 Copyright protects only original works but here again it is the form rather than the content which is important. The ideas need not be original provided the form in which they appear is. And this form will be original if it involves the use of some independent knowledge, skill, judgment or labour. There can be copyright in a list of football fixtures or Stock Exchange prices if skill was required in the selection or arrangement.

21–06   On the same principle there can be copyright in verbatim newspaper reports of public speeches. Neither the ideas nor the way of expressing them would be commonly regarded as the original work of the reporter, but the conversion of the spoken word into a written report involves the use of independent skill and labour on his part and the report is regarded as an original work for copyright purposes. If, however, the speaker hands the reporter a written copy of his speech and this is published verbatim by the newspaper then there would be no separate copyright in the report. There would be no conversion of the spoken to the written word and no exercise of independent skill or labour.

21–07   Another example will help to bring out the meaning of "originality" in copyright law. A translation is an "original" work for copyright purposes. The ideas and their arrangement are not original in the ordinary sense but the translation does involve independent knowledge and hard work on the part of the translator. It is therefore protected.

21–08   The type of copyright which is of most importance for journalists is that existing in "literary works". This term is much wider than might be thought. It certainly does not mean that a work must have literary merit before it is protected. An examination paper has been held to be a literary work for copyright purposes, the judge remarking: "In my view, the words, 'literary work' cover work which is expressed in print or writing irrespective of the question whether the quality or style is high.

21–09   The word 'literary' seems to be used in a sense somewhat similar to the use of the word 'literature' in political or electioneering literature, and refers to written or printed matter" (*University of London Press Ltd.* v. *University Tutorial Press Ltd.* [1916] 2 Ch. 601 at page 608).

21–10   In the case of "artistic works" too, paintings, drawings, engravings and photographs are protected irrespective of artistic quality. A tie-on business label has been held to be an artistic work for copyright purposes (*Walker* v. *British Picker Co.* [1961] R.P.C. 57).

21–11   It is clear that a "work" need not be very substantial, but a line must be drawn somewhere and in some instances protection has been refused on the ground that there was no "work". Advertising slogans consisting of a few words have been refused protection on this ground.

–12 It is probably for the same reason that titles of newspapers, books and periodicals are denied copyright. An established newspaper can, however, prevent another paper being sold under the same or a similar title by means of an action for "passing off". It must be proved that the other paper is so similar that it would be likely to deceive the public. The owners of the magazine *Punch* once failed for this reason to prevent the publication of a much cheaper magazine called *Punch and Judy*.

–13 "Could anyone", asked the judge, "be misled into buying this other paper instead, which has the words 'Punch and Judy' printed on it in distinct letters with a different frontispiece, and its price a penny? I am clearly of opinion that the mass of mankind would not be so misled" (*per* Malius V.C. in *Bradbury* v. *Beeton* (1896) 18 W.R. 33).

–14 The same considerations apply to a *nom de plume*. There is no copyright, but if the name has become well known the author can bring a passing-off action to prevent its use in ways likely to deceive the public.

–15 To sum up what has been said so far, copyright is a right to prevent copying, not a monopoly. It protects works, not ideas; form, not content. The works must be original, but need not be very original. In most cases, originality means the use of some independent skill, knowledge or labour. Merit is usually unimportant. Works can be small, but not too small. If, like newspaper titles, they are too small, they may nevertheless be protected by the law of passing-off.

Ownership and infringement

–16 The owner of copyright in a work has the exclusive right to copy it, issue copies to the public, perform, show or play the work in public, broadcast the work and make an adaptation of it. Copyright is infringed by anyone who reproduces the whole or a substantial part of the work without the permission of the copyright owner, but there are various exceptions which allow journalists to make use of copyright material for review, criticism and the reporting of current events.

Conversely, a newspaper or broadcasting organisation which owns copyright of material can prevent anyone else from reproducing it in public, recover damages and charge a fee for allowing the work to be published.

21–17   Under the 1988 Act, s.11(2), the person who first brings a work into existence is the owner of any copyright in it. However, where a literary (or dramatic or musical or artistic work) is made by an employee in the course of his work, the employer is the first owner of copyright unless there is some agreement to the contrary. Until the change in the law brought about by the 1988 Act, staff journalists retained residual copyright in their work which meant that it could be republished. For example, a columnist could publish an anthology of his best work in a book or use it for a broadcast or a film. Now the newspaper retains the entire copyright unless a special agreement has been reached. The newspaper also owns copyright in pictures taken by staff photographers.

21–18   The freelance journalist, not working under a contract of service or apprenticeship, is in a different position and owns the copyright in his or her work. This will apply even if a newspaper has ordered the freelance to write an article or series of articles. The position can be altered by a written agreement under which the freelance assigns his copyright. An assignation is different from a licence. An assignation actually transfers copyright: a licence merely gives permission to do something in spite of the copyright, which remains in the hands of the person granting the licence.

21–19   Before the 1988 Act, where a newspaper commissioned a picture from a freelance or commercial photographer the newspaper owned copyright in the picture. Now, unless there is an agreement to the contrary, copyright belongs to the photographer or his employer. If a member of the public submits a photograph for publication, he will retain the copyright, again subject to any agreement to the contrary.

21–20   However, under section 85 of the Act, a person who, for private and domestic purposes, commissions the taking of a photograph or the making of a film, has the right not to have copies issued to the public or shown in public or broadcast. This applies only to pictures taken after August 1, 1989, when the 1988 Act came into force. It may well create problems for the newspaper which borrows a wedding picture from a relative after the bride, groom or best man becomes headline news, perhaps years after the wedding. By publishing, the newspaper could be infringing the copyright of the photographer and of the groom who may have commissioned it and would have the right under section 85 not to have it issued to the public.

1–21 The solution for newspapers may be, if they accept commissions for pictures at weddings and christenings, to get a written undertaking that they can publish the pictures at any time.

1–22 An exceptional case where a man did object, understandably, to the publication of his wedding photograph was *Williams* v. *Settle* in 1960. The bridegroom's father-in-law was found murdered. Two national newspapers obtained from a freelance photographer, and published, a photograph of a group at the wedding which included the murdered man. The groom owned the copyright in the photograph in this case and recovered damages and costs from one newspaper and an apology and undertakings from the other. He also recovered substantial damages from the photographer.

Fair dealing

1–23 As we have seen, the owner of copyright in a work has the exclusive right to copy it, issue copies to the public, perform, show or play the work in public, or broadcast it. However, the 1988 Act, s. 30, contains a provision on "fair dealing" which allows the journalist to reproduce extracts from the work (other than a photograph for which permission would have to be obtained from the copyright owner) for reporting current events and for criticism and review. In the case of newspapers the use of the material must also be accompanied by a sufficient acknowledgment. No acknowledgment is needed in reporting current events by means of a sound recording, film, broadcast or cable programme.

1–24 If too much of a work was reproduced (for example lifting another newspaper's story or quotes word for word) that might not be held to be fair dealing. It is not possible to lay down a hard and fast rule on this. To quote a small but crucial part of a book might be regarded as an infringement of copyright, while the use of a longer but less important passage might not. In one case, the use of four lines from a Kipling poem was held to be an infringement of copyright when they were used in an advertisement.

21–25   In January 1991, in the High Court, Mr Justice Scott dismissed a breach of copyright action brought by the BBC against British Satellite Broadcasting over the use of BBC football highlights from the World Cup. The judge ruled that BSB's use of clips recorded from the BBC's live coverage was protected by the fair dealing defence allowing limited use of copyright material in reporting current events. The BBC contended that BSB's use of the "best bits" of its coverage was a breach of copyright.

The spoken word

21–26   One of the most important provisions for journalists was the introduction by the 1988 Act for the first time of copyright in the spoken word. Until then, if no notes had been made and the speech was completely off-the-cuff, the speaker had no copyright in his words. There was no "work" to which copyright could attach. Copyright came into existence only when the words were taken down by a reporter and it belonged either to the reporter or his employer. This meant, for example, that although the *Daily Mirror* could sue *Today* newspaper for allegedly "lifting" quotes from an interview with showbusiness personality Marty Caine, Miss Caine could not take action because she had no copyright in her words.

21–27   The Act gives the speaker a copyright which comes into existence as soon as the words are recorded by the journalist. Section 58 provides, however, that where a record of spoken words is made in writing or otherwise for reporting current events or broadcasting all or part of them, it is not an infringement of copyright in the words provided: (a) the record is a direct record of the spoken words; (b) the making of the record was not prohibited by the speaker; (c) the use made of the material is not of a kind prohibited by the speaker; and (d) the use is by or with the authority of the person lawfully in possession of the record.

21–28   The precise scope of this section, like many other parts of the Act, will not become clear until it has been tested by the courts, but it seems that if a speaker stands up before he makes his speech and makes it known that he does not wish it to be reported in any shape or form, the publisher who chooses to ignore this could be sued for breach of copyright. If the speaker decides after he has made the speech that he does not wish it reported, that will be too late. He must make it clear beforehand. The journalist may also be able to rely on the legal principle that there is no copyright in facts and ideas, and probably on a defence of fair dealing.

1–29   During the passage of the Bill, journalists also expressed concern as to how far back current events could be said to extend. What if evidence of some scandal emerged years after the event, as frequently happens, and, in the course of an investigation, a newspaper gained access to some documents protected by copyright? Would it be able to quote from the documents by saying it was reporting current events? The position is not clear.

1–30   The terms of section 58 also suggest that a speaker might be able to dictate in what form he wishes his words to appear. The section talks about the use of the material not being of a kind prohibited by the speaker. Suppose an MP was delivering a speech and made it clear that he wanted it reported by certain newspapers and not others? Or that he wished only part of the speech to be reported? The Act appears to give him the means to sue for breach of copyright if his wishes are ignored.

Moral rights

1–31   The Act also gives the author of a copyright literary work the moral right to be identified, not to have his work subjected to derogatory treatment, and not to have work falsely attributed to him. The treatment of a work is derogatory if it amounts to a distortion or mutilation of the work or is otherwise prejudicial to the honour or reputation of the author. Treatment is defined as any addition to, deletion from, alteration to or adaptation of the work.

1–32   The right to be identified and not subjected to derogatory treatment does not apply to work by employees or reports of current events or to a material made available to a newspaper or periodical by the author for publication.

1–33   There is no infringement of copyright in reporting proceedings in Parliament, the courts and public inquiries.

Duration

21–34 Copyright lasts for a very long time. In the case of the written word and photographs, copyright normally lasts for 50 years after the end of the year in which the author dies. For example, the UK copyright in *Ulysses*, claimed by some critics to be the greatest novel of the twentieth century, expired at the end of 1991, 50 years after the death of James Joyce.

21–35 Copyright in a computer-generated work lasts for 50 years from the end of the calendar year in which it was made. Copyright in a typographical arrangement, for example a cut-out from a newspaper, lasts for 25 years from the end of the year of publication. If, however, the work has not been published or otherwise exploited during the author's lifetime, there is an even longer period of protection—for 50 years after the end of the year of first publication or exploitation. After the expiry of copyright the work becomes public property and can be freely copied. In 1994 the government was preparing to implement an EC directive to increase the copyright protection period from 50 years after the death of the author to 70 years in the case of literary and artistic works and photographs.

21–36 The owner of copyright can sue for damages if his right is infringed, but the person alleged to have breached copyright has a defence if he can show that at the time of the infringement he did not know and had no reason to believe that there was copyright in the work. In that situation the copyright owner will not be entitled to damages but might still have some other form of remedy such as interdict or accounting of profits.

21–37 In an action for infringement, the court has power to award "such additional damages as the justice of the case may require"—looking at all the circumstances of the case, particularly the flagrancy of the infringement and any benefit gained by the guilty party.

21–38 It is not, of course, an infringement of copyright for a newspaper to print and publish letters or manuscripts sent to the editor. The fact that the author sends them implies a licence to publish. An interesting legal situation arises when a letter or article is sent to a newspaper for publication. In the absence of agreement, the position is that the author retains the copyright and the newspaper gets the property in the actual paper on which the words are written and, in addition, implied permission to publish. It is doubtful how far, if at all, the newspaper has implied permission to alter the letter or article. The view of the English courts is that in the absence of express or implied prohibition it has the right, as licensee, to make alterations. Also, a prohibition on reasonable alteration would probably not be implied in the case of ordinary letters and unsigned articles.

KEY POINTS

1–39 Copyright law exists to prevent original work such as litrerature, drama and music from being exploited without the owner's permission. The law is now contained in the Copyright Designs and Patents Act 1988.

Copyright in work produced by an employee such as a journalist belongs to his or her employer, unless there is an agreement to the contrary. A newspaper would also have copyright in pictures taken by a staff photographer.

Freelance journalists own the copyright in their own work. Where a newspaper commissions a picture from a freelance photographer the copyright belongs to the photographer or his employer.

The owner of a work has the exclusive right to copy it, issue copies to the public, show or play the work in public or broadcast it. However, the 1988 Act contains a provision on "fair dealing" which allows the journalist to reproduce extracts for reporting current events and for criticism and review.

Section 58 of the Act introduces copyright in the spoken word, and the journalist will infringe this copyright if a speaker makes it clear beforehand that he does not wish his words to be recorded. The Act also gives the copyright owner the moral right to be identified and not have his work subjected to derogatory treatment.

Copyright in the written word and photographs normally lasts for 50 years after the end of the year in which the author dies. A European directive proposed to increase this period to 70 years.

CHAPTER 22

BROADCASTING

CONTEMPT AND DEFAMATION GENERALLY

22–01 The legal principles governing the activities of journalists outlined in this book apply also to television and radio broadcasters, particularly in relation to contempt of court and defamation. Indeed, broadcasters, particularly television broadcasters, might expect more severe treatment from the courts than newspaper journalists in view of the higher public penetration of broadcasting and the higher authority which radio and TV appear to enjoy, according to statistical analysis, in the public mind.

22–02 The rules restricting publicity contained in the Contempt of Court Act 1981 apply to broadcasts as well as printed publications, but, because of the time factor, their effect may be different in practice. For example, in a case in 1992 a man who persistently refused to obey an order to demolish a building he had erected without necessary permission, was eventually confronted by the local planning officer and other officials, the police and television and press representatives. Millions of viewers saw the man fire several shots from a gun which killed one man and injured a TV cameraman. The reporters and cameramen from the press had time to consider whether, under the 1981 Act, it was safe for them to publish reports describing or showing what had in fact happened. Since a murder charge obviously was likely to follow, care had to be taken to avoid the kind of substantial risk of prejudice to court proceeding that the Act seeks to prevent. The TV crews had no such choice. They had no reason to anticipate that such an event would occur. It happened instantaneously and there was no time for any decision whether to publish. Yet, justice itself would have been strained beyond reasonable limits if the showing of the TV record of what actually happened had been made the basis of a criminal charge against the broadcasters.

2–03   As there have been so few cases concerning broadcasters in a Scottish court it is difficult to identify the approach of the Scottish judiciary to broadcasting. It is clear, however, that the transitory nature of a broadcast (unlike the written newspaper report which can be read and re-read) can be cited by the broadcasters' lawyers in court both as a defence and also as a mitigating factor in the event of a finding of guilt. Support for this approach can be found in England in the case *Attorney General* v. *ITN and Others* in May 1994. There the English Divisional Court accepted that a television broadcast was transitory and therefore less likely to cause a risk of prejudice than a newspaper article. The competing qualities of high penetration and the authority obtained by broadcasting on the one hand and the counterbalancing factor of its transitory nature have not been fully discussed in a Scottish case at the time of writing. It will suffice at present to warn broadcasters that the courts will undoubtedly attach weight to the argument that TV and radio broadcasts reach large audiences (which is their boast) and enjoy high authority and therefore a defamation or a contempt by a broadcaster could be regarded as more serious than that by a print journalist. If there is no sufficient counterbalancing argument available then it may be thought that the broadcasters expect a heavier sentence or fine for contempt or a higher award of damages for defamation.

CONTRAST BETWEEN BROADCASTS AND NEWSPAPERS IN CONTEMPT CASES AND DEFAMATION CASES

22–04   On the question of contempt some small degree of guidance might be obtained from the experience of newspapers and radio broadcasting in 1979 in the case of *Stuurman*. In that case the English police unfortunately put out a press release indicating that a Mr Stuurman, his wife and two other individuals arrested in Scotland and charged with crimes under the Misuse of Drugs Act were members of an international drugs running gang who had been sought by Interpol for many years. Some sections of the Scottish press carried this material and found themselves before the Scottish High Court of Justiciary for contempt.

22–05   The *Herald* was fined £20,000 for carrying the material, whereas Radio Forth was fined £10,000 for carrying basically the same material. It may be difficult to extract principles from one case but it is reasonable to suppose that the High Court took the view that the printed words in the *Herald* were more likely to reach and therefore affect potential jurors than the brief broadcast on Radio Forth.

22–06   Two cases which came before the Courts in 1992 do provide some guidance as to the Scots courts attitude to allegedly defamatory material which is broadcast rather than printed in a newspaper. In 1992, the case of Anthony Gecas against Scottish Television was finally decided. In that case Mr Gecas, a Lithuanian national living in Edinburgh, had sued STV in respect of their programme "Crimes of War" which alleged he was involved in the death squad extermination of many Lithuanian Jews. Gecas claimed £600,000. Lord Milligan's judgement was in favour of STV and accordingly, no award was made. Lord Milligan did however state that had he found in Mr Gecas's favour he would have awarded only £30,000. One has to remember that the programme alleged that Mr Gecas was a mass murderer.

22–07   At the time of writing another case which began before the Court of Session in 1992 and has not yet been determined. That is the case raised by Robert Henderson QC, against the Herald newspaper. At a preliminary motion which dealt with the question of caution Lord Abernethy took the view that damages of as much as a £100,000 might be due to Mr Henderson if he were to prove his case against The Herald.

22–08   Again, although it may be unwise to take too much from these two cases it would appear on the face of it the courts' approach is to regard newspaper articles as very much more damaging than television broadcasts despite the infinitely higher penetration by television.

INTERDICTS

22–09   In a few recent cases attempts have been made to obtain interim interdicts against radio or TV broadcasts on the basis that the material to be broadcast was defamatory. The first of cases was an application to the Court of Session by George Galloway, MP, in respect of a BBC Scotland programme which made reference to his activities whilst secretary of the charity, War on Want. The court refused interim interdict. So far as it is possible to elicit a principle from a case when no written judgment has been issued, it seems that the court's basis for refusing the application was that, if the material was defamatory, Mr Galloway had a remedy by suing BBC Scotland for damages. The application had been made when the broadcast was imminent. So too was an application by Touche Ross, chartered accountants, in connection with a BBC Scotland "Focal Point" programme on Glasgow's Year as European City of Culture in 1990. Touche Ross were accountants to the company formed in connection with the Glasgow Glasgow's Exhibition, which was part of the 1990 Year, and claimed that the programme defamed them by alleging that they had not carried out their work properly and professionally. BBC Scotland maintained that no such innuendo could be taken from the words used in the programme. In that case, with only minutes to go before transmission time, the Court of Session decided Touche Ross had not made out a *prima facie* case and interim interdict was refused. The case illustrated that to obtain an interim order the pursuer must at least demonstrate a *prima facie* case of defamation.

2–10   The English courts are very reluctant to grant what they call "prior restraint orders" when dealing with the media. Although there is no written constitution in Great Britain the European Convention to which the U.K. is a signatory recognises the principle of freedom of speech. Prior restraint orders could be said to offend against that principle. It is likely, as our laws become more unified within Europe, that prior restraint orders will be more difficult to obtain.

2–11   The Galloway case must, however, be contrasted with Sheriff Ewen Stewart's application for interim interdict against the "Focal Point" programme entitled "A law unto themselves". He presented a petition for interim interdict to the Court of Session less than one hour before the programme was due to start. Lord Penrose granted the interim interdict five minutes before the programme was due to go out. In so doing he stated that he felt that defamation damages were not an adequate remedy for the damage which might be done to Sheriff Stewart by the broadcast if it were untrue. A few days later (after seeing the programme) Sheriff Stewart consented to the interim interdict being lifted.

22–12   There is no authoritative Inner House decision laying down guidelines as to when interim interdict is appropriate against an allegedly defamatory broadcast. There have not been a sufficient number of cases to work out the principles on which our courts approach such situations. It is clear, however, that broadcasters would be foolish not to lodge *caveats* in the Court of Session to ensure that they have the chance of appearing to make representations against the granting of an interim interdict order. So, too, broadcasters should be prepared to defend controversial programmes in court (even, at the last minute). They must also be mindful of the fact that it seems likely that if an application for interim interdict were made and failed and later the programme was proved to be defamatory, the court would probably award higher damages against the broadcaster. Although the Scottish courts do not award exemplary damages, it seems reasonable to suppose that a judge would be sympathetic to a party who had in effect warned the broadcaster by applying for an interim interdict of the defamatory nature of material to be broadcast. If the broadcaster went ahead despite that warning it can be anticipated that the broadcaster would suffer more severe treatment from the court by way of damages.

SPECIAL PROBLEMS OF TELEVISION

22–13   The medium of television is an unusual form of communication in that it simultaneously conveys to the viewer words and visual images. This gives rise to particular legal problems. The juxtaposition of the pictures and commentary/script can frequently give rise to the broadcast becoming defamatory. Often this is accidental and completely unintentional. A recent example will illustrate the point.

In 1994 a BBC Television news broadcast on the Public Account's Committee's investigation into the activities of certain statutory bodies in Wales made reference to the PAC's findings of wasteful, fraudulent and corrupt behaviour on the part of the Welsh statutory bodies, particularly the Welsh Development Agency. During the course of these news reports the BBC used a Welsh Development Agency video which included pictures of a factory in North Wales run by a company called Sharp Electronics UK Limited. The company name and logo could be clearly seen. Sharp Electronics sued in the English courts for defamation claiming that there was an implication that their company was involved in the sort of activities the PAC was criticising. They succeeded in obtaining an apology, damages and payment of their costs.

The lesson to be learned for journalists working in television is that extreme care must be taken to prevent critical words in news reports which are aimed at one particular target from hitting another by accident.

Even in situations where an interviewee is intending to criticise one individual it is perfectly possible that as a matter of law his words are held to be defamatory of another individual. That will arise due to the television journalist 'cutting' the story in such a way that the interviewee's comments would be construed by the viewer in that (quite unintended) way.

It is undoubtedly good practice for a television journalist to have a colleague who has not been working on the story in question to view the television tape before transmission if there is doubt as to how the viewer would construe critical references in the report.

LIVE PROGRAMMES

22–14 Sadly, from a broadcaster's viewpoint live programmes enjoy no special legal protection whatsoever. So a robust remark in the course of an animated studio discussion can result in the broadcasting organisation finding itself on the wrong side of the law of contempt or, more likely, the law of defamation. It will not avail the broadcaster to say that vigorous comment was exactly what was wanted or that it is what the public wishes to hear. Nor will it help to point out that the U.K. is virtually alone in allowing its domestic law to stifle debate in this way. So in this situation in 1986 BBC Scotland were sued for £500,000 pounds by the late Robert Maxwell over a remark made by Arnold Kemp, editor of *The Herald* in the live discussion programme on Radio Scotland "Taking Issue with Colin Bell". Mr Kemp too was sued by Maxwell for £500,000. BBC Scotland as a matter of policy backed Mr Kemp financially as the case wended its way through the Scottish courts. They were, however, under no legal obligation to do so, which illustrates the difficulty anyone taking part in a broadcast in any capacity may face.

The law grants people protection against defamatory statements made about them on the air; the broadcaster takes the responsibility in putting out impromptu discussions for any harmful remarks giving ground for action made by the participants.

WHO MAY BE SUED/ACCUSED IN RESPECT OF A BROADCAST

22–15 Again this has never been judicially determined. On the analogy of newspaper cases, presumably the reporter, the editor, the producer and the broadcasting organisation itself could all find themselves involved in court proceedings.

In one contempt case in 1987 involving Radio Clyde, however, the fine of £20,000 imposed on the radio station's news editor, Colin Adams, by Lord Allanbridge at Paisley was reduced to nil on appeal by the High Court. (This case concerned a broadcast during a murder trial to the effect that the accused had offered to plead guilty to culpable homicide—an offer which the broadcast claimed had been rejected by the Crown.) This case should not be viewed by news editors as particularly comforting. Mr Adams' pleas that he relied on the expertise of the reporter had more force than normal in that the reporter in question was a freelance and had many years experience in the particular area of work (contemporaneous court reporting). If he had been a staff reporter under the control of Mr Adams the High Court's attitude would probably have been different. Lord Allanbridge refrained from fining the broadcasting limited company, Radio Clyde. It seems likely that such a fine would have received more support from the High Court than one of £20,000 imposed on an individual who the Judge was told earned £22,000 per annum and whose employers were by no means certain to back him financially in respect of the fine. (See also Chapter 9 on Contempt of Court).

It is interesting to note that the freelance reporter did not appeal the fine of £5,000 imposed on him by Lord Allanbridge, although the reporter's earnings at the relevant time were stated to be £7,000 per annum.

INDEPENDENT PRODUCERS AND CONTEMPT/DEFAMATION

-16 The foregoing paragraph has particular force nowadays when so much material broadcast comes from independent producers. It seems clear that Scots law allows the pursuer in a defamation action to sue the independent production company as well as the organisation which broadcast the material. It would be possible therefore to have several defenders when, for example, the programme broadcast was produced by an independent production company who employed a freelance reporter. It is suggested that the pursuer could sue all or any of the following:

(a) the broadcaster;
(b) the independent production company as producers;
(c) the reporter(s);
(d) possibly the editor of the programme;
(e) the contributor, if the alleged defamatory remarks were made by him.

There would be no need for the pursuer to sue the broadcasting organisation itself. He could choose to sue the independent producer alone or the reporter alone. In fact, normally a pursuer sues all concerned jointly and severally for the same amount of money. It is suggested that it would be wise for independent producers and reporters involved in such programmes to come to some sort of agreement before the broadcast as to who will be liable in a defamation situation. It must be emphasised, however, on the question of contempt, this is a quasi-criminal matter over which the court alone has jurisdiction. An agreement to pay each other's fines may be informally entered into but nobody can serve your jail sentence for you! Independent producers and their reporters should be mindful of this fact.

CONTEMPT OF COURT: PARTICULAR PROBLEMS FOR
BROADCASTERS

22–17   The ability of broadcasters to transmit up-to-the-minute
reports of developing news stories is one of the principal
strengths of TV and radio. But this very strength creates considerable dangers for broadcasters in the area of contempt of
court. If for example there were a dramatic bank raid in the
morning, the first newspaper report of the event would not
appear until the evening or perhaps in some cities until the
next day. But TV and radio could broadcast stories of the raid
within minutes of the event. The danger, however, of committing the serious offence of contempt of court in this situation
is extremely high. Reference is made to Chapter 9. The various
trigger mechanisms which cause the rules of the Contempt of
Court Act 1981 to commence operation should be in the fore-
front of the minds of broadcasters. The principal events which
would trigger the operation of the 1981 Act rules in such a
situation as envisaged here are (1) arrest or (2) the granting of
a warrant to arrest. A broadcaster reporting a bank raid would
have to check constantly with the police to see if either event
had taken place. If he received no information or received
wrong information to the effect that there had been no arrest
and no warrant granted, then he might well avail himself of
the defence of innocent publication which is set out in Section
3 of the Act. It is emphasised that the law requires that the
broadcaster must be able to show that he has "taken all reasonable care".

It is therefore suggested that broadcasters should operate a
working rule of keeping a record of all enquiries to the police
and the times they are made regarding the question of arrest
and the granting of arrest warrants in this sort of situation.

Broadcasters may, however, find that the police reaction to
requests from journalists for immediate information on arrests
and warrants can be less than helpful—at least in some forces.
Some police information services have been known to answer
journalists' enquiries as to whether or not an arrest has been
made by saying that the journalist and his legal advisers
should be able to work that out for themselves. It is submitted
that this unhelpful attitude would imperil the Crown's position in any petition for contempt against the broadcasting

organisation. The broadcaster could transmit in these circumstances with a reasonable prospect of adopting the innocent publication defence.

A very good example of developing a news story of dramatic proportions arose late in 1991 when a large number of armed police raided the home of the so-called gangland Godfather Arthur Thomson (Senior) in Provanmill, Glasgow in connection with an inquiry into the deaths of two Glasgow, gangland figures. Streets in the area were closed off as police surrounded the house and told the occupants via a loud hailer "to come out with their hands up". This they duly did. Later all were released. The police later put out the incredible statement that there had been no arrests and all concerned had attended voluntarily. The situation demonstrates the dangers for broadcast journalists. Had any of these "volunteers" become accused persons the court would undoubtedly have taken the view that they were arrested at Thomson's house and accordingly the terms of the Act operated from that point onwards.

That would have had a considerable effect on the way TV could cover the story. Pictures of those taken from the house could not have been used. Identity is almost always an issue in a Scottish criminal case. Once the rules of the 1981 Act operate pictures of the accused cannot normally be used unless there is specific permission from the Lord Advocate—and even then there could be dangers from the defence.

THREAT TO BROADCASTING FREEDOM: THE BROADCASTING ACT 1990

-18   A threat to broadcasting freedom may be seen by journalists to arise in Section 10 of the 1990 Act. That states that the Secretary of State can direct the Independent Television Commission to require the licenceholders to publish specific announcements. He may also require the ITC to direct their licenceholders to refrain from including any material specified in a Notice served by the Secretary of State or other Minister of the Crown.

Such power, which existed since before the 1990 Act, has been used by the Crown in relation to broadcasts containing material from Sinn Fein. For approximately six years it was possible to broadcast the content of a Sinn Fein's official speech/interview/press release but not to show him speaking the words. In the case of the BBC, the Crown used the terms of the Corporation's Charter to have the Corporation follow a similar practice.

Section 10 therefore has considerable potential for Government interference in broadcasting and it is unclear if the section and the provisions in the BBC's Charter comply with the terms of article 10 of European Convention on Human Rights for the protection of freedom of expression.

Article 10 of the Convention states:

"Everyone has the right to freedom of expression. This right shall include freedom to hold opinions and to receive and impart information and ideas without interference by public authority and regardless of frontiers. This Article shall not prevent States from requiring the licensing of broadcasting, television or cinema enterprises."

It would appear that the Convention, whilst accepting the principle of licensing broadcasting, does not make any exception in the case of broadcasting from the broad general principle of the right to freedom of expression. It therefore appears reasonable to anticipate that at some point a broadcasting organisation could challenge any use of Section 10 of the Broadcasting Act by the Crown in the European Court (it should be remembered that a challenge by BBC journalists to the Home Secretary's Order failed in the House of Lords).

It should be noted that part 2 of Article 10 of the Convention contains a proviso to the general right to freedom of expression, stating that:

"The exercise of these freedoms, since it carries with it duties and responsibilities, may be subject to such formalities, conditions, restrictions or penalties as are prescribed by law and are necessary in a democratic society, in the interests of national security, territorial integrity or public safety, for the prevention of disorder or crime, for the protection of health or morals, for the protection of the reputation or rights of others, for preventing the disclosure of information received in confidence, or for maintaining the authority and impartiality of the judiciary."

In any hearing before the Court of Human Rights the Crown could have been expected to claim that this proviso was applicable to ministerial control over broadcasting matter emanating from an organisation such as Sinn Fein.

POLICE POWERS

19 In terms of the Broadcasting Act 1990 Section 167, a Justice of the Peace may authorise a police constable to require a broadcaster to produce a visual or sound recording of any matter contained in a programme where there is reasonable ground for suspecting that a "relevant offence" has been committed, namely an offence under Section 51 of the Civic Government (Scotland) Act 1982 or under Section 22 of the Public Order Act 1986. Accordingly, if there were reasonable ground for suspicion that obscene or racially inflammatory material had been broadcast such authority could be given to a constable requiring compliance with any order made by a Justice of the Peace.

It would appear that the inclusion of this section in the Act indicates that, rather than finding themselves embarrassed by the controversy surrounding the Zircon raid on the Queen Margaret Drive premises of BBC Scotland in 1987, the Government has persuaded Parliament to grant powers to the police to obtain copies of material from broadcasters as a statutory right.

It is only fair, however, to say that Section 167 appears only to cover the situation where the material has already been broadcast. If the Crown wished to stop a broadcast being made on the basis that the suspected material might be obscene, racially inflammatory or might offend against some other statute or Scots common law, then it would require to proceed by way of interim interdict.

It is interesting to note that it is specifically said in terms of Section 167 (6)b that the reference to a Justice of the Peace shall include a reference to the Sheriff. Journalists may recall the considerable controversy at the time of the Zircon raid that the warrant had been signed by a Sheriff rather than a Justice of the Peace which appeared to offend against the terms of the Official Secrets Act 1911.

Finally, broadcasters should note that in terms of Section 145 (5) they have a duty to keep recordings of their programmes for the purposes of assisting the police under this section.

BROADCASTING COMPLAINTS COMMISSION

22–20   The Broadcasting Complaints Commission was set up in 1981 to consider and adjudicate upon certain specific types of complaint about radio or television programmes. The Commission's authority is now derived from the Broadcasting Act 1990.

COMPLAINTS WHICH THE COMMISSION CAN CONSIDER

22–21   The Commission is empowered to consider complaints only if they fall into either of the following two categories:
(a) Unjust or unfair treatment in radio or television programmes actually broadcast or included in a licensed cable or satellite programme service.
(b) Unwarranted infringement of privacy in, or on connection with the obtaining of material included in, such programmes.
Complaints may be made about any programme on BBC TV, BBC Radio, BBC World Service, ITV, Channel 4, Independent Radio or S4C or included in a licensed cable or satellite programme service, as well as advertisements or teletext transmissions.

WHO CAN COMPLAIN?

22–22   Complaints may be made by individuals or organisations. Complaints of unjust or unfair treatment must be made by someone who has been a participant in the programme, or who has a direct interest in the treatment of which they complain (or by someone authorised to complain on their behalf). It is not enough that an individual should simply feel that a subject was not fairly treated, or that a programme was unbalanced or misleading: there must be some direct personal interest.

How a Complaint is Made

23 Complaints must be in writing, either direct to the Commission or after a complainant has complained to the broadcasters and is not satisfied with their response.

Viewers or listeners who have a complaint which they wish the Commission to consider can write to the Secretary to the Commission giving the title of the relevant programme and the date and channel on which it was broadcast. They have to explain in what way they consider that the programme was unjust or unfair, or in what way they consider that their privacy was unwarrantably infringed. If they were not a participant in the programme, they also must explain what way they consider that they have some degree of direct interest.

The Commission's Handling of a Complaint

24 When the Commission receives a complaint, it decides whether it is within its jurisdiction and whether it is appropriate for it to entertain it. The Commission cannot entertain, or proceed with, a complaint if it appears to it that any of the following considerations apply:
1. The unjust or unfair treatment or the unwarranted infringement of privacy complained of is the subject of legal proceedings in the United Kingdom (not necessarily proceedings brought by the complainant);
2. The complainant has a remedy by way of legal proceedings, and in the particular circumstances it is inappropriate for the Commission to entertain the complaint;
3. The complaint is frivolous or for any other reason it is inappropriate.

The Commission may also refuse to entertain a complaint if it has not been made within a reasonable time of the broadcast in question, or it does not appear that the complainant has a sufficiently direct interest.

What happens when a complaint has been entertained?

22–25   If the Commission decides to entertain a complaint, it sends a copy of it to the broadcasters requiring them to provide a transcript of the programme and a written statement in answer to the complaint.

After the broadcasters' statement has been provided, the Commission may give the complainant the opportunity to respond in writing direct to the Commission. The response is sent to the broadcasters who may be invited to make a further written statement if they wish. Normally no further written comments are invited from either side. The Commission may, if appropriate, arrange a hearing in private to which the complainant and representatives of the broadcasters are invited. A main purpose of a hearing is to enable members of the Commission to ask questions about any matter which is in doubt. Alternatively, the Commission may invite each side to appear before them separately and in private in order that the written statements may be supplemented informally by discussion and in answers to questions put by the Commission. The hearings take place in London. The Commission then reaches its findings on the complaint, which are set out in a written adjudication. The same procedure is followed in respect of complaints about programmes on a cable service.

What happens after the Commission has adjudicated on a complaint?

22–26   When the Commission has considered and adjudicated upon a complaint, copies of its adjudication and a summary of it are sent at the same time to the complainant and the broadcasters. It is the Commission's normal practice, whether or not the complaint has been upheld, to direct the broadcasters to broadcast the summary and to publish it in the Radio or TV Times as appropriate. The summary of the Commission's adjudication is usually broadcast on the same channel as and at a similar time to the programme which was the subject of the complaint. This is the only sanction available to the

Commission; it cannot require the broadcasters to apologise to the complainant, to broadcast a correction or to provide a financial remedy.

Copies of the adjudication and summary are sent by the Commission to the national and provincial press, and the full adjudication is included in the Commission's Annual Report to the Home Secretary, which is laid before Parliament and published by H.M. Stationery Office.

Complaints which the Commission Cannot Deal With

-27 The Commission cannot consider complaints about any of the following:
  (a) the depiction of sex or violence
  (b) bad language or bad taste
  (c) background music
  (d) programme scheduling
  (e) a programme which is in the course of production or which has not yet been broadcast.

Any communication with the Broadcasting Complaints Commission should be addressed to the Secretary at Grosvenor Gardens House, 35 & 37 Grosvenor Gardens, London SW1W.

Broadcasting Standards Council

-28 This is a new (and controversial) body set up by the 1990 Act. The Act in terms of Section 151 gives the Secretary of State authority to appoint a Chairman, Deputy Chairman and at least four other members. Lord Rees-Mogg was the first Chairman. He was succeeded in 1993 by Lady Howe.

The Council's duty is to draw up a code of giving guidance for particular areas of broadcasting, as follows:
  (a) Practices to be followed in connection with the portrayal of violence in programmes to which this part of the Act applies;
  (b) Practices to be followed in connection with the portrayal of sexual conduct in such programmes;
  (c) Standards of taste and decency for such programmes generally.

The relevant part of the Act applies to:
(a) a television or sound programme broadcast by the BBC;
(b) any television programme by the Welsh Authority;
(c) any television or sound programme included in a licensed
    service—in effect to all U.K. television and radio broadcas-
    ters.
Basically it is the Council's duty to monitor the programmes
broadcast in relation to the portrayal of violence and sexual
conduct and on the question of the standards of taste and
decency maintained.

The Council whose functions are laid down by sections 151
to 161 of the Act, has the duty to consider complaints made
to it concerning the portrayal of violence or sexual conduct
and the attainment of standards of taste and decency. It must
make findings regarding such complaints. The complainer
must put his case in writing and the Council will not entertain
a complaint which is made more than two months after a television programme or three weeks after a sound programme
unless it appears to it that in the particular circumstances it is
appropriate to do so. It is suggested that "particular circumstances" might arise for example if the complainer was the
person mentioned in the programme and was absent from the
country for a while.

The Council has the power if appropriate to have a hearing
on a complaint. Normally such a hearing will be in private,
although the Council does have power to direct that it be in
public. A copy of the complaint must be sent to "the relevant
person" and, if the programme was included in a licensed
service, to the appropriate regulatory body. "The relevant
person" is defined as (a) in a case where the relevant programme was broadcast by a broadcasting body, that body;
and (b) in a case where the relevant programme was included
in a licensed service, the licence holder providing that service.
A broadcasting body is defined in the Act as meaning the BBC
or the Welsh Authorities.

Once the Council has considered and made findings in
respect of the complaint it will direct that a summary of the
complaint and its findings and any observations on it are
broadcast. The broadcaster must comply with any such direction.

The Council has a duty to produce an annual report which is laid before Parliament by the relevant Secretary of State.

BROADCASTING COMPLAINTS COMMISSION AND BROADCASTING STANDARDS COUNCIL: RECENT DEVELOPMENTS

29 In a White Paper in the summer of 1994 the Government indicated that they were considering amalgamating the Broadcasting Complaints Commission and Broadcasting Standards Council. If this proposal does become law it will be interesting to see to what extent the Broadcasting Standards Council's much criticised remit is restricted.

The very future of the BCC and the BSC has been called into question on a number of occasions in speeches by leading figures in the broadcasting industry. In September 1994, the BBC announced that they entirely rejected a BCC adjudication on the Panorama programme 'Babies on Benefit'. The BBC in a full frontal attack on the adjudication described the BCC decision as 'unsustainable and wrong'. They intend to seek judicial review in the English High Court of the BCC's decision.

Whatever the feeling in the industry, however, the BCC and the BSC (unlike the Press Complaints Commission) are creatures of statute. It would require an Act of Parliament to alter them or abolish them.

RACIAL HATRED: PUBLIC ORDER ACT 1986

30 Section 164 of the 1990 Act extends the law in the Public Order Act 1986 relating to incitement to racial hatred to apply to broadcasting.

So if a programme involves threatening, or abusive or insulting visual images then each of a group of persons will be guilty of an offence if—(a) he intends to stir up racial hatred, or (b) having regard to all the circumstances racial hatred is likely to be stirred up.

Those who may be guilty of an offence are:

(a) the person providing the broadcast,
(b) any person by whom the programme was produced or directed, and
(c) any person by whom offending words or behaviour are used.

It is a defence for the person providing the service, or a person by whom the programme was produced or directed, to prove that (a) he did not know and had no reason to suspect that the programme would involve the offending material, and (b) having regard to the circumstances in which the programme was broadcast it was not reasonably practicable for him to secure the removal of the material.

While this defence might well apply to the broadcasting organisation providing the service, it is difficult to see that either a producer or director is likely to be able to use it; by the nature of their job it would be difficult to claim ignorance. The decision of the European Court of Human Rights in *Jersild* v *Denmark* (23 September 1994) indicates that this statutory provision may well offend against Article 10 of the European Convention on Human Rights.

OBSCENITY

22–31 Section 163 of the 1990 Act modifies the terms of the Civic Government (Scotland) Act 1982 so as to allow prosecution of anyone responsible for the inclusion of any obscene material in a programme. The section appears wide enough to include the reporter, an independent production company (if there is one) and the broadcasting organisation itself, and possibly also the editor and producer of such a programme.

The Obscene Publications Act of 1959 (covering the broadcasting of obscene material in England) does not apply in Scotland.

Although Scottish journalists are in the same legal position as their English colleagues it may well be that the attitude of the Crown in Scotland to prosecution of obscenity was affected by the failure of the prosecution in the so-called "Glasgow Obscenity Trial" which took place in the early 1980s. This involved three men accused of running a "sex shop" selling allegedly obscene material. The trial lasted for many weeks in

Glasgow Sheriff court and the jury unanimously found the accused not guilty of all the charges.

BROADCASTING AT ELECTION TIME
THE REPRESENTATION OF THE PEOPLE ACT

32   At election time print journalists are entitled to be (and frequently are) extremely selective and biased in their reporting of events. Such an approach in the world of tabloid newspapers is the norm rather than the exception. In contrast broadcasters have to be particularly aware of the obligations imposed upon them to be impartial. As has previously been noted in the case of the BBC this arises in terms of the BBC's Charter. In the case of the independent broadcasting companies it arises in terms of the licence which they hold from the ITC.

Over the past few years there have been many complaints (principally from the Conservative Party Central Office) regarding alleged failure to be impartial in broadcasting on political issues. Broadcasters must therefore be specially alert and must ensure that they fulfil the obligations imposed on them.

Representation of the People Act

33   Certain duties are imposed by the Representation of the People Act 1983 on broadcasters, both in relation to parliamentary and local government elections. In the case of parliamentary elections, if we are dealing with a general election, the obligation arises from the date of dissolution of Parliament or from the announcement of the Queen's intention to dissolve Parliament. In the case of a parliamentary by-election the date of the issuing of the writ for the election imposes the obligation. In the case of a local government election the obligation arises five weeks before the date of the election.

The legal duty is that broadcasters must not transmit any item about the constituency or electoral area if any of the candidates at the election takes part in the item, unless that individual gives his consent. (Section 93 of the 1983 Act.)

Further, it is an offence to broadcast from outside the

United Kingdom with intent to influence voters. Broadcasts from outside the United Kingdom would, however, be permissible if they were for the purpose of supplying material to the BBC or if it were in the pursuance of an arrangement made with the ITC.

Decided cases

22–34　Journalists working in the field of broadcasting at election time should be aware of two court decisions which are instructive as to how to approach election broadcasts. The first case is English—*Marshall* v. *BBC* (1979) 3 A.E.R. page 80. In this case Mr Marshall (a Labour candidate in an English constituency) wished to prevent a broadcast which included reference to one of his rival candidates who was standing for the National Front. He indicated to the BBC he was unhappy about being involved in any broadcast which included reference to the National Front candidate. The BBC proposed a broadcast showing Mr Marshall taking part in electioneering—stopping people in the streets, calling at doors, etc. Initially he obtained an injunction against the BBC broadcast on the basis that he was refusing to give his consent to the transmission. On appeal, however, the Court of Appeal held that the 1983 Act, which gave a candidate a right of veto in respect of a programme in which he took part, did not entitle Mr Marshall to an injunction in this case, because the phrase "takes part in" in the context which it appeared in the Act meant an *active* part. Accordingly, TV pictures showing the candidate campaigning did not fall within the definition of "taking part in", and the injunction was lifted so that the programme could go ahead.

It is interesting to note that the Court of Appeal felt that if they had come to the opposite decision they would have been allowing Mr Marshall to compel the BBC to become partial in their reporting. He would have been able to veto any broadcast which referred to the National Front candidate and therefore would force the BBC to be partisan in their broadcasting on this particular parliamentary election. That, the Court of Appeal felt, was precisely what Parliament had intended to avoid. Parliament's intention was that broadcasters should be impartial and objective during the "run up" to an election.

The second case is an Irish one—*McAliskey* v. *BBC*—(1980)

Northern Irish Reports, page 44. It was brought by Bernadette McAliskey (formerly Bernadette Devlin) in connection with a European election. She claimed that the treatment she was to receive in a BBC programme indicated that she and various others who were standing for election to the European Parliament were more minor candidates than some of the other candidates. She made this claim on the basis that the BBC broadcast proposed to divide the candidates into two groups. In the case of one group (of which she was a member) less time would be allocated in the broadcast to their views and accordingly, she claimed, the impression would be given that they were less serious candidates.

She therefore refused her consent to the proposed broadcast and applied to the Irish Court for an injunction. She claimed that the BBC had a duty under its Royal Charter and licence to act fairly and impartially at election time. She also alleged that the proposed broadcast would constitute a breach of Section 9 (1) of the Representation of the People Act 1969.

In reply the BBC argued that the proposed broadcast did not breach the Act and so was not an unlawful broadcast. It also alleged that it had no obligation laid upon it in terms of its charter and licence to secure a fair balance.

Mr Justice Murray in the Irish High Court delivered a full and interesting judgment on this complex area of law. For present purposes suffice it to say that his conclusion was that the BBC had to get the consent of all 13 candidates before the item could be broadcast. If consent were not obtained from all candidates then the broadcast would become an illegal broadcast in terms of Section 9 of the Act.

The new law which is contained in section 93 of the Representation of the People Act 1983 is in the same terms as section 9 of the 1969 Act so the position remains as it was when the case of *McAliskey* was decided by Justice Murray.

THE STRUCTURE OF BROADCASTING
BROADCASTING ORGANISATIONS

The British Broadcasting Corporation

-35 The BBC is a Corporation incorporated by Royal Charter, the terms of which are subject to change. The charter is due for renewal in 1996. In 1994 the Government announced the BBC's Charter would be renewed for another 10 years. BBC's principal object under the charter is to provide broadcasting services for general reception at home and abroad. Alongside the charter the other constitutional document is the Licence and Agreement of April 2, 1981.

The powers, responsibilities and obligations laid upon the Corporation are vested in the Board of Governors who exercise them through a permanent staff headed by the Director General as the BBC's Chief Executive Officer, and the Board of Management. The 12 Governors—who include the Chairman, Vice-chairman and three who are respectively national Governors for Scotland, Wales and Northern Ireland are appointed by the Queen in Council (on the nomination of the Government of the day). The appointment is normally for five years. The Reverend Norman Drummond, headmaster of Loretto School, is currently the National Governor for Scotland. The management of BBC Scotland is controlled by its Chief Executive, Controller Scotland. The current Controller is John McCormick who succeeded Patrick Chalmers at the beginning of 1992.

The Government's Powers in relation to the BBC: In terms of Clause 13 (4) of the licence the Home Secretary "may from time to time by notice in writing require the Corporation to refrain at any specified time or at all times from sending any matter or matters of any class specified in such notice." Formally this clause confers on the Government absolute power to determine what the BBC may or may not broadcast. The clause has never been used to ban any specific programmes. In October 1988, however, the clause was used to restrict broadcast coverage of statements supporting terrorism in Northern Ireland. This was the first exercise of the Government's power under Clause 13 (4). The Home Secretary's decision has been vigorously challenged by journalists in the courts. The House of Lords, however, has refused to interfere with the notice. The notice was revoked in 1994.

The BBC's Obligations: In terms of Section 13 of the licence and Agreement the BBC is required to "broadcast an impartial account day by day prepared by professional reporters of the proceedings of both Houses of Parliament." The BBC is also required to broadcast official announcements whenever asked to do so by one of Her Majesty's Ministers. In reality this is achieved without ministerial intervention. Normally major Government announcements are reported naturally as a matter of news interest in BBC broadcasts.

The BBC is forbidden in terms of its licence to transmit television images of very brief duration which "might convey a message to influence the minds of an audience without their being aware, or fully aware, of what has been done". This is a safeguard against subliminal advertising or indoctrination.

In terms of its Licence the BBC is required to refrain from expressing its own opinion on current affairs or on matters of public policy other than broadcasting. This requirement underlines one of the major differences between the press and the broadcasting media in Britain. Newspapers are at liberty to express their own editorial views on any subject they choose. Broadcasting authorities are specifically prohibited from doing so.

Finance: The BBC relies on two principal sources of income:
1. The licence fees paid by the public;
2. A grant from the Treasury in respect of World Services provided for overseas listeners.

Broadcasting Councils: These are set up in terms of article 10 of the BBC's Charter. There is a National Broadcasting Council which was established in 1981. There is also a Broadcasting Council for Scotland which was established in 1952. The Councils' main functions are to control the policy and content of radio and television services of the BBC which are provided primarily for reception in the countries they represent. In this they are required to have full regard to the distinctive culture, language, interests and taste of the peoples of the respective country. They may also advise the Corporation on any other broadcasting matters which may affect the peoples in these countries. Constitutionally, the Councils' link with the Corporation is through their chairmen who are Governors of the BBC and are entitled National Governors. In the Broadcasting Council for Scotland the National Governor is assisted by 11 members of the Council, who are part-time appointees to reflect a reasonable cross-section of Scottish interests, and are appointed by the Corporation on the recommendation of a special panel.

The BBC is a legal entity and can sue and be sued in the courts. It does not enjoy any special rights or privileges, under the laws of defamation or contempt of court.

Independent broadcasters

22–36 In contrast, independent broadcasters, such as Granada and STV, are limited companies who enjoy the right to broadcast in terms of a licence held for a fixed period. The holders of licences in Scotland are STV and Grampian (Border TV based in Carlisle, broadcasts in the Lake District and the Scottish Border area). Their licences were awarded in 1991 and last for a 10-year period from January 1, 1993.

The Independent Television Commission

22–37 The Broadcasting Act of 1990 set up a new organisation—the Independent Television Commission, with headquarters at 70 Brompton Road, London SW3 1EY and a Scottish office at 123 Blythswood Street, Glasgow G2 4AN. The ITC has replaced the old IBA and Cable Authority. The ITC is not a broadcasting organisation but a licensing body with supervisory and regulatory powers. It issues licences for (a) terrestrial television, (b) satellite television and (c) cable television. There are eight to 10 members of the ITC, one of whom has to be Scottish. Members of the Commission are appointed for up to five years at a time.

The Commission, an independent body which is intended to be financially self-supporting, is accountable to the Secretary of State, to whom it must submit annual reports to be laid before Parliament.

The Commission's function is to regulate in accordance with the Act the provision of:

(a) Television programme services from places in the United Kingdom by persons other than the BBC and the Welsh Authority, and

(b) additional services from places in the United Kingdom. The Commission's duty is to discharge its functions in respect of the licensed services so as to ensure that a wide range of such services is available throughout the United Kingdom and to ensure fair and effective competition in the provision of such services. It is also its job in respect of licensing to ensure the provision of such services are of high quality and offer a wide range of programmes.

Principally therefore the Commission is an organisation which grants licences to television and radio broadcasters other than the BBC and Welsh Authority. The Commission has a discretion as to whom to award the licence and regarding the terms of a licence.

REQUIREMENTS AS TO LICENSED SERVICES

7-38 The ITC is required to do all that it can to ensure that every licensed service complies with certain requirements. These are listed in the Broadcasting Act 1990:

(a) That nothing is included in the programmes which offends against good taste or decency or is likely to encourage incitement to crime or lead to disorder or to be offensive to public feelings;

(b) That any news given (in whatever form) in its programmes is presented with due accuracy and impartiality;

(c) That due impartiality is preserved by the person providing the service on matters of political or industrial controversy or relating to current public policy;

(d) That due responsibility is exercised with respect to the content of any of its religious programmes; and

(e) That subliminal broadcasting does not take place.

7-39 For Independent Television broadcasters the ITC's regulatory function is extremely important. Journalists working in this area should familiarise themselves with the ITC Programme Code. In most cases Independent Television broadcasters will have in-house Compliance Officers who should be able to liaise and advise the working journalist in the field on aspects of the ITC Code. The current Code was promulgated in January 1993.

Perhaps the most important areas of the Code for journalists are that it covers filming and recording members of the public, the use of hidden microphones and cameras, interviewing of children and recognises the citizen's right to a degree of privacy. For the broadcaster the Code has something to say on the use of foul language, sex and nudity, bad taste in humour, the portrayal of violence, hypnotism, the portrayal of people with disabilities and a great deal to say on the scheduling of particular programmes. It contains rules on Party Political and Parliamentary broadcasting. It covers the reporting of terrorism, crime and anti-social behaviour.

If its Code is breached the ITC has the power to impose financial penalties on its licence holders. Currently, that penalty is 3% of 'qualifying revenue' (defining in The Broadcasting Act 1990 S19) for the first breach. For subsequent breaches the ITC can fine up to 5% of qualifying revenue.

The ITC can also require the licence holder to broadcast a correction or an apology. Finally, the licence holder can be required by the ITC not to repeat the offending programme.

The existence of the ITC as a regulatory body means that programme makers working in the independent sector are in the unenviable position of facing criticism and possible penalties from three regulatory bodies namely, the ITC, the BCC and the BSC. It is, of course, perfectly possible for one of these bodies to reject a complaint while another upholds it. Generally, the plethora of regulatory bodies is causing concern in broadcasting.

Establishment of Three new TV Channels

22–40 1. *Channel 3:* The 1990 Act by Section 14 established a new organisation called Channel 3. This is to be a nationwide system of television broadcasting structured on a regional basis and intended to replace the former ITV system. The Commission has a broad discretion to determine the structure of the new service, although it must have a regional form. There must be at least two Channel 3 regions in Scotland.

The Commission has to advertise for applications for licences to provide a Channel 3 service. It will charge a fee for the granting of a licence. It is the Commission's duty to ensure that a suitable amount of time is given in Channel 3 programmes to:

    1. Programmes of local interest;
    2. Religious programmes;

3. Programmes intended for children.
Channel 3 licences shall continue in force for ten years.

2. *Channel 4:* The 1990 Act also establishes the Channel 4 Television Corporation. The make-up of this body which came into being on January 1, 1993 is similar to that of the BBC. A licence is granted to the Corporation by the Independent Television Commission. The function of the Corporation is to secure the continued provision of the television broadcasting service known as Channel Four. In effect, it replaces the Channel Four television company which has to date provided the Channel Four service. However, the Channel Four television company was primarily a commissioning, purchasing and editing body rather than a programme making organisation. The Government decided that it was financially unviable for Channel Four to become an independent commercial company. Accordingly, the 1990 Act sets up what is in effect a public trust licensed by the ITC to continue the provision of the Channel Four services. The Commission is to fix the terms of the Channel 4 licence but these are to comply with the following requirements:
(a) That Channel 4 programmes contain a suitable proportion of matter calculated to appeal to taste and interests not generally catered for by Channel 3; and
(b) That innovation and experiment in the form and content of those programmes are encouraged. Channel 4 is to be a form of public service broadcasting; programmes are to maintain a high general standard in all respects and in particular in respect of their content and quality and a suitable proportion are to be of an educational nature. A sufficient amount of time is to be given to news and current affairs of high quality.
As in the case of Channel 4 there is a requirement that the broadcasting organisation will take material from independent producers.

3. *Channel 5:* The Commission is given a duty to secure the provision of a further television broadcasting service to be known as Channel 5 to take up broadcasting frequencies which may become available under the new system set up by the 1990 Act. Again the licence which the new organisation

will hold is to be held from the Independent Television Commission. The Channel 5 licence, as with the case of the Channel 3 licence, has to include conditions requiring the licenceholder:

(a) To broadcast from the licence services news programmes of high quality dealing with national and international matters; and

(b) To broadcast such programmes in that service at intervals throughout the period for which the service is provided at peak viewing times.

There have been many 'false dawns' on Channel 5. As yet, it appears that no suitable company has found the concept financially attractive.

In September 1994 the Government announced they were to invite application for the Channel 5 licence again.

Radio Authority

22–41 The Broadcasting Act 1990 established an entirely new regulatory body for independent radio. The Radio Authority established by Section 83 of the 1990 Act consists of a Chairman, Deputy Chairman and between four and ten other members. Appointments are made by the Secretary of State. No Governor or employee of the BBC, member or employee of Channel 4, member of the Welsh Authority, member of the BCC or the BSC can be a member of the Radio Authority. Appointments are made for a maximum period of five years. The Authority's function is to regulate the provision of independent radio services. Independent Radio has only been a phenomenon in this country since 1973, having been illegal (or pirate) before that time. The explosion in the market has meant that the Radio Authority, although a very new arrival on the broadcasting scene is an enormously important body.

The Radio Authority grants independent radio services licenses. It must be satisfied that a person applying for the licence is a fit and proper person to hold it. Licences can be transferred but the Radio Authority has to approve such transfers.

The 1990 Act in Section 87 lays down general conditions which apply to all licences granted by the Radio Authority. In terms of Section 90 the Radio Authority is placed under an obligation to do all it can to secure that every licensed service complies with the requirements that;

a) nothing is included in its programmes which offends against good taste or decency, is likely to encourage or incite crime, to lead to disorder or to be offensive to public feeling;
b) any news given (in whatever form) in its programmes is presented with due accuracy and impartiality;
c) its programmes do not include any technique which exploits the possibility of conveying a message to, or otherwise influencing the minds of, persons listening to the programmes, without their being aware of, or fully aware of, what has occurred (i.e. subliminal messages).

These, of course, are similar provisions to those found in the ITC's Code for Television.

If the Radio Authority is satisfied that the holder of a sound broadcasting licence has failed to comply with any licence condition, or with any direction, given by the Authority, then it may serve on him a notice. The independent radio broadcaster has a period within which to comply with the notice. If he fails to do so, the licence can be withdrawn.

For journalists it is important to note that in terms of Section 109(3) the Radio Authority has the power in the event of an independent radio broadcaster failing to comply with one of the terms of its licence to enforce the broadcasting of a correction or an apology. Further, by Section 110, the Radio Authority has the power to impose financial penalties or to suspend or shorten licence periods should the licence holder fail to comply with the conditions of the licence. A fine can be up to £50,000. The Secretary of State has power to increase this sum.

KEY POINTS

The law of defamation and contempt of court apply equally to journalists working in the field of radio or TV broadcasting.

In addition to the courts, journalists working in broadcasting have to concern themselves with regulatory bodies. In both the public and private sectors of broadcasting the Broadcasting Complaints Commission has jurisdiction in cases where there has been unfairness or a breach of privacy. Also, the Broadcasting Standards Council has jurisdiction where there has been deemed to be an improper use of material relating to violence, sexual matters or where material is offensive to taste and decency. The BCC and the BSC can direct broadcasters to publish their findings in a specified manner.

In addition, in the private or independent sector, broadcasters in radio must observe the Code promulgated by the Radio Authority. Similarly, in the independent television sector the ITC's Code must be obeyed. Both the Radio Authority and the ITC have the power to instruct the broadcasting of apologies and/or corrections. They have the power to modify or revoke licences. They have the power to fine.

CHAPTER 23

RIGHTS OF ACCESS

-01 With one or two exceptions, such as the right of admission to children's hearings, the journalist is in exactly the same legal position as any other member of the public. He can go to public places and public meetings. He cannot go to private places and private meetings. In many cases, of course, reporters are given special privileges such as reserved seats and free admission, but these are at the discretion of those who grant them and can be withdrawn at will. Privileges of this kind should not be confused with legal rights.

-02 Certain meetings must be held in public; certain places, such as streets and various open spaces in towns, are public places; certain places are private places to which the public are invited and most places are private places to which the public are not invited.

-03 Meetings and proceedings which must normally be held in public include court proceedings and certain local government meetings. Surprisingly, perhaps, they do not include proceedings in Parliament.

Court proceedings

-04 The general rule is that proceedings in a court of law must be in public, unless justice demands otherwise. The principal applications of and exceptions to this rule have been considered elsewhere in this book.

Quasi-judicial proceedings

-05 Most inquiries, tribunals and other quasi-judicial bodies must, as a general rule, meet in public, but there are numerous exceptions. These have been mentioned earlier when discussing the various bodies concerned.

Parliament

23–06 Both Houses of Parliament normally admit public and Press to their meetings, but this is merely practice and there is no legal right of admission. Both Lords and Commons have full power to regulate their own procedure and can hold secret sessions when they think it necessary. For example, many such sessions were held during the 1939–45 war. It is a breach of parliamentary privilege to publish any report of, or purport to describe the proceedings at, a secret session.

23–07 Each House has power to punish for breaches of privilege. These have been summarised as follows:

23–08 "Disrespect to any member of the House, as such, by a person not being a member; disrespect to the House collectively, whether committed by a member or any other; disobedience to the orders of the House or interference with its procedure, with its officers in the execution of their duty or with witnesses in respect of evidence given before the House or a Committee of the House" (Ansan, *Law and Custom of Parliament* (5th ed.), Vol. 1, p. 187).

23–09 Clearly, breach of privilege could be a real danger for newspapers. "Disrespect" is a word of wide meaning and leading journalists have criticised the law of parliamentary privilege on the ground that it curbs unduly the publication of information the public should know about.

23–10 Technically, to publish reports of debates in Parliament at all is a breach of privilege, and in the eighteenth century attempts were actually made to punish those who infringed. These led to such a public outcry that publication of reports has been allowed ever since. But false or perverted reports are regarded as punishable in practice as well as in theory.

23–11 To publish information derived from the reports of select committees before they have been laid before the House is a breach of privilege. The committee is reporting to the House in the first place and only indirectly to the public. To reveal the contents of a report before Members of Parliament have had a chance of reading it is dangerous. The same does not apply to Green and White Papers. They are addressed to the public in the first instance and, while the Government in practice communicates important matters to Parliament before publication, this is a matter of courtesy alone.

3–12   Complaints of breach of privilege are raised in the House by a member and are then usually referred to the Committee of Privileges for a report. The Commons can imprison an offender, although this is rare. The imprisonment can be during the pleasure of the House (*i.e.* for an indefinite period), but in this event the offender must be released at the end of the session. The House of Lords can imprison for a fixed term or impose a fine. Normally an offender is merely admonished or reprimanded. Proceedings were commenced in October 1994 against the *Guardian* editor Peter Preston over his sending of a fax which bore the House of Commons logo.

Local authorities

3–13   The Local Government (Access to Information) Act 1985 gives the public and duly accredited reporters of newspapers (which include any organisation "systematically engaged in collecting news for radio or television or for cable programme service') certain rights to attend meetings of regional, district and islands councils and their committees and sub-committees, with certain prescribed exceptions. These rights do not, however, extend to the taking of photographs at meetings or the recording of proceedings for later communication to anyone not attending. The meeting has a discretion to decide whether to permit taping or photography.

3–14   Press and public may be excluded for either of two reasons—that it is likely confidential information will be disclosed at the meeting or that the subject-matter of discussion is exempt from public access.

3–15   Confidential information is defined as information which has been furnished by a Government department on terms forbidding its disclosure or which is prohibited from being disclosed by any enactment or court order.

3–16   Exempt information is defined under a list of specific subjects, including such matters as adoption or fostering of particular children, financial affairs of named individuals, details of council contracts for acquisition or supply of goods or services, details of tenders for contracts and information about counsel's advice.

3–17   The list also includes "any protected informant", which means any person giving the local authority information about a crime or offence. Exclusion of press and public on the ground of exemption can take place only where a resolution to that effect has been passed identifying the particular subject on the list. The Act provides a right to challenge exclusion by application to the Court of Session for judicial review. The Secretary of State for Scotland has power to extend or curtail the exemption list.

23–18   A meeting also has power to exclude anyone to suppress disorder or other misbehaviour.

23–19   Press and public have a right to see copies of agendas, reports and other papers relating to meetings (but not those relating to confidential or exempt items). Papers must be supplied on request to the media and made open for public inspection for three days before a meeting, or, if it has been called at short notice, from the time it is convened. The papers remain open for public inspection for six years after a meeting. Where confidential or exempt information is concerned, an official of the local authority must provide instead a written summary indicating the nature of the matters considered in private without actually disclosing the confidential or exempt information. The authority is entitled to charge for the provision of these services and also for the supply of photocopies of extracts of documents.

23–20   Anything contained in any document supplied to the media which is defamatory is privileged under the Act unless published maliciously.

23–21   The Act leaves intact the rights of access by the media in Scotland to meetings authorised by earlier legislation. It does not, however, apply to community councils. Admission to certain other bodies is covered by the Public Bodies (Admission to Meetings) Act 1960, as amended by the Local Government (Scotland) Act 1973. The only bodies left in the 1960 Act so far as Scotland is concerned are health boards set up under the National Health Service (Scotland) Act 1972 (so far as their executive functions are concerned). Joint committees of two or more local authorities, and their sub-committees, are covered by the 1985 Act.

23–22   The Act does not cover Scotland's five new town authorities, but in November 1986 Glenrothes set a precedent by deciding to hold its monthly board meeting in public (though with certain confidential matters withheld from disclosure).

-23 The Water Act 1983 (as amended by the Water Act 1989 and the Water Industry Act 1991) reorganised water authorities, withdrew the right of media representatives and members of the public to attend meetings of such authorities, provided instead for news conferences to be held following meetings and set up consumer consultative committees for the water industry, which are to meet in public.

Other public meetings

-24 In the case of meetings held in public places the journalist has the same right to be present as any other member of the public—a right which may be limited by bye laws as well as by the law on such matters as breach of the peace. He cannot be singled out for exclusion by the organisers of the meeting. He has as much right to be in a public place as they have.

-25 In the case of meetings or other proceedings, such as most sports meetings, to which the public are invited but which are held on private property, the journalist's rights depend on the terms of the invitation. The organisers of such meetings may choose to exclude the media or impose conditions on entry, such as a ban on cameras. The whole question is really one of contract between those granting and those seeking admission and the terms of the contract may be express or implied. There may, for example, be an implied term that a person can be excluded if he does not behave in a proper manner. The Court of Session has upheld a right to exclude a known criminal from an enclosure at a race meeting. One of the judges observed that "there was an implied condition attaching to the right of entry that his character was such as warranted his presence in the enclosure".

KEY POINTS

3–26 Generally, the right of the journalist to attend meetings is the same as any other member of the public.

The Local Government (Access to Information) Act 1985 provides the right to attend meetings of councils and sub-committees. The media may be excluded if "exempt" information is to be discussed, but this can be done only after a resolution to that effect has been passed.

Copies of agendas and reports must be made available for inspection.

CHAPTER 24

PRIVACY

Property

4–01 As a general rule no one is entitled to enter private property without the owner's consent, but there are exceptions. Statutes give certain people, such as police officers with search warrants, rights of entry. And generally entry is allowed if it is necessary in the public interest—to put out a fire, for example, or continue the hot pursuit of a criminal. These exceptions will not normally benefit the journalist—and so for him the normal rule applies. He is infringing the owner's legal rights if he enters his property, whether it is enclosed or not, without permission.

4–02 Trespass is an infringement of rights, but until the Criminal Justice and Public Order Act 1994, was not normally a criminal offence in Scotland. The Act made some types of trespass criminal—for example for the purpose of holding a "rave" or setting up a "New Age" encampment. (Also see Calcutt Committee proposals later in this chapter.)

4–03 This does not mean, however, that the property owner has no remedies. He can order an intruder to leave. If met by a refusal, he can probably remove him by the use of reasonable force although there is some doubt about this in the case of property other than private houses. If the intrusion is likely to be repeated he can apply to the court for an interdict, which it is contempt of court to ignore. If the intruder has caused actual damage to the property, the owner can also sue for compensation.

4–04 In the normal case, then, where a trespasser is unlikely to repeat the trespass and has caused no damage, all that the owner can lawfully do is ask him to leave and, if he refuses, remove him by reasonable force. If too much force is used the trespasser can sue for assault, but he starts with the scales weighted against him. In the case of private houses the courts tolerate a certain amount of violence on the part of the houseowner who, after all, is entitled to suspect the worst if he finds a stranger on his premises.

Person

24–05   Unlawful interference with the person is assault. This may result in a criminal prosecution or a civil action for damages. The law on assault should not be of concern to the journalist but there have been instances of mobbing and manhandling by reporters on the trail of a story. To photograph a person is not by itself assault, even if he does not consent, but to force him to submit to being photographed in a certain place or in a certain pose probably would be assault.

24–06   Traditionally, the mere invasion of privacy has not in itself been actionable. It is not unlawful to photograph a person and expose his features to the public gaze even if the photograph is a bad one. Nor is it unlawful to expose a person's private life to the glare of publicity. But the courts do not look favourably on conduct of this kind and if there is any actionable wrong involved, such as defamation, infringement of copyright or breach of confidence, they are quite likely to take the invasion of privacy into account in assessing damages.

24–07   In the notorious *Argyll* divorce case (*Argyll* v. *Argyll* [1967] Ch. 302), the Duke of Argyll and *The People* were restrained from publishing certain intimate matters communicated to the Duke in confidence by his former wife during their marriage).

24–08   And in the case of *Williams* v. *Settle* [1960] 2 All E.R. 806, where a man's wedding photograph was published because it included a picture of his subsequently murdered father-in-law, it was said with reference to the amount of damages awarded against the photographer who had sold the picture, "it is the flagrancy of the infringement which calls for heavy damages because this was a scandalous matter in the circumstances. . . It is sufficient to say that it was a flagrant infringement of the right of the plaintiff, and it was scandalous conduct and in total disregard not only of the plaintiff's legal rights of copyright but of his feelings and his sense of family dignity and pride. It was an intrusion into his life, deeper and graver than an intrusion into a man's property".

24–09   We have seen too that the defence of fair comment in a defamation action may not be available if the comment is on a man's private life. The position can be summed up by saying that the courts at present give no redress for invasion of privacy by itself but they do not like it and are apt to take it into account if it is an element in a case before them. Journalists should also be aware of a case in 1989 in which a newspaper reporter in Scotland admitted a charge of fraud. She had gained access to a hospital patient by pretending to be his niece. The causing of distress to the patient would not be necessary to constitute the offence but could be regarded as an aggravating factor by the court.

The Calcutt Committee

10   Since at least the end of World War II there have been repeated calls for legislation to deal with what is seen as the invasion of privacy by the media. The Royal Commission on the Press in 1949 considered the possibility of introducing legislation but concluded that it would be difficult to frame a law which would be both effective and enforceable. In 1972 the Younger Committee on Privacy decided that it was impossible to devise any satisfactory yardstick by which to judge in finely balanced cases whether the public importance of a story should override the personal and private interest of the person involved.

11   A number of Private Members' Bills also fell by the wayside but a watershed was reached in June 1990 when the Report of the Committee on Privacy and Related Matters, chaired by Mr (later Sir) David Calcutt, Q.C., was presented to Parliament. It contained a number of major recommendations, the most important of which were the proposals to make certain activities carried out by the media a criminal offence and the abolition of the Press Council, to be replaced by a Press Complaints Commission.

12   The Calcutt Committee was appointed by the Home Secretary with the following terms of reference: "In the light of the recent public concern about intrusions into the private lives of individuals by certain sections of the Press, to consider what measures are needed to give further protection to individual privacy from the activities of the Press and improve recourse against the Press for the individual citizen, taking account of

existing remedies, including the law on defamation and breach of confidence". The background to the appointment of the committee was a general feeling, certainly amongst Members of Parliament, that Press standards were declining and that the intrusion into private lives, accompanied by highly dubious methods of gaining information, had gone too far.

24–13   While the committee was in the midst of its deliberations, a reporter and a photographer from the *Sunday Sport* managed to get into the hospital room in London where television actor Gorden Kaye was recovering from life-threatening brain injuries. Mr Kaye was interviewed and photographs taken of his injuries although medical evidence showed he was in no fit state to agree to what took place. Within 15 minutes of the journalists being ejected by security staff Mr Kaye had no recollection of what had taken place.

24–14   He was granted an injunction by the courts restricting what could be published and, in the Court of Appeal, Lord Justice Bingham described the newspaper's conduct towards the actor as "a monstrous invasion of his privacy". Lamenting the lack in English law of a proper remedy, the judge went on: "If ever a person has the right to be left alone by strangers with no public interest to pursue, it must surely be when he lies in a hospital recovering from brain surgery and in no more than partial command of his faculties".

24–15   This unfortunate incident reinforced what Calcutt called wide-ranging complaints made to the committee by individuals about general harassment, the planting of bugging devices, the publication of lurid sexual details, the denigration of homosexuals, sensationalism and inaccuracy. The committee referred to a MORI poll carried out for the *News of the World* in November 1989 which showed that 73 per cent of those questioned felt that the press intruded too much into the lives of public figures.

Criminal offences

24–16   The committee recommended that three of what it saw as the worst forms of physical intrusion such as door-stepping "bugging" and the use of long-range cameras should be criminal offences.

24–17   As we shall see in more detail later in this chapter these proposals were repeated in Sir David Calcutt's review of press self-regulation.

-18   The committee considered that the same categories of behaviour should also be a criminal offence in Scotland, but felt that because of the greater scope of common law, the same objective could be achieved by different means. It recommended that further consideration should be given to the extent to which the criminal law in Scotland needed to be extended to cover physical intrusion by journalists.

Press Complaints Commission

-19   The committee also received a number of criticisms of the Press Council, which for a number of years had been the main resort outwith the courts for individuals complaining about the media. The main complaint was that the council had proved neither effective nor impartial. Calcutt took the view that although the Press should be given one last chance to make voluntary self-regulation work the Press Council should not be retained as part of the system.

-20   The committee recommended that the Council should be disbanded and replaced by a Press Complaints Commission, consisting of press and lay members (who now form a majority), with the specific task of adjudicating on allegations of Press malpractice. The new body, said Calcutt, must be seen as "authoritative, independent and impartial. It must also have jurisdiction over the Press as a whole, must be adequately funded and provide a means of seeking to prevent publication of intrusive material".

-21   Calcutt rejected the notion that the new body should also continue with the twin rôle of defending press freedom. It was given the specific duty, similar to the Broadcasting Complaints Commission, to consider complaints of unjust and unfair treatment by the press and of unwarranted infringements of privacy. To provide the Commission with a clear idea of what amounted to unacceptable Press behaviour, Calcutt drew up a comprehensive code of practice for the guidance of both the Press and the public. A code was then drawn up by the newspaper industry which, in outline, followed that suggested by the Calcutt Committee. In his second report, however, Sir David Calcutt complained that the industry's code provided significantly less protection for individuals than the code drawn up by his committee. (The industry's code is reproduced as an appendix at the end of this book.)

24–22   Lord McGregor of Durris, the former chairman of the Advertising Standards Authority, became the first chairman of the Press Complaints Commission which is financed by a levy on newspapers and periodicals. The Commission held its first meeting in January 1991 to consider a complaint by Clare Short, the Labour MP, against the editor of the *News of the World*, who happened to be one of the Commission's members. Ms Short complained that she, her husband and friends had been harassed by the newspaper while it was in pursuit of a story about the MP's relationship with a man who was murdered in a gangland shooting. Her complaint was upheld by the Commission, which stated that two stories about Ms Short which had appeared in the *News of the World* gave rise to the inescapable suspicion that it was pursuing a vendetta against her in retaliation for her campaign against "page three" topless pictures.

24–23   In October 1991 the Commission ruled that the *Mail on Sunday* had "properly discharged the function of a responsible newspaper" in using subterfuge to obtain information from a therapist who went into private practice after being involved in the Cleveland child abuse inquiry. The story was headlined: "Expert condemned in Cleveland probe offers private therapy". The Commission stated: "In this case the newspaper was justified in using a pseudonym to get information unlikely to be obtainable by other means about what it believed might be a threat to the health of members of the public". In 1994 the Commission rejected a complaint that the Sunday Times newspaper was wrong when it used deception to show that at least one MP was willing to ask Parliamentary questions in the House of Commons for exchange for a payment of £1,000. The Commission took the view that the matter was of considerable public interest and the degree of deception used was permissible.

24–24   Calcutt made it clear that if the Commission was not seen to work then a statutory system for dealing with complaints should be introduced. It warned that this could happen if there was a serious breakdown of the system of self-regulation or persistent refusal by even one maverick publication to comply with the system.

25   In the event of a breakdown of this kind Calcutt recommended that the PCC should be replaced by a statutory Press Complaints Tribunal, headed by a Judge or senior lawyer appointed by the Lord Chancellor.

26   Calcutt ended with a warning: "Freedom of expression is vital in a democratic society. It is in everyone's interests that it should be upheld, provided that this is not at the expense of other important rights. All rights, however, carry responsibilities, especially when those exercising them have the potential to affect other people's lives.

27   "The record of the Press in this area has not always been good. It must now demonstrate that it can discharge its responsibility and that, through its own conduct and self-regulation, it can command the confidence of the public. If it is not prepared to put and keep its own house in order, further legislation must follow".

28   In May 1991, Lord McGregor warned members of the Scottish Newspaper Publishers' Association that the Press Complaints Commission had 18 months to prove it could curb the excesses of some newspapers, before a statutory body was set up which would restrict the freedom of the Press. He also warned of legislation "turning into criminal offences quite a chunk of the ordinary behaviour of journalists".

30   By May of the following year he felt confident enough to pronounce that self-regulation was working and that the need for a statutory tribunal had been eliminated. This confidence was, however, misplaced.

The Second Calcutt Report

31   In July 1992 Sir David Calcutt, as he now was, was asked by Mr David Mellor, Secretary of State for the Department of the National Heritage, to conduct a review of press self-regulation. Sir David recommended that the government set up a statutory Press Complaints Tribunal and confirmed the recommendations in his earlier report that certain forms of physical intrusion should now become criminal offences.

24–32   By this time the question of press invasion of privacy had become one of the burning national issues of the day, largely because of the publication of an extraordinary series of stories involving public figures—notably the Royal Family—and one in which Mr Mellor was the central figure.

24–33   Sir David Calcutt concluded that it was now too late for self regulation. He stated: "The Press Complaints Commission is not in my view an effective regulator of the press. It does not in my view hold the balance between the press and the individual. It is not the truly independent body which it should be.

As constructed it is, in essence, a body set up by the industry, financed by the industry, dominated by the industry, and operating a code of practice devised by the industry which is over-favourable to the industry."

24–34   He gave instances where, in his opinion, newspapers had treated the commission "with contempt" and talked of the commission's apparent lack of action in several cases involving public figures.

24–35   The PCC on the other hand described the second Calcutt Report as "particularly flawed." It claimed that Calcutt had failed to take into account the "considerable change" in press behaviour since the inception of the PCC and said of the second report: "It was preoccupied with the press reporting of the private lives of public figures and neglected to scrutinise what the PCC had achieved for people not in the public eye."

24–36   Calcutt recommended that a statutory Press Complaints Tribunal should have a number of functions and powers, including a power to draw up a code of practice, to receive complaints, restrain publication of material in breach of the code by a court order, require the printing of apologies and corrections, award compensation and impose fines.

24–37   Sir David correctly predicted: "I do not doubt that my recommendations will be met with claims that they will result in censorship and gagging of the press, that they will prevent responsible investigative journalism and that they will only serve as a shield for the wicked."

24–38   He insisted that his recommendations were not designed to suppress free speech, adding: "They are designed principally to ensure that privacy, which all agree should be respected, is protected from unjustifiable intrusion and protected by a body in which the public as well as the press has confidence."

–39   It quickly became clear, however, that although the Government was not happy with the Press Complaints Commission and felt it required reform, it was sensitive to arguments of press censorship, particularly where public figures were involved.

Following the publication of the second Calcutt report, National Heritage Secretary Mr Peter Brooke stated in the House of Commons that although the Government had not completely ruled out the case for a statutory tribunal it was "extremely reluctant" to take that path.

–40   Government sensitivity on the issue may have had something to do with the fact that one of the cases highlighted by Sir David Calcutt in his second report involved Mr David Mellor, the same Minister who had asked for a review of press self-regulation with a warning that the press was "drinking in the last chance saloon."

–41   In July 1992 *The People* newspaper had published details of an affair between Mr Mellor and actress Antonia de Sancha. The liaison came to light after a telephone conversation between the two had been recorded.

The Royal Family

–42   Arguments for a new statutory tribunal were also weakened when it emerged that at least one member of the Royal Family whose privacy was said to have been invaded had co-operated in providing information to the press.

–43   In June 1991 the *Sunday Times* had begun serialising a book by Andrew Morton which gave details of the "'loveless'" marriage between the Prince and Princess of Wales, suicide attempts by the Princess and an alleged relationship between the Prince of Wales and Mrs Camilla Parker-Bowles.

–44   Suggestions that the Princess of Wales had co-operated with Mr Morton were officially denied by a Palace spokesman, leading to the chairman of the Press Complaints Commission issuing a scathing condemnation of general press coverage of the state of the Royal marriage. Lord McGregor talked of "an odious exhibition of journalists dabbling their fingers in the stuff of other people's souls."

24-45   He then discovered that, despite the official denial, the Princess of Wales had indeed been helping to provide tabloid editors with information about the state of her marriage. For example, she had made herself available to be photographed with a friend who was known to be one of the sources of Andrew Morton's book. Lord McGregor said this situation had "seriously embarrassed" the Press Complaints Commission.

PHYSICAL INTRUSION

24-46   Sir David Calcutt's recommendation that the most blatant forms of physical intrusion by the press should become criminal offences in England and Wales received wider -support. The Heritage Secretary said that legislation would be brought forward "in due course" to bring the new offences into being and the Press Complaints Commission itself accepted the need for new laws on electronic "bugging."

24-47   When, in November 1993, the *Sunday Mirror* published "world exclusive" pictures (taken by a "peeping tom camera" hidden in the ceiling) of the Princess of Wales exercising in a London gym, Lord McGregor expressed his outrage. He described the newspaper's claim that the pictures raised issues of royal security as "one of the most hypocritical justifications for a breach (of the newspaper industry's code of conduct) that I have ever heard from an editor."

Privacy Commissioner

24-48   Following this incident, Professor Robert Pinker, a member of the PCC, was appointed as a Privacy Commissioner. He can investigate breaches of the industry's code of practice and if he finds that there has been a gross violation can recommend that the PCC asks the owner of the newspaper to take disciplinary action against the editor. In extreme cases, that can mean dismissal.

NEW OFFENCES

24-49   As in the earlier Calcutt report there were suggestions that any new statutory offences might not be necessary in Scotland

and that the existing law might be wide enough to cover the situation.

-50   Calcutt recommended that the following should become criminal offences in England and Wales:

(1) Entering or remaining on private property without the consent of the lawful occupant, with intent to obtain personal information with a view to its publication.

(2) (a) Placing a surveillance device on private property without the consent of the lawful occupant, with intent to obtain personal information with a view to its publication; or

(b) Using a surveillance device (whether on private property or elsewhere) in relation to an individual who is on private property, without the consent of an individual to such use, with intent to obtain personal information about that individual with a view to its publication.

(3) Taking a photograph, or recording the voice, of an individual who is on private property, without his consent to the taking or recording, with a view to its publication and with intent that the individual should be identifiable.

These offences would not apply to pictures taken outside the United Kingdom, for example the topless pictures of the Duchess of York published in some British newspapers, in 1992 but taken at a private villa in the south of France, or to nude pictures of the Prince of Wales, again taken in France and published in Germany. However, the individual involved would be able to apply for an injunction if the pictures were taken for publication in the UK.

-51   Calcutt recommended that private property should include any private residence, together with garden and outbuildings, hotel bedrooms, parts of a hospital or nursing home where patients are treated or accommodated and school premises.

-52   *Defences* It would be a defence to any of the proposed offences that the act was done:

(a) for the purpose of preventing, detecting or exposing the commission of any crime or other seriously anti-social conduct;

(b) for the purpose of preventing the public from being misled by some public statement or action of the individual concerned;

(c) for the purpose of informing the public about matters directly affecting the discharge of any public function of the individual concerned;

(d) for the protection of public health or safety;

(e) under any lawful authority.

24–53   Calcutt suggested that the courts should have the power, on an application by the individual concerned, to grant an injunction restraining the publication of any information, photograph or recording obtained by an act which constituted one of the offences.

24–54   He recommended that consideration should be given to the introduction of a new civil wrong of infringement of privacy and also asked the Government to look at the possibility of plugging gaps in legislation designed to protect private telephone conversations.

24–55   The second Calcutt Report was followed by a report of the National Heritage Select Committee (in March 1993) which endorsed criminal provisions similar to those proposed by Calcutt. It also recommended the enactment of a Protection of Privacy Bill with both criminal and civil provisions.

Electronic Bugging

24–56   In its first meeting after the publication of the second Calcutt Report the Press Complaints Commission also demanded new laws on electronic bugging.

24–57   The commission deplored the publication of a taped conversation alleged to have taken place between the Prince of Wales and Mrs Camilla Parker-Bowles.

24–58   Lord McGregror stated: "Bugging of private telephone calls is manifestly an invasion of privacy no matter who does it. As such it is contrary to the industry's code and the commission deplore the publication of the so-called Camillagate tapes.

We recognise, however, that unethically and illegally obtained material may still be published abroad and republished in Britain. For these reasons we think it essential there should be legislation defining the boundaries of the law."

24–59   At the same meeting, the commission said that it should consist of a majority of lay members to convince the public of its independence.

Infringement of Privacy

–60 In July 1993 the Lord Chancellor's Department and the Scottish Office published a consultation paper entitled Infringement of Privacy, which followed up Calcutt's suggestion and recommended the creation of a general civil remedy for breach of privacy, which would extend beyond the press. The Government took the view that the law as it stood did not afford enough protection for privacy.

–61 The Government proposal was in the following terms: A person shall have a cause of action in respect of conduct which causes an infringement of his privacy, causing him substantial distress, provided that distress would also have been suffered by a person of ordinary sensibilities in the circumstances of the complaint.

–62 A person's privacy shall be taken to include matters concerning his health, personal communications, family and personal relationships and a right to be free from harassment and molestation.

–63 The Government suggested that such a legal remedy of this kind would offer the ordinary citizen a means of preventing or obtaining redress for unwarranted intrusions into his or her private life. However, the consultation paper made it clear that legal aid would not be available to enable the ordinary citizen to pursue this new remedy.

–64 As the paper conceded, privacy is a complicated subject: "Sometimes, like Greta Garbo, we want to be alone; sometimes, like Mae West, we do not." But the Government pointed out that the law already protects a person's physical integrity, ownership of land and other possessions.

–65 It added: "It is suggested that the time has now come, as a matter of principle, to recognise in law another such interest, that aspect of personal integrity which we call privacy.

The right to privacy should now be seen as sufficiently important to justify its recognition per se, rather than leaving it to be dealt with piecemeal."

–66 As the Government also pointed out, under the European Convention on Human Rights (Article 8(1)), everyone has the right to respect for his faimly life, his home and his correspondence.

–67 It proposed that the new civil remedy would be used

against anyone who infringed a person's privacy intention-
ally, recklessly or negligently.

24–68   *Defences* A number of defences to a breach of privacy action—
namely, consent, lawful authority, absolute and qualified
privilege and public interest—were suggested in the consultation paper. The public interest defence would cover information relating to crime or seriously anti-social conduct; public
health or safety; discharge of a public function; and the correction of a misleading statement.

24–69   Just how far the public interest defence would extend is not
clear, because the consultation paper stated that any information of a personal nature, published allegedly in the public
interest, must be directly connected with the public function
of the individual concerned. For example, is there a legitimate
public interest in knowing that an M.P. is having an extra-
marital affair? Some would say that it is a private matter
between the individuals involved, others that it goes to the
heart of trust in public office.

24–70   At the time of publication of this book, the Government had
not made its intentions clear as to how many of the various
recommendations mentioned in this chapter would become
the subject of legislation and in what form.

KEY POINTS

The Calcutt Committee was appointed because of concern
about the intrusion into private lives by certain sections of the
media. It recommended that what it described as the worst
forms of physical intrusion by the media should be made
criminal offences.

Calcutt also led to the abolition of the Press Council and its
replacement by the Press Complaints Commission, whose
remit is to consider complaints of unjust and unfair treatment
by the Press and of unwarranted infringements of privacy. It
also led to a code of conduct for journalists. (See appendix.)

Calcutt warned that if the commission did not work it
would be replaced by a statutory Press Complaints Tribunal
with wide-ranging powers to order not only the publication
of corrections and apologies but also compensation.

His review of self regulation, published in January 1993, concluded that the press had failed to put its own house in order. He repeated his call for a Press Complaints Commission, and for the most blatant forms of privacy invasion, such as doorstepping, bugging and use of long-range cameras to become criminal offences. He called for a review of the law on the interception of telephone calls and asked the government to consider introducing a new civil wrong of infringement of privacy.

A Government consultation paper adopted the latter suggestion and recommended the creation of a civil action for a breach of privacy which caused the ordinary person substantial distress. Private matters would include health, personal communications, family and personal relationships. There would also be a right to be free from harassment and molestation. A public interest defence would be available.

CHAPTER 25

THE REHABILITATION OF OFFENDERS ACT 1974

Purpose of Act

25–01 The purpose of this Act is to enable people with criminal convictions to wipe certain old offences off their records and continue their lives free from the constant threat of disclosure. The Act achieves its purpose by prohibiting the telling of the truth and legalising lying. It uses two key concepts, the "rehabilitated person" and the "spent conviction.

Restriction of information about spent convictions

25–02 From the journalist's point of view one of the main effects of the Act is that it restricts the availability of information about the spent convictions of a rehabilitated person. A rehabilitated person is, in general, to be treated for all purposes in law as if he had not committed the offence in question or been charged, prosecuted, convicted or sentenced as a result. Evidence of spent convictions is not normally admissible in any judicial proceedings in Great Britain and a person is not, in such proceedings, liable to be asked or bound to answer any question relating to his past which cannot be answered without acknowledging or referring to a spent conviction.

25–03 However, there are important exceptions to these rules. The Act does not affect the admission of evidence as to a person's previous convictions (a) in any criminal proceedings before a court in Great Britain, (b) in service disciplinary proceedings, (c) in most proceedings (such as children's hearings, or adoption, guardianship or custody proceedings) relating to children under 18. A party or witness in any proceedings can also waive the protection of the Act and consent to the admission of evidence about his spent convictions or the determination of an issue involving such evidence.

25–04 In most non-judicial contexts too, such as applying for a job or filling in a proposal form for an insurance policy, a person is not bound to disclose spent convictions in answer to any question about his past and is not to be subjected to any legal liability or prejudice for his non-disclosure. The Secretary of State has power to make orders excluding or modifying the application of these provisions in particular circumstances.

-05 It is also an offence for a person, such as a court official, police officer or civil servant, who in the course of his duty has access to official records, to disclose, "otherwise than in the course of those duties", information about spent convictions. There is a defence which covers disclosure to, or at the express request of, the rehabilitated person.

-06 The phrase "otherwise than in the course of those duties" probably relates to disclosure by one official to another, and is probably not intended to cover, for example, disclosure by a Press officer to the Press. If such disclosure to the Press were regarded as covered by the phrase, the further question would arise whether the journalist receiving the information was a "person who, in the course of his official duties ... had custody of or access to any official record of the information contained there". It would be difficult to argue that he was. He would receive the information in the course of his job but he would not have custody of or access to it in the course of his official duties.

-07 On a proper reading of the Act the obligation would seem to be on court officials, police officers and other officials to hold back the relevant information and not on the Press. This view is supported by section 9(4), which makes it an offence to obtain information about spent convictions from any official record by means of any fraud, dishonesty or bribe. The purpose of section 9 of the Act, in short, is to keep information on spent convictions within the confines of official records, and the effect of sections 4 and 9 is to restrict the information available to the Press and public.

Effects on law of defamation

-08 The other main effect of the Act from the point of view of the media is that it limits the availability of certain defences to an action of defamation. First, a defender in such an action cannot rely on the defence of *veritas* in relation to a spent conviction if the publication is proved to have been made with malice.

25–09   It is not clear exactly what is meant by "malice" in this context. It cannot include, as it does in some other areas, the lack of any honest belief in the truth of the statement made. On the other hand it probably includes an intention to injure wholly or mainly for the gratification of personal spite or ill will. A newspaper which published details of a rehabilitated person's spent convictions because it was annoyed by his unco-operative attitude over some other matter would, if its malice could be proved, be unable to rely on the defence of *veritas*.

25–10   Secondly, a defender in an action for defamation cannot rely on the privilege attaching to a fair and accurate report of judicial proceedings if it is proved that the report contained a reference to evidence which was ruled to be inadmissible in the proceedings because it related to a spent conviction. This provision does not apply to *bona fide* law reports and reports or accounts of judicial proceedings "published for *bona fide* educational, scientific or professional purposes, or given in the course of any lecture, class or discussion given or held for any of these purposes".

25–11   These are the only two areas in which the law of defamation is altered by the Act, which expressly provides that spent convictions can be referred to in other respects to enable a defender to rely on any defence of *veritas* or fair comment or of absolute or qualified privilege which is available to him. Moreover, the law of defamation is not in any way altered by the Act if the publication complained of took place before the conviction was spent.

Sentences subject to rehabilitation

25–12   Some sentences are excluded from rehabilitation under the Act. The convictions to which these sentences relate accordingly never become spent convictions and the person on whom they are imposed never becomes a rehabilitated person in relation to them. These sentences excluded from rehabilitation are as follows:

(a) a sentence of imprisonment for life;

(b) a sentence of imprisonment or corrective training for a term exceeding 30 months;

(c) a sentence of preventive detention; and

(d) a sentence of detention during Her Majesty's pleasure or for life, or for a term exceeding 30 months, passed under section 53 of the Children and Young Persons Act 1933 or under section 57 of the Children and Young Persons (Scotland) Act 1937 (section 5).

All other sentences are subject to rehabilitation.

Effect of subsequent conviction

-13   A subsequent conviction after the rehabilitation period does not revive the earlier conviction: it remains spent.

-14   The effect of a subsequent conviction during the rehabilitation period depends on its nature. If it is a conviction for a minor offence (in Scotland, an offence within the jurisdiction of the district courts) it has no effect on rehabilitation. If it is a more serious offence but does not involve a sentence excluded from rehabilitation (*i.e.* heavier than 30 months' imprisonment or detention) it delays the expiry of the rehabilitated period until the end of the rehabilitation period applicable to the new offence or the old offence whichever ends later. If the subsequent conviction involves a sentence excluded from rehabilitation then it precludes rehabilitation altogether and the old offence never becomes spent.

Rehabilitation periods

-15   The Act provides for different rehabilitation periods depending on the gravity of the sentence and the age of the offender. In the case of adult offenders the scale is as in Table A.

Table A

Sentence	Rehabilitation Period
Imprisonment or corrective training for 6–30 months	10 years
Imprisonment for a term not exceeding 6 months	7 years
Fine or other sentence subject to rehabilitation	5 years

25–16   In the case of persons under 17 these periods are reduced by half and there is a special scale for certain sentences confined to young offenders (Table B).

Table B

Sentence	Rehabilitation Period
Borstal training	7 years
Detention for 6–30 months under s.53 of the Children and Young Persons Act 1933 or s.57 of the Children and Young Persons (Scotland) Act 1937	5 years
Detention for not more than 6 months under either of the above provisions	3 years
Detention in a detention centre under s.4 of the Criminal Justice (Scotland) Act 1963	3 years

25–17   The rehabilitation period applicable to an order discharging a person absolutely for an offence is six months from the date of the conviction and the same period applies to a discharge by a children's hearing under the Social Work (Scotland) Act 1968. If a person is put on probation the rehabilitation period ends one year after the date of the conviction or when the probation order ceases to have effect, whichever is the later. The same rule applies if a person is conditionally discharged, or bound over to keep the peace or be of good behaviour.

25–18   A similar rule—one year or the duration of a period of care, residential training or supervision, whichever is the longer—applies in relation to various orders dealing with children and young persons, including a supervision requirement under the 1968 Act. If a convicted person is made the subject of a hospital order under the Mental Health Act 1959 or the Mental Health (Scotland) Act 1983 or the Mental Health (Scotland) Act 1984 (with or without an order restricting discharge) the rehabilitation period ends five years after the date of the conviction or two years after the hospital order ceases to have effect, whichever is later.

25–19   Finally, if a convicted person has any disqualification imposed on him (such as a disqualification from driving) the rehabilitation period ends when the disqualification ceases to have effect. The same rule applies to a "disability, prohibition or other penalty'.

25–20   These are the main rules on rehabilitation periods but the Act contains other provisions and also empowers the Secretary of State to make orders varying the periods. The result is a complex piece of legislation. It will often be difficult to know whether a conviction is spent. Fortunately, as we have seen, the main sanction of the Act lies in the law of defamation and, so long as there is no malice, and no reference in a report of judicial proceedings to evidence actually ruled to be inadmissible under the Act, the journalist has the protection of the usual defences and privileges and has nothing to fear from the Act.

"Rehabilitated person" and "spent conviction"

-21 On the expiry of the relevant length of time, the person concerned becomes a rehabilitated person and the conviction becomes a spent conviction. This is subject to the rules on subsequent conviction considered above, since rehabilitation under the Act is designed for those who do not commit other serious offences during the rehabilitation period. It is also subject to the sentence being served, at least in the case of imprisonment and other custodial sentences. Non-payment of a fine does not prevent rehabilitation; nor does failure to comply with any requirement of a probation order, suspended sentence or supervision order). The escaped convict does not become a rehabilitated person.

Application to service disciplinary proceedings

-22 Findings of guilt by army, navy or air force courts-martial or other competent authorities are treated as convictions for purposes of the Act but only if (a) the offence is also a civil offence or comes within a specified list of service offences or (b) the punishment is imprisonment; cashiering, discharge with ignominy or dismissal with disgrace from Her Majesty's service; dismissal from Her Majesty's service; or detention for a term of three months or more. The rehabilitation period for cashiering, discharge with ignominy or dismissal with disgrace from Her Majesty's service is 10 years; for dismissal from Her Majesty's service, seven years; and for a sentence of detention, five years: these periods are halved if the person sentenced was under 17 years of age when found guilty.

Application to children's hearings

25–23 Children's hearings do not convict or sentence the children who come before them. Their approach is intended to be therapeutic rather than punitive. Nevertheless it was thought desirable that people brought before them on an offence ground should have the chance of becoming rehabilitated persons under the Act. If that were not the case, a boy sent to a residential school for stealing lead from a roof would be denied the opportunity of living down his offence.

25–24 Accordingly, the Act provides that if a child is referred to a children's hearing on an offence ground and that ground is either accepted by the child (and, where necessary, his parent) or established to the satisfaction of the sheriff on a referral to him, then the acceptance or establishment of the ground shall be treated for the purposes of the Act as a conviction and any disposal of the case by a children's hearing as a sentence.

Application to foreign courts

25–25 The Act applies to convictions by or before courts outside Great Britain. In calculating rehabilitation periods in relation to such convictions a sentence is treated as if it were the nearest British equivalent. But a conviction by a court outside Great Britain does not delay or preclude rehabilitation in relation to a previous conviction.

KEY POINTS

25–26 The aim of the Rehabilitation of Offenders Act is to allow people with convictions to live without the constant threat of having their past dredged up. The rehabilitated person is generally to be treated as if he had never committed the offence. After a certain period of time, the conviction is regarded as "spent".

Evidence of previous convictions is, however, admitted in criminal proceedings.

In a defamation action involving a spent conviction a journalist cannot rely on a defence of *veritas* if the publication is proved to have been made with malice. Sentences of imprisonment or detention of more than 30 months are not subject to rehabilitation.

CHAPTER 26

PRINTER AND PUBLISHER

26–01 There are various Acts of Parliament which apply primarily to the editorial or managerial side of the newspaper business but which journalists should know. These provisions apply to both Scotland and England unless otherwise stated.

Name of printer

26–02 The name and address of the printer must be printed on the first or last page of every newspaper, periodical and most other printed matter in Scotland or England (the Newspapers, Printers and Reading Rooms Repeal Act 1869; the Printers Imprint Act 1961). If this is not done, printers, publishers and distributors can be fined up to £50 for each offending copy. Prosecutions must be brought in the name of the Lord Advocate in Scotland.

Registration

26–03 Newspapers must register annually with the General Post Office in London to enjoy the benefit of reduced rates of postage.

Keeping copies

26–04 The printer of a paper (if it is printed for hire, reward, gain or profit—which covers most cases) must keep at least one copy, showing on it the name and address of the person for whom it was printed. He must preserve it for six months and show it to any justice of the peace requiring to see it in that time. Failure to comply may result in a fine (Newspapers, Printers and Reading Rooms Repeal Act 1869).

Delivering copies to museums and libraries

05 The publisher of every newspaper, periodical or book published in the United Kingdom must within a month of publication deliver a copy to the British Library, at his own expense (Copyright Act 1911).

06 On written demand within 12 months of publication, he must also deliver a copy to the Bodleian Library, Oxford; the University Library, Cambridge; the National Library, Scotland; the Library of Trinity College, Dublin and in certain cases the National Library of Wales. A separate demand need not be made for each copy of a newspaper. One demand can cover all numbers subsequently published.

07 There is a fine and the value of the paper, book or magazine, for failure to comply with these provisions.

Obscene matter

08 Section 51 of the Civic Government (Scotland) Act 1982 makes it an offence to display any obscene material (any book, magazine, bill, paper, print, film, tape, disc or other kind of recording, photograph, drawing or painting) in a public place, which means a place to which the public are allowed access, whether on payment or otherwise. It bans the publication, reproduction, sale, distribution, printing and keeping of obscene material.

09 The penalty for contravention is, on summary conviction, a fine not exceeding £2,000 or imprisonment for up to three months, or, on indictment, a fine of no stated limit or imprisonment for up to two years, or both in each case. There is a defence where it can be proved all due diligence was used to avoid an offence.

10 The section was extended to television and sound broadcasts by the Broadcasting Act 1990.

CHAPTER 27

ADVERTISEMENTS

27–01 The publication of certain advertisements is illegal and can result in a fairly heavy fine or imprisonment or both.

Medical advertisements

27–02 It is an offence to take part in the publication of an advertisement containing an offer to treat any person for cancer, or to prescribe a remedy or give advice on the treatment of that disease (Cancer Act 1939, s. 4).

27–03 The Medicines Act 1968 introduced a set of offences concerning medical advertisements generally. Under the Act it is an offence to issue, at the request or with the consent of "a commercially interested party" (a term which includes most manufacturers and suppliers of medicines), a false or misleading advertisement relating to medicinal products.

27–04 An advertisement is false or misleading for this purpose if it falsely describes the medicinal products or if it is likely to mislead as to their nature, quality, uses or effects.

27–05 In the case of certain medicinal products which are subject to a licence it is also an offence to issue an advertisement containing recommendations other than those authorised by the licence. In both cases, however, it is a defence for an accused person to prove that he did not know, and could not with reasonable diligence have discovered, that the advertisement was false or misleading or contained unauthorised recommendations.

27–06 Where a product licence is in force for medicinal products of a particular description only the holder of the licence can authorise advertisements relating to such products. Accordingly, it is an offence under section 94 of the Medicines Act 1968 to issue any such advertisement at the request or with the consent of any other commercially interested party. It is, however, a defence for an accused person to prove (a) that he exercised all due diligence to secure that the section would not be contravened, and (b) that the contravention was due to the act or default of another person.

27–07   The Medicines Act 1968 also empowers the appropriate Ministers to make regulations prohibiting, or regulating, particular types of advertisements for medicinal products. The regulations may, for example, prohibit the advertising of treatments for particular diseases, or prohibit advertisements containing particular misleading words or phrases, or require medical advertisements to take a certain form and contain specified particulars. The defence mentioned in paragraph 27–06 above is available where a contravention of these regulations is alleged.

Food advertisements

27–08   It is an offence to be a party to the publication of an advertisement giving a false or misleading description of any food or drug (Food and Drugs (Scotland) Act 1956). There are special provisions for margarine advertisements designed, it seems, to prevent all possibility of confusion with butter (Labelling of Food (Amendment) Regulations 1955). However, it is a defence to prove that the advertisement was published in the ordinary course of business by a person whose business it is to publish or arrange for the publication of advertisements. This will normally protect newspapers.

Experiments on animals

27–09   It is an offence to publish an advertisement of a public exhibition of an experimental or scientific procedure on an animal which may have the effect of causing the animal pain, suffering, distress or lasting harm (Animals (Scientific Procedures) Act 1986).

Fraudulent advertisements

27–10   It is a serious offence to distribute circulars which to one's knowledge fraudulently induce or attempt to induce people to invest money. This will not involve a newspaper proprietor, publisher or distributor in liability unless he knows of or is a party to the fraud (Prevention of Fraud Investments Act 1958).

Consumer credit advertisements

27–11 The Consumer Credit Act 1974 contains provisions on consumer credit advertisements, such as most advertisements of hire-purchase facilities and most moneylenders' advertisements. Regulations will provide for the form and content of such advertisements to ensure, among other things, that they give a fair indication of the credit or hire facilities offered and of their true cost. The Act itself makes it an offence to publish a consumer credit advertisement which conveys information which is misleading in a material respect. It also prohibits certain advertisements of credit facilities for goods or services which are not available for cash. There are similar restrictions on advertisements by credit brokers, debt adjusters and debt counsellors.

27–12 All these provisions apply expressly to the publisher of an advertisement as well as to the advertiser, but newspapers and others are protected by a provision that it is a defence for a person charged to prove (a) that the advertisement was published in the course of a business carried on by him, and (b) that he received the advertisement in the course of that business, and did not know and had no reason to suspect that its publication would be an offence.

Adoption and care of children

27–13 It is an offence to publish knowingly an advertisement indicating that a parent or guardian wants a child adopted, or that a person wants to adopt a child or that any person other than a registered adoption society or local authority is willing to make arrangements for the adoption of a child (Adoption (Scotland) Act 1978).

27–14 The Children Act 1958 makes it an offence to publish knowingly an advertisement that a person will undertake or will arrange for the care and maintenance of a child, unless the advertisement truly states the person's name and address.

Licensed betting office advertisements

27–15 It is an offence to publish or permit to be published an advertisement of a particular licensed betting office or of licensed betting offices in general. But it is a defence for a person to prove that he did not know and had no reasonable cause to suspect the nature of the advertisement and that he had taken all reasonable steps to ascertain that it did not infringe the Betting, Gaming and Lotteries Act 1963. An advertisement breaks the law if it indicates where a licensed betting office can be found, even although it does not state that it is a licensed betting office. To publish an advertisement in the form "A. Smith, Commission Agent, 12 High Street, Greentown" would be an offence if the premises were in fact a licensed betting office.

Lotteries

-16   A lottery is a scheme for distributing prizes by lot or chance. With certain exceptions, all lotteries are unlawful. It is an offence to print or advertise lottery tickets; to print, publish or distribute any advertisement of a lottery, or any list of lottery winners, or anything concerning a lottery calculated to induce people to participate in it or in other lotteries (Lotteries and Amusements Act 1976). It is, however, a defence to prove that the lottery in question was one of the few types of lawful lotteries mentioned below and that the person charged believed, and had reasonable ground for believing, that none of the statutory conditions applying to the lottery had been broken.

-17   The five types of lawful lottery mentioned above are as follows:

(1) Small lotteries incidental to certain entertainments such as bazaars, sales of work, fêtes, dinners, dances and sporting or athletic events. There must be no money prizes and tickets must be sold and the result declared only at and during the entertainment in question. The lottery must not be the only, or the only substantial, inducement to people to attend the entertainment. The whole proceeds of the entertainment (including the proceeds of the lottery), less expenses and a small sum for the purchase of prizes, must be devoted to purposes other than private gain. This exception would cover, for example, an announcement in an advertisement of a football match that a bottle of whisky would be raffled.

(2) Private lotteries. These are lotteries held by and for people belonging to the same society, working on the same premises or living on the same premises. The main

conditions applying to this kind of lottery are that the sale of tickets must be restricted to the people mentioned, the net proceeds must be devoted only to the provision of prizes or the purposes of the society holding the lottery and there must be no outside advertisement. The tickets must contain certain information and must all be the same price. This exception would cover, for example, an announcement in a newspaper that So-and-so had won the local golf club's Derby sweepstake.

(3) Lotteries promoted by societies established and conducted wholly or mainly for charitable, sporting, cultural or other purposes not for private gain or any commercial undertaking. A society must register with the appropriate district or islands council if it wishes to promote lawful lotteries, and it must keep within certain financial and other limits.

(4) Local lotteries promoted by local authorities in accordance with an approved scheme.

(5) Art union lotteries. Art unions are societies which purchase works of art or raise money for their purchase and distribute works of art or money among their members by lot or otherwise.

Amusements with prizes

27–18 None of the restrictions relating to lotteries apply to amusements with prizes provided as an incident to entertainments such as a bazaar, sale of work, fête, dinner, dance or sporting or athletic event. The proceeds must be devoted to purposes other than private gain and the opportunity to win prizes must not be the only substantial inducement to attend the entertainment. The restrictions on lotteries do not apply to amusements with prizes provided on premises authorised by the local authorities or at funfairs held by travelling showmen.

27–19 A newspaper will generally be quite safe in advertising fêtes, bazaars, funfairs, etc., even if the advertisement states that certain amusements with prizes will be provided.

Prize competitions

27–20 It is an offence to conduct in or through any newspaper, magazine or other periodical (a) any competition in which prizes are offered for forecasts of the result of a future event or of a past event the result of which is not yet ascertained or not yet generally known, or (b) any other competition, in which success does not depend to a substantial degree on the exercise of skill.

21   In 1973 the House of Lords decided that the *News of the World's* "Spot-the-ball" competition did not infringe this provision. The paper published a photograph of an actual incident in a football game but with the ball eliminated. Competitors were asked to mark with a cross the position where the ball was most likely to be. The winning entry was that which corresponded most closely with the opinion of a panel of experts as to the logical position of the ball in the circumstances (which might not be the same as the true position of the ball in the original photograph). The court took the view that competitors were being asked to use their skill and judgment and not just to forecast a future event (the decision of the panel of experts).

Advertisements of foreign betting

22   It is an offence, subject to certain limited exceptions, to advertise foreign pool betting or coupon betting or betting with a bookmaker outside Great Britain (Betting and Gaming Duties Act).

Gaming advertisements

23   The Gaming Act 1968 defines gaming as "the playing of a game of chance for winnings in money or money's worth, whether any person playing the game is at risk of losing any money or money's worth or not". The term is wide enough to include shove-halfpenny and bingo as well as the more sophisticated games normally played in casinos.

24   The Act makes it an offence to publish any advertisement informing the public that any premises in Great Britain are premises on which gaming takes place or inviting the public to take part in such gaming. It is also an offence to publish advertisements inviting the public (a) to apply for information about taking part in any gaming in Great Britain, or (b) to subscribe money or money's worth to be used in gaming anywhere, or (c) to apply for information about facilities for such subscriptions.

27–25   There are, however, exceptions for advertisements of certain kinds of gaming. The first relates to gaming as an incident of a bazaar, sale of work, fête, dinner, dance, sporting or athletic event or other entertainment of a similar character. The second relates to games played at an entertainment promoted otherwise than for purposes of private gain and complying with certain stringent conditions. This exception could cover, for example, advertisements of a bingo session held to raise funds for a football supporters' club. The third exception relates to gaming at amusement arcades or similar premises which are used wholly or mainly to provide amusements by means of gaming machines and which have a permit from the local authority to do so. The fourth exception covers gaming at any travelling showmen's pleasure fair.

27–26   The Gaming Act 1968 provides for the licensing of certain gaming premises including bingo clubs. The mere fact that premises are licensed to carry on gaming does not mean that they can be advertised (other than by a sign or notice displayed on the premises themselves). However, there is a specific provision allowing the publication in any newspaper of a notice stating that a licence under the Gaming Act has been granted. The notice must be published not later than 14 days from the date when the licence was granted or from such later date as the licensing board may specify and provided it is in a form approved by the licensing board. The Act also requires applications for licences to be advertised in a newspaper, so there can clearly be no objection to publishing these.

27–27   The provisions restricting gaming advertisements do not apply to the publication of an advertisement in a newspaper which circulates wholly or mainly outside Great Britain.

27–28   Finally, it is a defence to a prosecution under these provisions for the accused to prove that he is a person whose business it is to publish or arrange for the publication of advertisements and that he received the offending advertisement for publication in the ordinary course of business and did not know and had no reason to suspect that its publication would amount to an offence.

False trade descriptions

27–29   The Trade Descriptions Act 1968 prohibits false trade descriptions (as defined in the Act) and various other misstatements, such as false indications that goods are being offered at a cut price. The Act also gives the Department of Trade power to require certain advertisements to include certain particulars if they think this is necessary or expedient in the interests of consumers. Although the Act is aimed primarily at misstatements by those supplying goods and services, certain of its provisions apply to publishers of advertisements. If a newspaper knew that an advertisement contained a false trade description (e.g. that goods advertised as new were in fact second-hand or reconditioned) it would be guilty of an offence under the Act if it published it. Obviously, however, newspapers cannot be expected to investigate the accuracy of every statement made in their advertising columns. The Act therefore provides that it shall be a defence for the publisher of an advertisement to prove that he is a person whose business it is to publish or arrange for the publication of advertisements and that he received the advertisement for publication in the ordinary course of business and did not know and had no reason to suspect that its publication would amount to an offence under the Act.

Pirate radio stations

30 Under the Marine etc. Broadcasting (Offences) Act 1967 it is an offence to publish the times or other details of broadcasts to be made from pirate radio stations or to publish advertisements calculated to promote their interests.

Cars

31 An advertisement for new cars which contains any statement about fuel consumption must include information about results of relevant official tests.

Surrogacy arrangements

32 The Surrogacy Arrangements Act 1985 makes it an offence to publish any advertisement containing an indication (a) that any person is or may be willing to enter into a surrogacy arrangement or to negotiate or facilitate the making of a surrogacy arrangement or (b) that any person is looking for a

woman willing to become a surrogate mother or is looking for persons wanting to carry a child as surrogate mother.

Obscene publications

27–33   Obscenity is an offence at common law in Scotland. The broad test is whether the publication complained of is calculated to deprave and corrupt those who are likely to read it. The Indecent Advertisements Act 1889 deals mainly with placing indecent advertisements on walls and similar places and the distribution or exhibition of indecent matter in the streets. The Civic Government (Scotland) Act 1982 makes it an offence to publish any advertisement to the effect that the advertiser distributes or intends to distribute an indecent photograph of a child under 16.

Harmful publications

27–34   It is an offence to print, publish, sell or hire "horror comics" (Children and Young Persons (Harmful Publications) Act 1955). This will not affect the average newspaper as the statute applies only to works which consist wholly or mainly of picture stories portraying the commission of crimes or acts of violence or cruelty or incidents of a repulsive or horrible nature in such a way that the work as a whole would tend to corrupt a child or young person into whose hands it might fall. It would apply, *e.g.* to "video nasties". A child is defined as someone under 14 and a young person as someone under the age of 17.

Election matter

27–35   It is an offence to incur expense without the written authority of the election agent in issuing advertisements, circulars or publications with a view to promoting or procuring the election of a candidate at an election (Representation of the People Act 1983). This does not prevent newspapers commenting on an election with complete freedom and presenting a candidate or his views or disparaging another candidate. It has been held that there was an offence when a publication advised electors to vote against a candidate but did not advise them to vote for his opponent. It nevertheless tended to promote the opponent's election.

7–36   But to offend, the publication must tend to promote or procure the election of a particular candidate and not merely a political party as a whole. This was decided in a case in 1952 (*R. v. Tronoh Mines Ltd.*) in which the proprietors of *The Times* and others were prosecuted over an advertisement condemning the financial policy of the Labour Party and saying that an election would give an opportunity of saving the country from being reduced to bankruptcy through the policies of a socialist government. The judge observed that no reasonable jury could find that this advertisement presented to the electors of any particular constituency any particular candidate.

7–37   It is also an offence to print, publish, post or distribute any bill, placard or poster referring to an election unless the name and address of the printer and publisher appear on its face (Representation of the People Act 1983). This provision might apply, for example, to newspaper posters proclaiming "Vote for Blogg".

Accommodation agencies

7–38   It is an offence under the Accommodation Agencies Act 1953, to issue any advertisement describing any house as being to let without the authority of the owner of the house or his agent. It is also an offence under the Act to demand or accept certain illegal commissions for registering people seeking tenancies or for supplying particulars of houses to let. However, the Act expressly provides that "a person shall not be guilty of an offence under this section by reason of his demanding or accepting any payment in consideration of . . . the publication in a newspaper, of any advertisement or notice, or by reason of the . . . publication . . . of an advertisement or notice received for the purpose in the ordinary course of business".

Sex Discrimination Act 1975

7–39   Under section 38 of this Act it is unlawful to publish or cause to be published an advertisement which indicates, or might reasonably be understood as indicating, an intention by a person to do any act which is or might be unlawful discrimination on grounds of sex in the employment field or in other fields. This provision does not apply to an advertisement if the intended act would not in fact be unlawful. For example, the 1975 Act does not apply to employment for the purposes of a private household or where the number of persons employed by the employer does not exceed five. A private householder or, say, a solicitor employing only three people could therefore lawfully advertise for a male gardener or a female secretary respectively even though such advertisements are in general unlawful.

27–40   The section provides that for its purposes the use of a job description with a sexual connotation (such as "waiter", "salesgirl", "postman" or "stewardess') shall be taken to indicate an intention to discriminate, unless the advertisement contains an indication to the contrary. It would obviously be impossible for newspapers and others in a similar position to check the lawfulness of each advertisement submitted to them. They could not be expected, for example, to carry out independent inquiries into the number of people employed by a particular advertiser. The section therefore provides a defence for the publisher of an advertisement if he proves (a) that the advertisement was published in reliance on a statement made to him by the person who caused it to be published to the effect that the intended act would not in fact be unlawful and (b) that it was reasonable for him to rely on the statement.

Equal opportunities

27–41   In 1981 the Equal Opportunities Commission issued guidance notes on the advertising provisions of the Act which included points for the guidance of advertisers. These included the following: "Watch out for words like salesman, storeman/ woman. If these are used, make sure the ad clearly offers the job to both sexes. Make sure that advertisements for jobs which have in the past been done mainly by men or women only (*e.g.* mechanic, typist) could not be understood to indicate a preference for one sex. If the ad contains words like he, she, or him, make sure that they are used as alternatives, *e.g.* he or she, or him/her, and are consistent throughout the advertisement. In one way or another the ad must make it clear that the vacancy is open to both men and women. Pictures can give a biased impression too. If they are used, ensure that men and women are shown fairly, in both numbers and prominence. Otherwise a bold disclaimer should be placed as close to the illustration as possible".

Advertising standards

7–42   Publishers should be familiar with the British Code of Advertising Practice, administered by the Advertising Standards Authority. Although the code is not statutory, the Authority has power, where an advertisement is found to have contravened the code, to order the advertiser to amend or withdraw it from publication. The aim of the code is to protect consumers from unacceptable or misleading advertising, its philosophy, in brief, being that "if an advertiser can't prove it, he can't say it"; and the Authority summarises its message thus: "All advertisements should be legal, decent, honest and truthful".

7–43   The code, which is under constant review, makes special provision for political and religious advertising, to avoid undue suppression of freedom of speech. Publishers of newspapers and periodicals are entitled to withdraw any advertisement they think is contrary to the code. There are separate codes dealing with television, radio, cable and satellite broadcasting.

7–44   In December 1990, the Advertising Standards Authority ruled that a leading research charity, the Imperial Cancer Research Fund, had exaggerated its rôle in pioneering a new breast cancer therapy and had made misleading claims about the therapy.

7–45   In the same month a former boxing champion Tony Sibson threatened to take legal action after an advertisement for Audi cars used a picture of his bruised and battered face accompanied by the words: "In our eyes, it's better to avoid a hit than take one". Mr Sibson said that the advertisement, which had been published without his permission and without warning, had caused distress to his whole family and carried the implication that his only talent had been to endure punishment.

27–46   The Advertising Standards Authority said that its code of practice did not require advertisers to seek the permission of people in the public eye although they were advised to do so. It pointed out however, that it had recently endorsed a complaint by Mr Arthur Scargill, President of the National Union of Mineworkers, over an advertisement for an anti-perspirant which used his picture with the caption: "For when you're really sweating". The authority described this as "highly distasteful" at a time when Mr Scargill was involved in an inquiry over missing union funds.

27–47   The British Code of Advertising Practice says advertisements should contain nothing which might cause children physical, mental or moral harm, or which exploits their credulity, lack of experience or sense of loyalty and should not encourage them to be a nuisance to their parents or anyone else with the aim of persuading them to buy an advertised product.

Key Points

27–48   A fine and/or imprisonment can be imposed for the publication of certain types of illegal advertisement. For example, it is an offence to publish false or misleading advertisements about medicines or medical treatment, food and drugs.

There are also strict rules governing advertisements on consumer credit, betting and lotteries.

Advertisements are supposed to be "legal, decent, honest and truthful" and the Advertising Standards Authority has power to order an advertiser to amend or withdraw an advertisement which fails to meet these criteria.

CHAPTER 28

RACE RELATIONS

3-01 It is an offence under section 19 of the Public Order Act 1986 to display, publish or distribute written material which is threatening, abusive or insulting if the intention is to stir up racial hatred or, taking all the circumstances into account, racial hatred is likely to be stirred up. The penalties for a breach of the Act are up to six months' imprisonment or a fine or both for summary conviction and up to two years' imprisonment or a fine or both on indictment. The Broadcasting Act 1990 extended these provisions to radio and television broadcasts (see also chapter 22).

3-02 The important point to note is that an offence can be committed under the Act without any intention of stirring up racial hatred. An editor could be prosecuted for publishing a racist speech, just as an extremist politician could be for making it. The editor would have to decide whether in all the circumstances racial hatred was likely to be stirred up. He might have to consider toning down the language of the original by taking the controversial parts out of direct speech so that they were no longer threatening, abusive or insulting in terms of the Act.

3-03 Under section 22 of the 1986 Act journalists involved in television or radio broadcasts may be guilty of an offence if the programme involves the use of threatening, abusive or insulting visual images or sounds in circumstances in which racial hatred is likely to be stirred up. The offence covers each of the people providing the programme service; any person by whom the programme is produced or directed and any person by whom the offending words or behaviour are used. (see 22–30).

3-04 The Act defines racial hatred as hatred against a a group of people in Great Britain by reference to colour, race, nationality (including citizenship) or ethnic or national origins. This can include a particular racial group such as Jews, Sikhs or Romanies. In October 1991 the Dowager Lady Birdwood was conditionally discharged and ordered to pay £500 towards prosecution costs after being convicted of distributing anti-Jewish leaflets intended to stir up racial hatred.

28–05   In a test case in 1983, the House of Lords, overruling the English Court of Appeal, decided that Sikhs qualify for protection under the Race Relations Act Act 1976 as a racial group. The Court of Appeal had held that they were a religious community and did not enjoy such protection. The Lords ruled that a Birmingham headmaster unlawfully discriminated against a Sikh pupil in refusing to allow him to wear a turban in the school. Lord Fraser of Tullybelton (a Scottish Lord of Appeal), said the Sikhs were a group defined by reference to ethnic origins for the purposes of the Act. The court laid down a test of whether a group regarded itself and was seen by others as a distinct community because of certain characteristics such as a long shared history, a cultural tradition of its own, a common ancestry, common language and literature, a common religion and being a minority.

28–06   In a case in April 1991 an employment appeal tribunal decided that Rastafarians were a religious sect but not a racial group defined by ethnic origin within the meaning of the Race Relations Act. In allowing an appeal from an employer from a finding of racial discrimination by an industrial tribunal, the employment appeal tribunal stated that Rastafarians were not sufficiently distinguishable from the rest of the Afro-Caribbean community. It also took the view that as a movement which went back only 60 years, the Rastafarians did not possess a long shared history, one of the tests for establishing a racial group.

28–07   It is a defence for someone who is not shown to have intended to stir up racial hatred to prove that he was not aware of the content of the material or did not suspect, and had no reason to suspect that it was threatening, abusive or insulting. The defence must be proved on a balance of probabilities.

28–08   The Act does not apply to fair, accurate and contemporaneous reports of public hearings before any court or tribunal exercising judicial authority, or to reports of proceedings in Parliament.

28–09   During 1986 the Press Council dealt with a series of complaints about the practice of some newspapers of specifying the skin colour or race of the offender or defendant in reports of cases of violence or serious crime—dubbed by some writers "adjectival racism". Its decisions had no legal force, but they at least gave editors a basis for considering how to proceed in this sensitive area. One of the grounds of complaint was that while reports sometimes described offenders as black, no mention was made of the fact, in other similar kinds of case, that the offenders were white.

3–10   The council upheld a complaint against the *Daily Telegraph* over its description of a rape gang as black, and held that this was an irrelevant, prejudicial description which tended to exacerbate hostility against minority groups. The then editor, William Deedes, maintained that there would always be differences on what was or was not relevant in a particular case.

3–11   The council ruled that reference to race or colour was objectionable where it was both irrelevant to the report and in a prejudicial context. There might be cases where it would be relevant to refer to race or colour without substantial risk of prejudice. Where, however, the reference was to a person convicted or accused of violent crime as black, this was both irrelevant and prejudicial. It tended to exacerbate hostility against minority groups, who were at risk of serious prejudice within the community. Accepting that there were different views on the matter, the council believed that its view served the interest of better community race relations and should be respected.

3–12   In another case the council heard a complaint that the same paper reported that a 16-year-old white girl told the Old Bailey she was raped "about 30 times" by a gang of black youths. The council held that no evidence was reported that the crimes had been racially motivated and the paper should not have introduced the defendants' colour or race into the story. But it was held not improper that the paper failed to identify the colour or race of defendants or victims in other reports cited.

3–13   The council rejected a complaint against the *Daily Telegraph* that in reporting the Tottenham riots it specified that alleged offenders later brought before the court in connection with the disturbances were black. The editor, Max Hastings, said he was determined to preserve editorial discretion as to whether or not it was appropriate to mention the colour of a person named in news items. The council took the view that the colour of those involved in the Tottenham riots was relevant to the reports of the court cases covered by the paper. The *Daily Telegraph*, it may be noted, in other reports of violent crimes during the year, specified the colour of assailants where this was not black.

28–14 In another case, the council found it was not improper or irrelevant for the *Daily Telegraph* to refer to the colour of two armed burglars in a report of their trial. It said counsel's description of one of the accused as black was relevant to the trial. It was the way in which a principal witness distinguished between the two in her evidence of what they did and said. The complaint in this case also was rejected.

28–15 In February 1989 the Press Council decided that a newspaper's reference to a man's dreadlocked hairstyle and his white girlfriend clearly implied his race or colour, which was irrelevant to the report. The council upheld a complaint that by describing a rapist as "dreadlocked" the *Daily Mail* had improperly identified his race and religion. The complaint stated that the use of the word dreadlocked was a description of the man as a black Rastafarian, although it might be that he was neither.

28–16 In April 1990 the Press Council upheld a complaint against the *Sun*, *Star* and *Daily Mail* that their coverage of a trial had unnecessarily identified the defendant as a black ballet dancer. The man denied the charge and was acquitted. The Press Council ruled that the newspapers should have avoided revealing the man's colour "in the interests of avoiding unjustified discrimination in the minds of the readers".

28–17 The following month the Press Council upheld a complaint that the *Sun* had improperly identified the colour of the white victim of a rush-hour knife attack. The complaint against the newspaper was that although it was acceptable to describe the attacker as black, since this could help in his capture, reference to the colour of the white victim suggested a racial motive and was likely to exacerbate racism. The managing editor of the newspaper had argued that it was a fact that a black man had stabbed a white man and that the colour of the victim was relevant to the story.

28–18 The subject of discrimination was dealt with in a Code of

Practice drawn up by the newly-established Press Complaints Commission. The Code, which came into effect on January 1, 1991, stated:

(1) The Press should avoid prejudical or pejorative reference to a person's race, colour, religion, sex or sexual orientation or to any physical or mental illness or handicap.

(2) It should avoid publishing details of a person's race, colour, religion, sex or sexual orientation, unless these are directly relevant to the story.

KEY POINTS

–19 It is an offence to publish threatening, abusive or insulting material with the intention of stirring up racial hatred, or if racial hatred is likely to be stirred up (Public Order Act 1986). Racial hatred is defined as hatred against a group of people by reference to colour, race, nationality or ethnic or national origins.

Guidelines for dealing with issues of race and colour are contained in the Code of Practice drawn up by the Press Complaints Commission.

CHAPTER 29

OFFICIAL SECRETS

The Official Secrets Acts

29–01　In the pursuit of news the journalist may come up against the Official Secrets Acts which make it an offence to be in or around a prohibited place for any purpose prejudicial to the safety or interests of the State (Official Secrets Act 1911, s. 1). Prohibited places include Her Majesty's arsenals, naval or air force establishments, factories, stations, dockyards, camps, ships and aircraft. They also include places where the Crown has munitions or models or papers relating to munitions. Various other places may be specifically declared to be prohibited. A journalist can be convicted if his conduct or the circumstances of the case indicate that his purpose was prejudicial to the interests of the State. This purpose need not be expressly proved by the prosecution.

29–02　It is also an offence under the Act to make sketches, photographs or notes which might be useful to an enemy. The same applies to obtaining, communicating or publishing documents or information which might be useful to an enemy. In these cases a purpose prejudicial to the safety or interests of the State is usually presumed unless the contrary is proved (Official Secrets Act 1911, s. 1).

29–03　Under the all-embracing provisions of section 2 of the 1911 Act it was an offence for anyone with access to official secrets to communicate them to unauthorised persons. Of more importance to journalists was the provision that a person who knowingly and willingly received a communication of this kind was also guilty of an offence (s. 2). Under a strict interpretation of section 2 it was an offence to disclose how many cups of tea were drunk each week in the Ministry of Defence or how much toilet paper was used.

29–04　However, in a number of English cases in the 1960s and 1970s juries could not be persuaded to convict people charged under section 2, and the Official Secrets Act 1989 was introduced to replace the "catch-all" approach of section 2 with a series of measures to deal with specific types of official information.

–05   The information protected by the Act falls into one of the following categories: security and intelligence; defence (including the size, organisation, deployment and training of the armed forces and defence policy and strategy); international relations; crime (information which, if disclosed, does or is likely to result in the commission of a crime, assist an escape from custody or impede the prevention or detection of offences); information entrusted in confidence to other States or international organisations; special investigation powers (information on State telephone-tapping, interception of letters or other communications). The offence of deliberate disclosure carries a maximum penalty of two years' imprisonment.

–06   The Act is primarily aimed at unauthorised disclosures of protected information by members of the security and intelligence services, Crown servants and government contractors, but also applies to disclosures by anyone, including journalists. However, if a journalist disclosed information connected with security, intelligence, defence or international relations, the prosecution would have to prove that the disclosure was "damaging", and that the journalist knew or had reasonable cause to believe it to be damaging.

–07   Where a journalist disclosed information relating to crime and special investigation powers, the Crown would not have to prove damage (damage is assumed) or that the journalist knew or had reasonable cause to believe the disclosure to be damaging. A disclosure would be regarded as damaging if, for example, it harmed the capability of the armed forces or endangered the interests of the United Kingdom abroad.

–08   It is not a defence under the 1989 Act that the disclosure was made in the public interest, for example that it revealed the existence of criminal conduct. Nor is there a prior publication defence—that the information is no longer secret because it has already been published—although, as the *Spycatcher* case illustrates, this plea would be likely to succeed in the European Court of Human Rights. In the case of the journalist, however, the fact that information was already in the public domain could provide the basis for an argument that further publication could no longer cause any damage.

29–09   In certain cases a police officer above the rank of inspector can require a person to give information relating to an offence or suspected offence under the Official Secrets Acts. It is an offence to fail to comply with such a requirement or knowingly to give false information. But the officer must have the authority of the chief officer of police and, except in emergencies, a Secretary of State must have given his express permission (Official Secrets Act 1939, s. 1).

The Zircon case

29–10   As was illustrated by the Zircon case in 1987, section 9 of the 1911 Act remains of considerable significance to journalists, as it gives the police wide powers to carry out searches. If satisfied that an offence under the Act has been or is about to be committed, a magistrate may grant a warrant authorising police to enter premises named in the warrant, to search the premises or anyone found on them and to seize material which is evidence of an offence under the Act. Armed with the warrant, detectives searched and removed from the BBC's offices in Glasgow, material connected with a programme on the Zircon intelligence-gathering satellite. It was to be one of a six-part series, *The Secret Society*, produced by BBC Scotland and presented by the journalist Duncan Campbell. The programme claimed that the Government had deceived Parliament by concealing the fact that it was spending £500 million on the Zircon project.

29–11   One of the many controversial aspects of the Zircon case was that the warrant was in fact granted by a sheriff rather than a magistrate. The Broadcasting Act 1990 made it clear that a sheriff as well as a magistrate can grant a warrant authorising the seizure of film and other material from a broadcasting organisation.

The DA-notice system

29–12   The system of "DA-notices" formerly known as "D notices" is important in the field of official secrets, although it is a matter of practice, not law. The system is administered by the Defence, Press and Broadcasting Advisory Committee which has both media and civil service representatives. The service departments bring cases before the committee and make known their wishes as to whether the information should be published. The committee considers the case and then sends DA or Defence Advisory notices to the participating sections of the media. The notices indicate what information should not be published. Doubts about the interpretation or application of notices are generally resolved by consulting the secretary of the committee. The whole system is a voluntary one.

–13   The system has operated for more than 80 years and is generally thought to have worked well, apart from one or two isolated incidents. The most notable of these was the "D-notice affair" of 1967 which arose out of the disclosure by the *Daily Express* that cables sent out of Britain were regularly made available to the security authorities for scrutiny. The Government said this was a breach of D notices: the *Express* maintained it was not. A committee of inquiry found for the *Express*, but the Government purported to "reject" this finding.

–14   The system was subjected to careful examination but survived. It was revised in 1982 after a lengthy examination, and four subjects were dropped—advice on Royal Navy warship construction and equipment; aircraft and aero-engines; prisoners of war and evaders; and the whereabouts of the former K.G.B. chief in Canberra, Vladimir Petrov, and his spy wife, who defected to Australia in 1954.

–15   Terrorism figured in the revised list. The introduction to the up-dated set of notices, presented in simpler and more general terms than before, stated: 'Dissemination of sensitive information . . . can also be of value to terrorist groups who lack the resources to obtain it through their own efforts". The system then covered: (1) Defence plans, operational capability, state of readiness and training; (2) Defence equipment; (3) Nuclear weapons (this item bears the warning that publication of design information could assist nuclear weapon states to improve their nuclear capability and non-nuclear states to acquire one or sub-national groups to produce explosive nuclear devices); (4) Radio and radar transmissions; (5) Cyphers and communications (with the request that extreme discretion should be used in reporting ostensible disclosures of information published at home or overseas about British codes and cyphers and that such information should not be elaborated upon without reference to the secretary of the committee); (6) British security and intelligence services (the names "security service" (MI5) and "secret service" (MI6) were dropped); (7) War precautions and civil defence; (8) Photographs of defence establishments, installations, dockyards and factories.

29–16 In 1988 Press representatives on the Defence, Press and Broadcasting Committee expressed their concern over a number of incidents in which the Government had pursued legal action against the Press although the information in question had been referred to the secretary of the D-Notice Committee and no further action had been taken. The chairman replied to these concerns by reaffirming the Government's commitment to the D-notice system and by pointing out that questions of breaches of the duty of confidentiality owed to the Crown by members and former members of the security and intelligence services were outwith the remit of the D-Notice Committee.

29–17 The first D notice for six years was issued in December 1990 shortly before the bombing of Iraq. It requested the media not to publish any details about the theft from an RAF officer's car of a lap-top computer and classified documents containing information about the Gulf. The machine was returned to the Ministry of Defence in January, apparently by the thief, after a nationwide search. In October 1992 the Defence, Press and Broadcasting Committee announced a thorough review of the system. This was said to be as a result of Prime Minister John Major's insistence on more government openness and the end of the Cold War.

In July 1993 an update of the system was announced reducing the number of DA notices to six.

They now cover "operations, plans and capabilities", "non-nuclear weapons and operational equipment," "nuclear weapons and equipment", "cyphers and secure communications", "identification of specific installations" and "United Kingdom security and intelligence services."

D Notices were renamed DA Notices or Defence Advisory Notices, and the D-Notice Committee, the Defence Press and Broadcasting Advisory Committee.

Scots law and *Spycatcher*

-18 Ban a book and make it a best-seller: that was the bitter lesson facing the British Government as it pursued its relentless efforts through the English civil courts, and elsewhere, including New South Wales and Hongkong, in 1987 to stop publication of extracts from the book *Spycatcher* written in retirement in Australia by Peter Wright, a former MI5 officer. A more pointed lesson for Scottish journalists was the impotence of the English interim injunctions north of the Border. While the English proceedings were going through all stages to the House of Lords the book was published in the USA and copies entered Britain and were put on sale unhindered.

-19 The understandable object of the Government, through the Attorney-General, was to stop Wright's breach of a lifelong obligation of confidence which he owed it. The legal mechanisms available to it proved, however, unequal to the task outside the jurisdiction of the English courts. Scottish editors were alive to the fact that orders made by English courts did not rule in Scotland. Some of them, having taken legal advice, published extracts from the book and reports of the court proceedings in Sydney, all prohibited to English editors by interim injunctions.

-20 The House of Lords decision was intended to preserve the ban in the interests of national security, pending a full hearing of the case, and to prevent future repetition of Wright's breach of duty by other members of the British secret service. Although the Lord Advocate issued a warning that he would take proceedings in the Court of Session against any Scottish publication which breached the House of Lords ban, no action was in fact taken in the Scottish courts—tacit confirmation that the legal advice on which Scottish editors decided to publish was well founded, and a tribute to the special care taken to ensure that nothing they printed or broadcast reached across the Border.

-21 Nothing could have better illustrated the special place of Scottish editors under their separate and independent legal system. The alleged relevations made by Wright about the internal workings of MI5, and the issues raised by the efforts to have him silenced, were of undoubted public interest—having been already published in the USA and also circulating in other countries. Had he been living in the United Kingdom he could have been prosecuted under the Official Secrets Acts.

29–22   The final decision of the House of Lords on a full hearing of the case was in fact that due to extensive prior publication of the information in the book in other jurisdictions, further publication in England would not pose a threat to national security. All the injunctions were lifted and the court ruled that anyone could now publish the information.

29–23   In November 1991 the 24 judges of the European Court of Human Rights ruled unanimously that the Governnment had been in breach of the European Human Rights Convention by banning the media from publishing material from *Spycatcher* between July 1987 (when the book was published in the USA) and October 1988 (when the House of Lord lifted the injunctions). The Court upheld claims by the *Sunday Times*, *Observer* and *Guardian* that the Government had infringed Article 10 of the Convention governing freedom of expression. In assessing whether a ban had been "necessary in a democratic society" the European Court said confidentiality in *Spycatcher* had been destroyed by publication abroad. However, the European Court also decided, by a narrow majority, that the Government had not violated Article 10 when it obtained the original injunctions against publication in 1986, because at that time no information had been published in the United States.

Inside Intelligence

29–24   The case of *Lord Advocate* v. *The Scotsman Publications Ltd.* (The *Inside Intelligence* case) is the closest Scottish equivalent to *Spycatcher*. It involved a petition by the Lord Advocate for interdict against *The Scotsman* and "any other person having notice" of the interdict, to ban publication of any of the information contained in the book *Inside Intelligence*, written by former MI6 member Anthony Cavendish. The Scottish case followed the granting of an injunction in England banning further publication after extracts from the book appeared in the *Sunday Times*.

29–25   As in *Spycatcher*, the final decision of the House of Lords in *Inside Intelligence* was in favour of publication, although on different grounds. In this case, the Law Lords' decision hinged more on the fact that the Lord Advocate had failed to establish that further publication would do any significant damage to the public interest.

26   This may seem to be another victory for freedom of speech and the press, but in fact the judgments of the Lords laid down a number of categories in which the Crown could succeed in an action to restrain publication of information, provided they could fit the case into one of these categories. These include the situation where the specific information concerned is shown to pose a direct threat to national security (provided there has not been extensive prior publication) and of course the court pointed out that the chances of an interdict being granted were greater if there had been no prior publication at all.

27   As we have seen earlier in this chapter, the Official Secrets Act 1989 has now gone further in setting out the specific categories of information in which disclosure is prohibited.

28   Another important issue for the media, which was discussed in the course of *Inside Intelligence* although not decided by the House of Lords, was the scope of the interdict sought by the Crown. The Lord Advocate's attempt to gain an interdict effective against the world in general (not just *The Scotsman* but any person having notice of the interdict) was rejected by the Court of Session as contrary to Scots law. However, there was no decision on whether an action of contempt of court (rather than breach of interdict) would be available in Scotland in the case of a third party disclosing information subject to a court order banning publication. Such an order was granted by the Court of Appeal in England and approved by the House of Lords in the *Spycatcher* case and might prove persuasive in Scotland (see also Chapter 9 on Contempt of Court).

29   The ineffectiveness of an English injunction in Scotland was also underlined when the *Herald* published the contents of a confidential despatch from H.M. Ambassador to Saudi Arabia in 1986. An injunction had been granted by the English courts to prohibit publication of the despatch by the *New Statesman*, but the editor of the *Herald* took the view that the order had no application north of the Border. Similarly, *The Scotsman* published a story concerning an extra-marital affair by Liberal

Democrat leader Mr Paddy Ashdown in 1992 when an injunction existed in England banning publication of the information. Ineeed, the English injunction banned mention of the fact that the injunction existed!

29–30   In the Saudi Arabian letter case the Government did seek an interim interdict in the Court of Session against the *Herald*. However, by the time an interdict was granted by Lord Davidson at his home in the early hours of the morning, the paper was already on the streets with the despatch reproduced in full.

KEY POINTS

29–31   The Official Secrets Act 1911 makes it an offence to be in and around certain areas such as dockyards, naval or air force establishments for purposes prejudicial to the interests of the State. It is also an offence to take pictures or make sketches or notes which might be useful to an enemy.

The "catch-all" section 2 of the 1911 Act, under which a journalist risked prosecution for receiving secret information however trivial, was repealed in the 1989 Official Secrets Act. In most cases, the journalist will now be guilty of an offence only where the disclosure of specific types of classified information is damaging.

The Defence Press and Broadcasting Advisory Committee provides guidance to the media on publication of national security matters through the "DA-Notice" system. The system is voluntary and has no legal authority.

An injunction granted by the English courts is not effective in Scotland. In the *Inside Intelligence* case, the Court of Session refused to grant an interdict aimed at all sections of the media, not just the newspaper named in the court action.

However, the question of whether an action for contempt of court (rather than breach of interdict) might be brought in Scotland against a third party who disclosed information subject to a court order was not decided.

CHAPTER 30

REPORTS OF ENGLISH COMMITTAL PROCEEDINGS

01 Scots lawyers have often in the past been critical of the English system of holding a preliminary public inquiry before examining justices to decide whether or not someone should be committed for trial on an indictable offence. It was pointed out that this could result in publicity which might prejudice potential jurors against the accused. The system was contrasted with the Scottish system of private preliminary proceedings.

02 The Criminal Justice Act 1967 has introduced special rules designed to prevent prejudicial pre-trial publicity in relation to English committal proceedings. The proceedings are still generally held in public but the rules make it unlawful to publish anywhere in Great Britain a report of any committal proceedings in England and Wales if the report contains any matter other than certain permitted particulars. The prohibition ceases to apply, however, after the conclusion of the defendant's actual trial. If there are two or more defendants the prohibition normally lasts until the conclusion of the trial of the last one to be tried. However, if the magistrates proceed, during the inquiry, to try one or more of the defendants summarily (as they are entitled to do under certain statutory provisions) while committing the other defendants or any of them for trial, it is permissible to publish a report of the summary trial which includes material from the preceding committal proceedings. The purpose of this last concession is no doubt to enable newspapers to publish enough to make a report of the summary trial intelligible.

03 Should the magistrates decide not to commit the defendant(s) for trial the prohibition no longer applies. The permitted particulars, which may be included in a report even though it is published before the trial, are as follows:

(a) the identity of the court and the names of the examining justices;

(b) the names, addresses and occupations of the parties and witnesses and the ages of the defendant or defendants and witnesses;

(c) the offence or offences, or a summary of them, with which the defendant or defendants is or are charged;

(d) the names of counsel and solicitors engaged in the proceedings

(e) any decision of the court to commit the defendant or any of the defendants for trial, and any decision of the court on the disposal of the case of any defendants not committed;

(f) where the court commits the defendant for trial, the charge or charges, or a summary of them, on which he is committed and the court to which he is committed;

(g) where the committal proceedings are adjourned, the date and place to which they are adjourned;

(h) any arrangements as to bail on committal or adjournment;

(i) whether legal aid was granted to the defendant or any of the defendants.

(j) any decision of the court to lift or not to lift reporting restrictions

30–04   It will be noted that the prohibition is on publishing a report, not on making a report. It would, therefore, be possible for a Scottish newspaper to obtain a report of committal proceedings quite legitimately from an English correspondent. In such a case the newspaper would have to be careful not to publish anything other than the permitted particulars until it was lawful to do so. In the normal case this would be after the conclusion of the trial.

30–05   One effect of the Criminal Justice (Amendment) Act 1981 is that reporting restrictions are no longer automatically lifted at the request of one of several defendants. If one or more defendants object to the restrictions being lifted the court can lift them only if satisfied this is "in the interests of justice". The kind of consideration the court may have to have in mind is whether one defendant wants publicity in the hope of encouraging an important witness for his defence to come forward.

-06   The coverage of committal proceedings can be further affected by the operation of section 4(2) of the Contempt of Court Act 1981, which gives courts power to postpone publication of reports of proceedings to avoid prejudicing other proceedings which are pending or imminent. In an appeal against an order made by Horsham magistrates under the section in 1981 the English High Court ruled that magistrates must not make an order that is wider than necessary to secure the desired end, namely to prevent prejudice to the administration of justice. Holding that the magistrates' order was too wide, the court said it should have been limited to sensitive matters disclosed during the committal hearing.

-07   In February 1994 Home Secretary Michael Howard announced his intention to abolish committal hearings. He said he would table amendments to the Criminal Justice and Public Order Bill to allow cases to go straight to the Crown Court, although defendants would still be allowed to make written submissions to a magistrate that there was no case to answer.

The idea was to cut the time defendants had to wait for trial and reduce stress on victims and witnesses by avoiding the possibility of having to give evidence twice.

The decision stemmed from a recommendation of the Royal Commission on Criminal Justice in England and Wales which received evidence that most committal proceedings served little useful purpose.

CHAPTER 31

BREACH OF CONFIDENCE

31–01   Journalists should be aware of the existence of the law of confidence. The legal complexities will almost inevitably require that legal advice is taken in a case where there is a question of breach of confidence.

31–02   The law of confidence is not fully developed in Scots law, but recent events have made it clear that the law is sufficiently advanced for courts to grant remedies against journalists, when they attempt to use information which the court decides should be protected by the law of confidence. The *Spycatcher* litigation in England and the *Cavendish* litigation in Scotland both involved the law of confidence. It is commonly supposed by journalists that these cases are of limited relevance because they involved the use by journalists of material obtained by Peter Wright and Anthony Cavendish when both were working for the security services as spies.

31–03   The law of confidence is not restricted to matters involving State secrets. Nor is it restricted to cases, such as *Spycatcher* and *Cavendish*, in which the duty of confidence is owed to the Government.

31–04   In fact, the legal principles involved in these cases have a much wider application. Basically, the law protects information which is given in confidence by one person (the confider) to another (the confidant). Examples would be communication between husband and wife, employer and employee, from business to business on contractual matters and between the Government and civil servants. The obligation of confidentiality is not confined to the two parties to the confidential communication. It extends to third parties who come into possession of confidential information. As the *Cavendish* litigation made clear, the obligation will extend even to situations where the third party comes into possession of the confidential information without any positive steps on his part. The law of confidence will apply just as much to the journalist who receives the confidential information anonymously in a brown paper parcel as to the journalist who, in the course of an investigative piece of work, uncovers the confidential information by his own efforts. The law, of course, requires that there is knowledge that the material is of a confidential nature. However, it seems clear that the courts will take the view that certain material, by its very nature, must put the recipient on his guard that it is confidential. The approach the courts will take is basically a commonsense one. If, applying common sense, it is obvious that the material is of a confidential nature, then the journalist should be alert and takes a risk if he publishes without making further inquiries.

5   In England it was the law of confidence that enabled Princess Diana to obtain an injunction against the *Daily Mirror* newspaper from further publication of photographs of her working out in a health club gym in London in November 1993. It may also be possible for her to obtain damages against the *Mirror* newspaper for profits they obtained from the use of these pictures which were obtained and published in breach of the obligation of confidence which existed between the Princess and the owners and operators of the health club. The right to claim damages was affirmed in the *Spycatcher* litigation by the House of Lords where it awarded damages to the Attorney-General against *The Times* newspaper for the profits that newspaper obtained by increased circulation when it published part of Peter Wright's book.

6   Similarly, in Scotland, the parents of the children removed by the Social Work Department from Orkney had been successful in November 1992 in obtaining an interim interdict in the Court of Session against the BBC "Panorama" programme from using tapes of the disclosure sessions between the children and officials of the Royal Scottish Society for the Prevention of Cruelty to Children. The interim interdict was granted by Lord Cameron, despite the fact that the BBC had given an undertaking that the children could not be seen in the interview and their voices would be disguised.

7   The law of confidence is presently a developing area, particularly in view of the courts' current interest in protecting the privacy of private citizens. On the other hand, it is clearly part of the journalists' trade to make some material public

despite the fact that it was communicated in confidence. For example, journalists would hardly be doing their work properly if they failed to expose wrongdoings simply because the communication between the wrongdoers was confidential.

31–08   Generally speaking, the law of confidence allows the parties to the confidential communication to ask the court to grant an interim interdict against publications of the confidential information. If there are counterbalancing interests such as the public interest in being informed on certain matters then journalists can, quite properly, have their legal representatives make these points in court.

31–09   Journalists should be mindful of the fact that although public interest may well provide a defence to an action of breach of confidence, the courts define "public interest" in a way quite different from that of journalists. Judges have repeatedly told the Press that public interest in law does not mean *that in which the public has an interest*. For example, there might be a wide (prurient) interest amongst the public at large in seeing the pictures of Princess Diana in the gym. But in law, that sort of interest is not deemed to be the public interest. In law, the public interest in this context is confined to the likes of exposure of fraudulent activity, discovery of a crime or revelation of political hypocrisy.

31–10   It is suggested that, particularly where sensitive commercial information comes into the hands of journalists, they would be wise to seek legal advice as to the remedies which might be sought by confider/confidant as the publication of such information could open the door to claims for substantial damages.

31–11   The courts will apply the balance of convenience test in cases involving the law of confidence. The pursuer need only show that he has a *prima facie* case against the defender and that the balance of convenience favours an interim interdict being granted.

31–12   This is a lower test than that applied by the courts in the law of libel. There, the courts are more likely to permit publication on the premise that damages can correct most defamatory publications. In cases involving confidential information, however, it is of the essence that damage will be done if the information is made public. The mere fact of publication means that the information loses its confidential quality. A

Judge may well feel that damages would be an inadequate remedy for a breach of confidence.

–13   Journalists are only too aware of the fact that although an interim interdict can be overturned once the court has heard all the evidence, that this will usually be of no comfort as the newsworthiness of the material will not endure until the court hears the evidence (this can be a year or two later). So victory at the interim stage is vital for the media. For this reason journalists should be mindful of the fact that the standard the courts will apply when considering an application for interim interdict in confidence cases is lower than in defamation cases.

KEY POINTS

Material passing between individuals (including corporate individuals) who owe a duty of confidence to each other will still have the quality of confidence if it comes into the hands of the journalist as third party. To use such information is a breach of confidence and can give rise to an application to the court by one of the original parties to the confidential communication for interdict preventing publication. An action for damages to recover any profits received from a publication made in breach of confidence could follow.

CONTEMPT OF COURT ACT 1981

Strict liability

1. In this Act "the strict liability rule" means the rule of law whereby conduct may be treated as a contempt of court as tending to interfere with the course of justice in particular legal proceedings regardless of intent to do so.

2.—(1) The strict liability rule applies only in relation to publications, and for this purpose "publication" includes any speech, writing, broadcast or other communication in whatever form, which is addressed to the public at large or any section of the public.

(2) The strict liability rule applies only to a publication which creates a substantial risk that the course of justice in the proceedings in question will be seriously impeded or prejudiced.

(3) The strict liability rule applies to a publication only if the proceedings in question are active within the meaning of this section at the time of the publication.

(4) Schedule 1 applies for determining the times at which proceedings are to be treated as active within the meaning of this section.

3.—(1) A person is not guilty of contempt of court under the strict liability rule as the publisher of any matter to which that rule applies if at the time of publication (having taken all reasonable care) he does not know and has no reason to suspect that relevant proceedings are active.

(2) A person is not guilty of contempt of court under the strict liability rule as the distributor of a publication containing any such matter if at the time of distribution (having taken all reasonable care) he does not know that it contains such matter and has no reason to suspect that it is likely to do so.

(3) The burden of proof of any fact tending to establish a defence afforded by this section to any person lies upon that person.

(4) Section 11 of the Administration of Justice Act 1960 is repealed.

4.—(1) Subject to this section a person is not guilty of contempt of court under the strict liability rule in respect of a fair and accurate report of legal proceedings held in public, published contemporaneously and in good faith.

(2) In any such proceedings the court may, where it appears to be necessary for avoiding a substantial risk of prejudice to the administration of justice in those proceedings, or in any other proceedings pending or imminent, order that the publication of any report of the proceedings, or any part of the proceedings, be postponed for such period as the court thinks necessary for that purpose.

(3) For the purposes of subsection (1) of this section and of section 3 of the Law of Libel Amendment Act 1888 (privilege) a report of proceedings shall be treated as published contemporaneously—

    (a) in the case of a report of which publication is postponed pursuant to an order under subsection (2) of this section, if published as soon as practicable after that order expires;

    (b) in the case of a report of committal proceedings of which publication is permitted by virtue only of subsection (3) of section 8 of the Magistrates' Courts Act 1980, if published as soon as practicable after publication is so permitted.

(4) Subsection (9) of the said section 8 is repealed.

5. A publication made as or as part of a discussion in good faith of public affairs or other matters of general public interest is not to be treated as a contempt of court under the strict liability rule if the risk of impediment or prejudice to particular legal proceedings is merely incidental to the discussion.

6. Nothing in the foregoing provisions of this Act—

    (a) prejudices any defence available at common law to a charge of contempt of court under the strict liability rule;

    (b) implies that any publication is punishable as contempt of court under that rule which would not be so punishable apart from those provisions;

    (c) restricts liability for contempt of court in respect of

conduct intended to impede or prejudice the administration of justice.

. . . . .

Other aspects of law and procedure

8.—(1) Subject to subsection (2) below, it is a contempt of court to obtain, disclose or solicit any particulars of statements made, opinions expressed, arguments advanced or votes cast by members of a jury in the course of their deliberations in any legal proceedings.

(2) This section does not apply to any disclosure of any particulars—

(a) in the proceedings in question for the purpose of enabling the jury to arrive at their verdict, or in connection with the delivery of that verdict, or

(b) in evidence in any subsequent proceedings for an offence alleged to have been committed in relation to the jury in the first mentioned proceedings,

or the publication of any particulars so disclosed.

9.—(1) Subject to subsection (4) below, it is a contempt of court—

(a) to use in court, or bring into court for use, any tape recorder or other instrument for recording sound, except with the leave of the court;

(b) to publish a recording of legal proceedings made by means of any such instrument, or any recording derived directly or indirectly from it, by playing it in the hearing of the public or any section of the public, or to dispose of it or any recording so derived, with a view to such publication;

(c) to use any such recording in contravention of any conditions of leave granted under paragraph (a).

(2) Leave under paragraph (a) of subsection (1) may be granted or refused at the discretion of the court, and if granted may be granted subject to such conditions as the court thinks proper with respect to the use of any recording made pursuant to the leave; and where leave has been granted the court may at the like discretion withdraw or amend it either generally or in relation to any particular part of the proceedings.

(3) Without prejudice to any other power to deal with an act

of contempt under paragraph (a) of subsection (1), the court may order the instrument, or any recording made with it, or both, to be forfeited; and any object so forfeited shall (unless the court otherwise determines on application by a person appearing to be the owner) be sold or otherwise disposed of in such manner as the court may direct.

(4) This section does not apply to the making or use of sound recordings for purposes of official transcripts of proceedings.

10. No court may require a person to disclose, nor is any person guilty of contempt of court for refusing to disclose, the source of information contained in a publication for which he is responsible, unless it be established to the satisfaction of the court that disclosure is necessary in the interests of justice or national security or for the prevention of disorder or crime.

11. In any case where a court (having power to do so) allows a name or other matter to be withheld from the public in proceedings before the court, the court may give such directions prohibiting the publication of that name or matter in connection with the proceedings as appear to the court to be necessary for the purpose for which it was so withheld.

. . . . .

13. . . . . (4) In any case where a person is liable to be dealt with for contempt of court during the course of or in connection with Scottish proceedings he may be given legal aid, and the Legal Aid (Scotland) Act 1967 shall have effect subject to the amendments set out in Part II of Schedule 2.

(5) This section is without prejudice to any other enactment by virtue of which legal aid may be granted in or for purposes of civil or criminal proceedings.

Penalties for contempt and kindred offences

. . . . .

15.—(1) In Scottish proceedings, when a person is committed to prison for contempt of court the committal shall (without prejudice to the power of the court to order his earlier discharge) be for a fixed term.

(2) The maximum penalty which may be imposed by way of imprisonment or fine for contempt of court in Scottish proceedings shall be two years' imprisonment or a fine or both, except that—

    (a) where the contempt is dealt with by the sheriff in the course of or in connection with proceedings other than criminal proceedings on indictment, such penalty shall not exceed three months' imprisonment or a fine of level 4 on the standard scale or both; and

    (b) where the contempt is dealt with by the district court, such penalty shall not exceed sixty days' imprisonment or a fine of level 3 on the standard scale or both.

(3) Section 207 (restriction on detention of young offenders) and sections 175 to 178 (persons suffering from mental disorder) of the Criminal Procedure (Scotland) Act 1975 shall apply in relation to persons found guilty of contempt of court in Scottish proceedings as they would apply in relation to persons convicted of offences, except—

    (a) where subsection (2)(a) applies, when sections 415 and 376 to 379 of the said Act shall so apply; and

    (b) where subsection (2)(b) above applies, when section 415 of the said Act and subsection (5) below shall apply.

(4) Until the commencement of section 45 of the Criminal Justice (Scotland) Act 1980, in subsection (3) above for the references to section 207 and section 415 of the Criminal Procedure (Scotland) Act 1975 there shall be substituted respectively references to sections 207 and 208 and sections 415 and 416 of that Act.

(5) Where a person is found guilty by a district court of contempt of court and it appears to the court that he may be suffering from mental disorder, it shall remit him to the sheriff in the manner provided by section 286 of the Criminal Procedure (Scotland) Act 1975 and the sheriff shall, on such remit being made, have the like power to make an order under section 376(1) of the said Act in respect of him as if he had been convicted by the sheriff of an offence, or in dealing with him may exercise the like powers as the court making the remit.

. . . . .

Supplemental

. . . . .

19. In this Act—

"court" includes any tribunal or body exercising the judicial power of the State, and "legal proceedings" shall be construed accordingly;

"publication" has the meaning assigned by subsection (1) of section 2, and "publish" (except in section 9) shall be construed accordingly;

"Scottish proceedings" means proceedings before any court, including the Courts-Martial Appeal Court, the Restrictive Practices Court and the Employment Appeal Tribunal, sitting in Scotland, and includes proceedings before the House of Lords in the exercise of any appellate jurisdiction over proceedings in such a court;

"the strict liability rule" has the meaning assigned by section 1;

"superior court" means the Court of Appeal, the High Court, the Crown Court, the Courts-Martial Appeal Court, the Restrictive Practices Court, the Employment Appeal Tribunal and any other court exercising in relation to its proceedings powers equivalent to those of the High Court, and includes the House of Lords in the exercise of its appellate jurisdiction.

20.—(1) In relation to any tribunal to which the Tribunals of Inquiry (Evidence) Act 1921 applies, and the proceedings of such a tribunal, the provisions of this Act (except subsection (3) of section 9) apply as they apply in relation to courts and legal proceedings; and references to the course of justice or the administration of justice in legal proceedings shall be construed accordingly.

(2) The proceedings of a tribunal established under the said Act shall be treated as active within the meaning of section 2 from the time when the tribunal is appointed until its report is presented to Parliament.

. . . . .

SCHEDULE 1

1. In this Schedule "criminal proceedings" means proceedings against a person in respect of an offence, not being appellate proceedings . . .; and "appellate proceedings" means proceedings on appeal from or for the review of the decision of a court in any proceedings.

2. Criminal, appellate and other proceedings are active within the meaning of section 2 at the times respectively prescribed by the following paragraphs of this Schedule; and in relation to proceedings in which more than one of the steps described in any of those paragraphs is taken, the reference in that paragraph is a reference to the first of those steps.

Criminal proceedings

3. Subject to the following provisions of this Schedule, criminal proceedings are active from the relevant initial step specified in paragraph 4 until concluded as described in paragraph 5.

4. The initial steps of criminal proceedings are—
- (a) arrest without warrant;
- (b) the issue, or in Scotland the grant, of a warrant for arrest;
- (c) the issue of a summons to appear, or in Scotland the grant of a warrant to cite;
- (d) the service of an indictment or other document specifying the charge;

. . . . .

5. Criminal proceedings are concluded—
- (a) by acquittal or, as the case may be, by sentence;
- (b) by any other verdict, finding, order or decision which puts an end to the proceedings;
- (c) by discontinuance or by operation of law.

6. The reference in paragraph 5(a) to sentence includes any order or decision consequent on conviction or finding of guilt which disposes of the case, either abolutely or subject to future events, and a deferment of sentence under section . . . 219 or 432 of the Criminal Procedure (Scotland) Act 1975 . . .

7. Proceedings are discontinued within the meaning of paragraph 5(c)—

. . . . .

- (b) in Scotland if the proceedings are expressly abandoned by the prosecutor or are deserted *simpliciter*;

. . . . .

8. Criminal proceedings before a court-martial or standing civilian court are not concluded until the completion of any review of finding or sentence.

. . . . .

10. Without prejudice to paragraph 5(b) above, criminal proceedings against a person cease to be active—

>   (a) if the accused is found to be under a disability such as to render him unfit to be tried or unfit to plead or, in Scotland, is found to be insane in bar of trial; or
>
>   (b) . . ., in Scotland where a transfer order ceases to have effect by virtue of section 73(1) of the Mental Health (Scotland) Act 1984,

but become active again if they are later resumed.

11. Criminal proceedings against a person which become active on the issue or the grant of a warrant for his arrest cease to be active at the end of the period of twelve months beginning with the date of the warrant unless he has been arrested within that period, but become active again if he is subsequently arrested.

Other proceedings at first instance

12. Proceedings other than criminal proceedings and appellate proceedings are active from the time when arrangements for the hearing are made or, if no such arrangements are previously made, from the time the hearing begins, until the proceedings are disposed of or discontinued or withdrawn; and for the purposes of this paragraph any motion or application made in or for the purposes of any proceedings, and any pre-trial review in the county court, is to be treated as a distinct proceeding.

. . . . .

14. In Scotland arrangements for the hearing of proceedings to which paragraph 12 applies are made within the meaning of that paragraph—

>   (a) in the case of an ordinary action in the Court of Session or in the sheriff court, when the Record is closed;
>
>   (b) in the case of a motion or application, when it is enrolled or made;
>
>   (c) in any other case, when the date for a hearing is fixed or a hearing is allowed.

Appellate proceedings

15. Appellate proceedings are active from the time when they are commenced—
>   (a) by application for leave to appeal or apply for review, or by notice of such an application;
>   (b) by notice of appeal or of application for review;
>   (c) by other originating process,

until disposed of or abandoned, discontinued or withdrawn.

16. Where, in appellate proceedings relating to criminal proceedings, the court—
>   (a) remits the case to the court below; or
>   (b) orders a new trial or a *venire de novo*, or in Scotland grants authority to bring a new prosecution,

any further or new proceedings which result shall be treated as active from the conclusion of the appellate proceedings.

CODE OF PRACTICE

The Press Complaints Commission is charged with enforcing the following Code of Practice which was framed by the newspaper and periodical industry and ratified by the Press Complaints Commission in April 1994.

All members of the press have a duty to maintain the highest professional and ethical standards. In doing so, they should have regard to the provisions of this Code of Practice and to safeguarding the public's right to know.

Editors are responsible for the actions of journalists employed by their publications. They should also satisfy themselves as far as possible that material accepted from non-staff members was obtained in accordance with this Code.

While recognising that this involves a substantial element of self-restraint by editors and journalists, it is designed to be acceptable in the context of a system of self-regulation. The Code applies in the spirit as well as in the letter.

It is the responsibility of editors to co-operate as swiftly as possible in PCC enquiries.

Any publication which is criticised by the PCC under one of the following clauses is duty bound to print the adjudication which follows in full and with due prominence.

---

1. Accuracy

i) Newspapers and periodicals should take care not to publish inaccurate, misleading or distorted material.

ii) Whenever it is recognised that a significant inaccuracy, misleading statement or distorted report has been published, it should be corrected promptly and with due prominence.

iii) An apology should be

published whenever appropriate.

iv) A newspaper or periodical should always report fairly and accurately the outcome of an action for defamation to which it has been a party.

2. Opportunity to reply

A fair opportunity for reply to inaccuracies should be given to individuals or organisations when reasonably called for.

3. Comment, conjecture and fact

Newspapers, whilst free to be partisan, should distinguish clearly between comment, conjecture and fact.

4. Privacy

Intrusions and enquiries into an individual's private life without his or her consent including the use of long-lens photography to take pictures of people on private property without their consent are not generally acceptable and publication can only be justified when in the public interest.

Note—Private property is defined as any private residence, together with its garden and outbuildings, but excluding any adjacent fields or parkland. In addition, hotel bedrooms (but not other areas in a hotel) and those parts of a hospital or nursing home where patients are treated or accommodated.

5. Listening devices

Unless justified by public interest, journalists should not obtain or publish material obtained by using clandestine listening devices or by intercepting private telephone conversations.

6. Hospitals

i) Journalists or photographers making enquiries at hospitals or similar institutions should identify themselves to a responsible executive and obtain permission before entering non-public areas.

ii) The restrictions on intruding into privacy are particularly relevant to enquiries about individuals in hospital or similar institutions.

7. Misrepresentation

i) Journalists should not generally obtain or seek to obtain information or pictures through misrepresentation or subterfuge.

ii) Unless in the public interest, documents or photographs should be removed only with the express consent of the owner.

iii) Subterfuge can be justified only in the public interest and only when material cannot be obtained by any other means.

8. Harassment

i) Journalists should neither obtain nor seek to obtain information or pictures through intimidation or harassment.

ii) Unless their enquiries are in the public interest, journalists should not photograph individuals on private property (as defined in the note to Clause 4) without their consent; should not persist in telephoning or questioning individuals after having been asked to desist; should not remain on their property after having been asked to leave and should not follow them.

iii) It is the responsibility of editors to ensure that these requirements are carried out.

9. Payment for articles

Payment or offers of payment for stories, pictures or information, should not be made directly or through agents to witnesses or potential witnesses in current criminal proceedings or to people engaged in crime or to their associates—which includes family, friends, neighbours and colleagues—except where the material concerned ought to be published in the public interest and the payment is necessary for this to be done.

10. Intrusion into grief or shock

In cases involving personal grief or shock, enquires should be carried out and approaches made with sympathy and discretion.

11. Innocent relatives and friends

Unless it is contrary to the public's right to know, the press should generally avoid identifying relatives or friends of persons convicted or accused or crime.

12. Interviewing or photographing children

i) Journalists should not normally interview or

photograph children under the age of 16 on subjects involving the personal welfare of the child, in the absence of or without the consent of a parent or other adult who is responsible for the children.

ii) Children should not be approached or photographed while at school without the permission of the school authorities.

13. Children in sex cases

1) The press should not, even where the law does not prohibit it, identify children under the age of 16 who are involved in cases concerning sexual offences, whether as victims, or as witnesses or defendants.

2) In any press report of a case involving a sexual offence against a child—

i) The adult may be identified.

ii) The term "incest" where applicable should not be used.

iii) The offence should be described as "serious offences against young children" or similar appropriate wording.

iv) The child should not be identified.

v) Care should be taken that nothing in the report implies the relationship between the accused and the child.

14. Victims or crime

The press should not identify victims of sexual assault or publish material likely to contribute to such identification unless, by law, they are free to do so.

15. Discrimination

i) The press should avoid prejudicial or pejorative reference to a person's race, colour, religion, sex or sexual orientation or to any physical or mental illness or handicap.

ii) It should avoid publishing details of a person's race, colour, religion, sex or sexual orientation, unless these are directly relevant to the story.

16. Financial journalism

i) Even where the law does not prohibit it, journalists should not use for their own profit, financial information they receive in advance of its general publication, nor should they pass such information to others.

ii) They should not write about shares or securities in whose performance they know that they or their close families have a significant financial interest, without disclosing the interest to the editor or financial editor.

iii) They should not buy or sell, either directly or through nominees or agents, shares or securities about which they have written recently or about which they intend to write in the near future.

17. Confidential sources

Journalists have a moral obligation to protect confidential sources of information.

18. The public interest

Clauses 4, 5, 7, 8 and 9 create exceptions which may be covered by invoking the public interest. For the purposes of this code that is most easily defined as:

i) Detecting or exposing crime or a serious misdemeanour.

ii) Protecting public health and safety.

iii) Preventing the public from being misled by some statement or action of an individual or organisation.

In any cases raising issues beyond these three definitions the Press Complaints Commission will require a full explanation by the editor of the publication involved, seeking to demonstrate how the public interest was served.

Comments or suggestions regarding the content of the Code may be sent to the Secretary, Press Standards Board of Finance, Merchants House Buildings, 30 George Square, Glasgow G2 1EG, to be laid before the industry's Code Committee

Sept 94

Ab ante	before, previously
ab initio	from the beginning
absolvitor	decree absolving defender
actus Dei	act of God
ad factum praestandum	obligation to perform an act other than payment of money
adhere	(court) affirm; (spouse) live with
ad hoc	for this purpose
ad interim	in the interval; meantime
Adjournal, Acts of	procedural rules made by High Court
ad litem	as regards the action
adminicle	piece of supporting evidence
ad valorem	according to value
advise	give judgment
advocation	form of criminal appeal usually by prosecution at preliminary stage
a fortiori	all the more
agnate	related through father
alibi	elsewhere (special defence plea)
aliment	maintenance enforceable by law
aliquot	integral factor
aliunde	from a different source
a mensa et thoro	from bed and table (separation)
ante omnia	first of all
apparent insolvency	insolvency which has become public
a posteriori	reasoning from effect to cause
appoint	to order, direct
a priori	reasoning from cause to effect
arbiter	one chosen by parties to settle difference (in England—arbitrator)
as accords (of law)	in conformity with the law

assize	jury
assoilzie (z silent)	absolve
aver	to state in written pleadings
a verbis legis non est recedendum	the words of a statute must be strictly adhered to
avizandum	to be considered (reserved judgment)
Back letter	document qualifying another which purports to give an absolute right
bairns' part of gear	(see legitim)
barratry	acceptance of bribes by a judge
before answer (allowance of proof)	before the law of the case is determined
bill of suspension	form of appeal to Justiciary Appeal Court
bona fide	in good faith
brevi manu	short cut; summarily
brutum fulmen	harmless thunderbolt; vain attack
Calling	first step in civil action
calumny, oath of	formerly oath (in divorce cases) that facts pleaded are believed to be true
Candlemas	February 2, quarter-day
casual homicide	blameless killing
caution (pronounced "cay-shun")	security
caveat	"let him take care"; legal document lodged by part to ensure no order passes against him in his absence
certiorate	give formal notice of a fact
champerty	offence of assisting a party in a suit without having an interest except to share in any pecuniary outcome
circumvention	dishonest taking advantage of a facile person for gain
cite	to summon to court
cognate	related through mother

commit	consign to prison to await further procedure
compear	to appear and participate in an action
compos mentis	of sound mind
conclusion	relief sought in an action
condescendence	statement of averred facts or contentions
conditio si testator sine liberis decesserit	principle by which a will not dealing with children is revoked by birth of a child
consanguinean	relationship between brothers or sisters who have the same father but different mothers
consistorial	relating to questions of status, such as matrimonial proceedings
continue	adjourn (case) to later date
contra bonos mores	in breach of moral law
contumacy	failure to obey court order
courtesy	widower's liferent of his wife's heritage (now obsolete)
crave	formally ask court (as in petition)
curator ad litem	officer appointed by court to assume responsibility for interests of litigant
curator bonis	officer appointed by court to manage a person's estate
cy-près	as near as possible (applied to necessary variation of terms of trust, will, etc.)
Damnum	harm, loss
damnum fatale	loss due to act of God
data	statements acknowledged as true
decern	give formal, final decree
declarator	binding statement of rights of a party issued by court
declinature	refusal of judge to take jurisdiction because of his interest or relationship

de die in diem	from day to day
de facto	in point of fact; actual
deforcement	offence of resisting officer of law to prevent him carrying out his duties
de futuro	in the future
de jure	in point of law; legal (as opposed to actual)
delectus personae	choice of person who is thereby excluded from delegating his duty
delict	a wrong
de minimis (non curat lex)	the law ignores trifles
de novo	of new; afresh
de plano	summarily; simply; without further procedure
de presenti	now
desert	to abandon (diet)
design	to set forth person's occupation and address
dies non	a non-legal day
diet	date fixed for a hearing of a case
diligence	execution against a debtor; procedure for recovery of document
disentail	release from entail (q.v.)
dispone	to convey (land)
DA-notice	Defence Advisory (see Chapter 29)
dominus litis	person controlling lawsuit who is not actually a party to it
Edictal citation	method of citing persons who are furth of Scotland or sheriffdom
effeir	to correspond, appertain
embracery	attempt to corrupt a jury, or acceptance of bribe by juror
entail	restriction of heritage to prescribed line of heirs (incompetent since 1914)
eo ipso	by the thing itself

ergo	therefore
error calculi	error in calculation
escheat	forfeiture of a person's estate
esto	assuming; let it be assumed
ex adverso	opposite to; adjacent
ex animo	willingly; intentionally
excambion	contract for exchange of one piece of land for another
ex concesso	from what has been admitted
executor-dative	executor appointed by court
executor-nominate	executor appointed by testator
ex facie	on the face of it
ex hypothesis	by the hypothesis
ex justa causa	for just cause or sufficient reason
ex officio	by virtue of office
ex parte	in absence of a party; one-sided; partisan
expenses	payment for legal services (in England—costs)
expose	put up for sale
ex post facto	after the event; retrospectively
ex proprio motu	on (the court's) own initiative
ex re	arising in the circumstances
ex tempore	without premeditation
extract	authenticated copy of decree, etc.
Facsimile	exact copy
fee	full right of property (as opposed to liferent, *q.v.*)
fiar	owner of a fee
fiars (prices)	average prices of grain fixed annually to determine ministers' stipends
filiation	determination by court of paternity
force and fear	duress vitiating a contract
force majeure	something beyond the control of man; that cannot be prevented
forisfamiliation	departure of child from family on becoming independent
forum (or fora)	platform; court; tribunal

fugitation	outlawry
fulmen brutum	vain threat
fund in medio	amount under dispute in action of multiplepoinding (*q.v.*)
furtum grave	theft which formerly merited death penalty
furth	outside (*e.g.* the country)
Garnishment	order not to pay creditor(s) before first settling debt to third party holding judgment against his creditors
gift	bequest
glebe	land in parish to which minister has right apart from stipend
grassum	single payment made in addition to periodic one, such as rent
Habeas corpus	writ releasing person from prison (English law)
habile	apt
habit and repute	reputation of being married without formal ceremony, entitling parties to declarator of marriage
hamesucken	assault upon man in his own home
haver	person holding documents he is required to produce in court
heritage	land and buildings passing to an heir on owner's death
holograph	wholly handwritten and signed by the author
homologate	approve and thereby validate
horning	ancient procedure for public denunciation of a debtor
hypothec	security for debt, such as right of landlord over tenant's goods in premises let to him
Impeachment	special defence accusing another of the crime charged (known also as incrimination)

impetrate	procure, to another's prejudice
in camera	behind closed doors
in causa	in the case (of)
incompetent	in conflict with the law applicable
indictment	accusation of a crime made in name of Lord Advocate
induciae	time limit
in extenso	in full
in faciendo	in doing
in favorem	in favour
infeft	having a feudal title to heritage
in forma pauperis	in the character of a pauper
in foro	in court
in futuro	in the future
in gremio	in the body (of a deed etc.)
in hoc statu	at this stage; in the present state of affairs
in initio litis	at the outset of the action
in jure	in right
in limine	at the outset (threshold)
in litem	in the case
in loco parentis	in the place of a parent (*e.g.* guardian)
in mala fides	in bad faith
Inner House	appellate department of Court of Session comprising First and Second Divisions
in re	in the case of
in rem suam	in one's own affairs
in rem versum	to one's own account
in retentis	kept for the record
in solidum	for the whole sum
instruct	to vouch or support
inter alia	among other things
inter alios	among other persons
interdict	judicial prohibition (in England—injunction)
interlocutor	formal minute of court decision
interpone authority to joint minute	give court's approval to agreement between parties

interrogatories	written questions put to witness excused from attending court
in toto	totally
inter vivos	between living persons (with reference to deeds)
intromit	to handle, deal with, funds, property, etc.
ipse dixit	bare assertion
ipso facto	by the fact itself
ipso jure	by the force of law alone
irritancy	forfeiture of a right due to neglect or contravention (*e.g.* lease)
irrelevant	even if proved, would not justify remedy sought
ish	termination, usually of lease
Judicial factor	person appointed by court to manage affairs of another
jus mariti	right of husband to part of wife's moveable property (now abolished)
jus quaesitum tertio	contractual right of a person arising out of a contract between two others to which he is not a party
jus relictae	widow's right to share of husband's moveable property
jus relicti	widower's right to share of wife's moveable property
jus tertii	right of a third party
Justiciar	ancient term for Lord Justice-General
justifiable homicide	killing in exercise of public duty
justo tempore	in due time
Lammas	August 1, quarter-day
lawburrows	ancient process for security against apprehended molestation
legitim	children's right to share of parent's moveable property at death

legitimation per subsequens matrimonium	rendering child legitimate by subsequent marriage of parents
lenocinium	procuring by husband of his wife's adultery
lesion	detriment, loss, injury
lex loci contractus	law of the place where contract was made
lex patriae	law of one's own country
lien	right to retain property of a debtor until he pays
liferent	right entitling a person for life to use of another's property
light	property owner's obligation not to obstruct neighbour's light
liquid (sum)	of ascertained amount
List D	category of school which replaced "special" school
loco parentis, in	in the place of a parent (*e.g.* guardian)
locus	place
locus standi	right to be heard in court
Mala fides	bad faith
mala in se	bad in itself
Martinmas	November 11 or 28, quarter-day
medio tempore	in the meantime
medium concludendi	ground of action
medium filum	centre line of river
minute	document by which party defines his position to the court
misfeasance	doing of an act in an unlawful manner
missives	writings exchanged by parties negotiating for a contract
modus	mode, manner
Moorov doctrine	the principle that, where an accused is charged with a series of similar offences closely linked in time and circumstances, the evidence of

	one witness as to each offence will be taken as mutually corroborative
mora	delay in making claim
mortis causa	to take effect after death
muirburn	seasonal burning of heather
multiplepoinding	action raised nominally by one party but in which a number of conflicting claims are made to a fund in medio
murmur (a judge)	to slander him
Necessitas juris	by necessity of law
nemo	no one
next-of-kin	relatives entitled to succeed to moveable property under common law
nihil novit	he knows nothing
nobile officium	equitable jurisdiction of High Court of Justiciary or Inner House of Court of Session by which strictness of common law may be mitigated, or a remedy given where not otherwise available
nolle prosequi	decision by prosecutor to stop proceedings
nomine damni	in name of damages
nominal raiser	holder of fund in a multiplepoinding when another initiates proceedings
non compos mentis	not of sound mind
non constat	it is not evident, not agreed
nonfeasance	omission to do a legal duty
notour bankruptcy	insolvency which has become public, a prerequisite in most cases of sequestration now, apparent insolvency
Obiter dictum	judge's expression of an opinion not forming part of court's decision

obtemper	obey (court order)
onerous	granted for value
onus	burden (*e.g.* of proving case)
oppression	use of office or process of law to commit injustice
Outer House	department of Court of Session exercising jurisdiction of first instance
outputter	one who passes counterfeit coins
Pactum illicitum	unlawful contract
panel, pannel	prisoner at bar
paraphernalia	woman's clothes and adornments which remained her own on marriage (obsolete)
pari passu	share and share alike; side by side
parole (evidence)	oral (term borrowed from England)
particeps criminis	accomplice
patrimonial	pertaining to property; pecuniary
party-minuter	party entering proceedings by lodging a minute
penal action	one in which not only damages are sought, but also a sum as penalty
per capita	divided equally among persons
per incuriam	by mistake
per se	of itself; by himself
per stirpes	division among children of the shares that would have been their parents' (as opposed to per capita)
plagium	child-stealing
poind (pronounced "pind")	to take debtor's moveable property by way of execution
praepositura	wife's implied agency to purchase household supplies on husband's credit (obsolete)
precognition	statement from witness of evidence he is prepared to give

prescription	restriction of a right owing to passage of a specific period of time
prima facie	at first sight
primo loco	in the first place
probable cause	case satisfactory on the face of it
probative document	one which by its nature appears to afford proof of its contents
process	documentary course of an action from first step to final judgment
pro confesso	as if conceded
pro forma	as a mere formality
pro hac vice	for this occasion
pro indiviso	undivided
pro loco et tempore	for the place and time
proof	hearing of evidence by a judge
pro rata	proportionately
prorogate	extend time allowed; or submit to court's jurisdiction
pro tanto	to that extent
pro tempore	for the time being
protestation	procedure whereby defender compels pursuer to proceed with his case or end it
prout de jure	by all the means known to the law
pro veritate	as if true
punctum temporis	point of time
Quantum lucratus	as much as he has profited
quantum meruit	as much as he has earned; what is due
quantum valeat	for what it is worth
Queen's and Lord Treasurer's Remembrancer	administrator of Crown revenues in Scotland
quid pro quo	exchange of equivalents
quoad ultra	otherwise; with regard to other matters
Rank	to admit a claimant to his rightful place (*e.g.* in multiplepoinding)

ratio decidendi	line of reasoning; basis of judgment
real raiser	party who, holding fund in medio, initiates action of multiplepoinding
reclaim	to appeal to Inner House of Court of Session against Outer House judgment
record	statement by parties to an action of their claims and answers; document containing these
reduce	annul; rescind; set aside (by action of reduction)
regalia majora	Crown rights, *e.g.* to hold seashore in trust for public (inalienable)
regalia minora	Crown rights, such as salmon fishing, which may be subject of grant
rei interventus	rule barring a party, who knowingly permits another to depart from form, to challenge the resulting contract
relevant	applied to case where, if facts stated are proved, pursuer would be entitled to remedy he seeks
relocation	re-letting
repel	reject (a plea or objection)
repone	to restore a party as a litigant
res gestae	things done
res judicata	matter already judicially decided
res noviter	information newly discovered
res publicae	things owned by the state
resting-owing	unpaid (debt)
respondentia	money lent on ship's cargo subject to certain conditions
review	revision by appeal court
rider	addition by jury to its verdict; claim lodged in multiplepoinding

rolls	list of cases to be heard in court
roup	auction
rubric	head-note; summary given at head of law report
Saevitia	legal cruelty (obsolete)
sanctuary	protection against claims once enjoyed by debtor (*e.g.* by taking refuge in Holyrood Abbey)
sasine	a putting into possession of land
scienter	knowledge of animal's dangerous tendency
Sederunt, Acts of	procedural rules made by Court of Session
separatim	separately
sequestrate	render bankrupt (strictly it is the estate which is sequestrated)
seriatim	singly, in regular order
serve	to deliver (a court document)
servitude	burden or obligation on a piece of land
simpliciter	simply, absolutely, without qualification
sine die	without a date being fixed
sine qua non	indispensable condition
Single Bill	motion in the Inner House of the Court of Session
singular successor	person obtaining property otherwise than as heir
sist	to stay or stop a process; to summon or call a party
sleep	a civil action may fall asleep after a year without any step of procedure being taken; it may be revived by a minute of wakening
socius criminis	accomplice in a crime
solatium	damages for injured feelings, grief, pain
solum	ground, foundation, bed of river

special case	method of obtaining legal opinion of Inner House of Court of Session where facts are agreed
spei emptio	purchase of a chance (*e.g.* succession)
spes successionis	hope of succession (as heir apparent)
status	standing, rank
status quo	existing situation
subjects	property, usually heritable
subpoena	under penalty
sui generis	of its own kind
summons	court writ bearing royal mandate; document served on defender by which pursuer initiates civil action
superior	grantor of a feu
supersede	postpone
superinduction	unwarranted alteration of a deed
supra	above
suspension	stay of diligence
Tacit relocation	implied re-letting
taciturnity	keeping silent about a debt leading to inference of payment
tailzie (z silent)	entail (*q.v.*)
teind	tithe, tenth part of annual produce of land
tender	offer in settlement made by defender to pursuer
tenor, proving the	establishing the effect of a document (*e.g.* will) the principal copy of which has been lost
terce	widow's liferent of one-third of husband's heritage (abolished)
thole an assize	undergo trial, after which no further trial on same charge may take place
tinsel of feu	forfeiture for non-payment of feu duty

title to sue	legal right to bring an action
tocher	dowry
trepass	temporary intrusion on land without owner's consent or permission
trial	hearing of a case before a jury
Truck Acts	legislation limiting payment of wages in kind (now repealed)
tutor	guardian of child
Ultimus haeres	last heir (the Crown), to whom estate falls when all other claims fail
ultra valorem	beyond the value
ultra vires	beyond (one's legal) powers
unum quid	one thing; single unit
upset price	price at which property is exposed for sale by auction
uterine	born of same mother but different father
utter	to put false writing or currency into circulation
Veritas	truth (defence to action of slander)
vice versa	conversely
vis et metus	force and fear (*q.v.*)
viva voce	orally
volenti non fit injuria	no injustice is done to a party by an act to which he consents (defence to action for damages)
Wakening	step taken to revive action which has gone to sleep (*q.v.*)
warrandice	guarantee of a right contained in a deed, usually disponing heritage
white-bonnet	one who bids at auction to enhance price
Whitsunday	May 15 or 28, quarter day
writ	a writing possessing legal significance
writer	old name for solicitor

(All references are to paragraph numbers)

PARLIAMENT,
  breaches of privilege, 23.06–12
  European Union, 01.07
  rights of access, 23.06–12
  sovereignty, 01.07
PARTY LITIGANTS,
  court reporting, 07.39–43
PETITION,
  See also COURT DOCUMENTS
  petitioner, 04.23
  procedure, 08.54–56
  scope, 08.55
  summons, comparison, 08.54
PHOTOGRAPHY,
  See also CONTEMPT OF COURT;
    CONTEMPT OF COURT ACT
    1981; TELEVISION
  "assault by photography",
    10.36–10.39
  captions, 10.13
  care, need for, 10.01 *et seq.*
  cases, 10.04 *et seq.*
  children, protection, 10.40–42,
    12.01 *et seq.*
  civil proceedings, 10.14
  common law, 10.02 *et seq.*
  copyright, 21.19–22
  court precincts, 10.24–26
  Criminal Justice Act 1925,
    10.16–23
  English courts, comparison,
    10.03 *et seq.*
  fair trial, 10.05–12
  fatal accident inquiries, 10.43–44
  inside the court, 10.15–17
  intimidation by photography,
    10.36–39
  official secrets, 10.45
  open space, 10.34–35
  outside court, 10.34–35
  precincts of court, 10.24–26
  privacy, 24.05–08
  publications, scope, 10.01
  television. *See* TELEVISION

POLICE,
  See also CRIMINAL JUSTICE
    (SCOTLAND) ACT 1980
  broadcasting, 22.19
  investigation, 03.28
  media help, 03.29
  powers, 03.34–36, 22.19
POLICE COURT. *See* DISTRICT
  COURT
PORNOGRAPHY. *See* OBSCENITY
PRECEDENT,
  case law, 01.10
PRESS COMPLAINTS
  COMMISSION,
  See also PRESS COUNCIL;
    PRIVACY
  Calcutt Committee. *See*
    CALCUTT COMMITTEE
  cases, 24.22–23
  chairman, 24.22
  investigation, 24.21
  jurisdiction, 24.20
  Press Council, abolition,
    24.19–20
  press freedom, 24.21
  press record, 24.27
  race relations, 28.18
  self-regulation, 24.19, 23.24
  warning for future, 24.26
PRESS COUNCIL,
  See also PRESS COMPLAINTS
    COMMISSION; PRIVACY
  abolition, 24.19–20
  cases, 28.09–18
  race relations, 28.09–17
PRINTING. *See* PUBLISHING
PRISONERS, ESCAPED,
  contempt of court,
    09.132–135
PRIVACY,
  See also RIGHTS OF ACCESS
  Calcutt Committee. *See*
    CALCUTT COMMITTEE
  person, 24.05–09
  photography, 24.05–08